~ FREEDOM ROAD ~

Freedom Road

*For Keith & Lorraine
With very best of everything
James
05-09-2008*

James Millette

EDITOR

ARAWAK publications
KINGSTON · JAMAICA

Arawak publications
17 Kensington Crescent
Kingston 5   Jamaica W I

© 1988, 2007 by James Millette
All rights reserved. First edition 1988
Second edition 2007
ISBN-10 976 8189 89 4
ISBN-13 978 976 8189 89 9

11 10 09 08 07   6 5 4 3 2

NATIONAL LIBRARY OF JAMAICA CATALOGUING-IN-PUBLICATION DATA

Millette, James
   Freedom road / James Millette, editor. - 2nd. ed.
       p. ; cm.
   Includes bibliographical references
   ISBN 978-976-8189-89-9 (pbk)
   1. Slavery - Caribbean Area - History
   2. Slaves - West Indies, British - Emancipation
   3. Women slaves - Caribbean Area
   4. Maroons - Suriname

   I. Millette, James

   306.362   dc 22

Book and cover design by Annika Lewinson-Morgan
Set in 10.5/13pt Book Antiqua with Casablanca AntiqueBT

for the slaves who made us free

Contents

Introduction to the Second (2007) Edition 1

Introduction to the First (1988) edition 8

Chapter 1 ~ **James Millette** 17
Labour and Capital under Slavery: Trinidad, 1783-1838

Chapter 2 ~ **Margaret D. Rouse-Jones** 47
Freedom before Emancipation: Manumission in Trinidad, 1808-1830

Chapter 3 ~ **Hilary M. Beckles** 67
The Struggle of Blacks and Free-coloureds for Freedom in Barbados, 1800-1833

Chapter 4 ~ **Kusha Haraksingh** 102
Free Workers and Sugar Estates in Trinidad, 1838-1845

Chapter 5 ~ **H.A.M. Essed** 121
Freedom without Emancipation: the Rise of Large Maroon Communities in Suriname

Chapter 6 ~ **Lloyd King** 136
Slavery and Literature in Cuba

Chapter 7 ~ **Rhoda E. Reddock** 152
Women and Slavery in the Caribbean: a Feminist Perspective

Chapter 8 ~ **Selwyn Carrington** 170
Economic Determinism vs. Humanitarianism: a Look at the William Hypotheses

Chapter 9 ~ **Bridget Brereton** 192
Caribbean History in the Schools: a Critical Assessment of Recent Writing for Secondary Schools in Anglophone Caribbean

Chapter 10 ~ **James Millette** 213
Labour vs. Capital after Emancipation, 1838-1897

Biographies 255

Introduction

TO THE SECOND EDITION

The first and second editions of *Freedom Road* are separated by two important events in the unfolding of the experiences of the people of the African Diaspora. The first edition was intended to appear in 1984 on the 150th anniversary of the abolition of slavery in the British Empire. The second edition has been stimulated by the celebration of the bicentennial of the abolition of the British slave trade in 1807 and the observances associated with that event. The first edition missed the mark by about four years and appeared in 1988; the second edition appears within the ambit of the celebrations which are now taking place and comes about two decades after the appearance of the first.

Thereby hangs a tale. For many reasons, one of which had to do with the state of the Caribbean publishing industry in the early 1980s, and the other with the perspective of the book itself, *Freedom Road* was offered for publication and accepted by the José Martí Publishing House in Havana, Cuba in late 1983. Hopes were high that the book would be available by or soon after August 1st, 1984, but that was not to be. Larger issues were involved, and for one reason or the other the publication did not emerge until 1988. It also emerged in a very limited edition with the result that the book has not generally been available in the English language in the years that have intervened between the first edition and the edition that now appears.

In a real sense, therefore, *Freedom Road* has been in existence for just about 20 years, but it has not been effectively published, and is in many important respects unknown to the audience for which it was intended. It was clear soon after the first appearance of the work that a second edition needed to be done and, in many important respects, the intervening years have been committed to that prospect.

There were however many difficulties in the way of a second edition. For one thing the book had been published, and the publisher had copyright claims which could not be ignored. For sure, those claims were not ignored by prospective publishers who very often took one look at a volume published in Havana, Cuba of all places and decided to have nothing further to do with it. Secondly, the first edition was marred by many textual errors, omissions, and other problems which needed to be corrected before a second edition could appear. Thirdly, there were the interests of the authors, some of whom wanted nothing more than to leave their chapters alone while others wished to revise their chapters significantly.

Finally, there were problems associated with the reproduction of a book which needed to be retyped almost from scratch. Here, the rapidly changing technology was both friend and foe. Friend, in that the increasingly widespread emergence of word processing technologies helped to facilitate the reproduction of the text. Foe, in that the rapidly changing technologies did themselves at times imperil the continuation of the reproduction of the second edition. For example, the first attempt to reproduce the material was by way of scanning which did help and was certainly cheaper and less burdensome than typing. The scanned material was saved onto 3.5 inch floppy disks which were themselves, in due course, scheduled to become obsolete and virtually useless. Computers themselves were undergoing rapid transformations which sometimes complicated the writing process. For example, the first computer to whose hard drive the full text of the second edition was saved was an AT&T 486, which duly crashed in much the same way that the AT&T venture into the computing world collapsed in the early nineties. A second retyping was necessary, and this was partly completed with the assistance of students and staff at Oberlin College, where I was by that time located. The product we now have is to a large extent the result of their efforts.

Even so, the appearance of the second edition would not have been possible at this time without the tremendous improvements of word processing, printing and publishing, and the mastery of the new techniques by the modern Caribbean publishing industry. I was truly impressed when Arawak publications in Jamaica and their partners The Blue Edition in Trinidad began to discuss with me as a serious proposition the possibility of actually publishing the second edition within a few months of talking about it. In fact, Arawak publications took the project successfully and spectacularly from start to finish in the space of about three months, with such retyping as was necessary (and retyping is always necessary) completed with the assistance of freelance staff in the final weeks of the project. The printing and binding of the book was done in Trinidad by SCRIP-J.

Along the way I decided to abandon what was an impediment in the way of the second edition for a long time. Instead of trying to keep up with the literature and to 'modernise' the material, I decided

Introduction

to reproduce the material basically as it was written in the early 1980s with such corrections as were necessary and imperative. So that the chapters are not exactly what they were in the first edition, but they are close. The references are not entirely the same as they were in the first edition, but they are not very different. In fact I have resisted the temptation to update the references with the inclusion of new notes on material that has emerged since the first edition was published. Sometimes this includes the omission of references to works that have appeared in a more mature form than when first cited. For example, some of the material which first saw the light of day as theses and dissertations for higher degrees and have now been published as books and monographs have been referred to in the original form only. This is not entirely because I am reluctant to acknowledge the new work that has been done, but because I think that the new work is already sufficiently well known without me having to proselytise on its behalf.

The chapters that appear in this edition essentially cover the period 1783-1897, that is to say the period leading up to and leading away from the emancipation of the slaves in the British West Indian territories.

Chapter 1, "Labour and Capital Under Slavery: Trinidad 1783-1838", the first of the two chapters that I have contributed, deals with the rise and collapse of the slave system in Trinidad and the general strategy for abolition and emancipation in the wider West Indian community. Emphasis is placed on the emergence of the imperial strategy for realising abolition while generally leaving the social, political and economic system unchanged by that major development.

In Chapter 2, "Freedom Before Emancipation: Manumission in Trinidad, 1808-1830", Margaret Rouse-Jones deals with the issue of manumission in Trinidad and explores what seems to be a more favourable environment for manumission in Trinidad as a contributory factor in the creation of a significant free coloured and black population in the period preceding emancipation.

In Chapter 3, "The Struggle of Blacks and Free-Coloureds for Freedom in Barbados, 1800-1833", Hilary Beckles interrogates the notion that Barbados was more placid than most other slave societies in the run up to abolition and emancipation. His chapter deals specifically with the April 1816 revolt in Barbados and estimates the extent to which that revolt intimidated and troubled the ruling class in the island and instructed the imperial government about where slavery was really heading in the West Indies.

Chapter 4, "Free Workers and Sugar Estates in Trinidad, 1838-1845", written by Kusha Haraksingh, reexamines the dynamics of the survival of the sugar plantations in the aftermath of emancipation, provides a nuanced account of what the flight from the estates really meant, and concludes that the introduction of Indian indentureship was inspired by planter insistence, contrary to the evidence that "labour was inadequate and not continuous".

Chapter 5, "Freedom Without Emancipation: the Rise of Large Maroon Communities in Suriname", discusses the signal achievement of the maroon communities in Suriname, who freed themselves without waiting for formal emancipation from the colonial regime. In the chapter H.A.M. Essed queries some of the extant literature on the maroons and offers an explanation of the processes that governed their emergence and survival.

In Chapter 6, "Slavery and Literature in Cuba", Lloyd King discusses the intersection between slavery and the hierarchies of race and colour in Cuba in pre- and post-emancipation Cuba. He reviews the writings of some of the most prominent novelists in nineteenth century Cuba and focuses on the contradictions in their work engendered by their handling of the slave question.

Rhoda Reddock in Chapter 7, "Women and Slavery in the Caribbean: a Feminist Perspective", discusses the experience and influence of women in the Caribbean slave system and offers a feminist perspective on the role played by women in this central Caribbean institution.

Over the years, Selwyn H.H. Carrington (Chapter 8) has distinguished himself as the most robust and informed defender of the Eric Williams hypotheses articulated in his classic work *Capitalism and Slavery*. This essay, "Economic Determinism vs. Humanitarianism: a Look at the Williams Hypotheses", marks the beginning of Carrington's engagement with this issue and is remarkable as an episode in opening up the modern historiographical debates that have taken place over the years.

In Chapter 9, "Caribbean History in the Schools: a Critical Assessment of Recent Writing for Secondary Schools in the Anglophone Caribbean", which is published as written in 1984, Bridget Brereton offers a critical review of the history texts being written for schools in the Anglophone Caribbean in that time, elucidates their shortcomings, and draws attention to the contributions and deficiencies made by this important emerging literature on the Caribbean.

In Chapter 10, "Labour vs Capital after Emancipation, 1838-1897",

Introduction

I return to the contradictions between labour and capital in the post-emancipation period in colonial Trinidad and focus in particular on the growth of dominant capitalist enterprises and the emergence of nascent popular organisations which marked the inception of the anti-colonial and working class struggles in Trinidad and Tobago and the broader Caribbean.

With respect to the issue that stimulated the publication of the second edition, namely, the abolition of the British slave trade, the question might well be asked: What was its importance?

We all know that the slave trade did not come to an end with the British abolition, which incidentally was duplicated in the United States with an abolition which was far less meaningful. The organised slave trade continued for about another 60 years and only came to an end as an important factor in the perpetuation of the slave plantations with the actual abolition of slavery in the United States. Thereafter, the trade gradually withered away even though Cuba and Brazil continued to be major destinations for those hardy smugglers who still attempted to engage in the commerce.

But even if ineffective, the abolition of the slave trade was significant in that it was the first clear declaration by a major imperial power of the illegality and the barbarism of a traffic in human beings which had previously been widely supported in the highest circles of European society. Great Britain was also, at the time of the abolition, the rising superpower of the day. Notwithstanding the evidence of numerous ambiguities in its suppression initiatives, it was able to bring to the task diplomatic and material resources which other powers did not possess. In the event, it was able to use slave trade abolition as a major diplomatic weapon in the period marking the rise of free trade imperialism. The abolition of the slave trade, and thereafter the abolition of slavery itself, allowed Britain to use these achievements as bludgeons against its rivals and to clothe the imperialism of *Pax Britannica* in moral dress.

For the slaves, the abolition of the slave trade was at once a disappointment and a harbinger of the total emancipation which was to come. In the competitive dialectic that developed between masters and slaves, the slaves chose to believe and often to assert that not only the slave trade but slavery itself had been abolished. In doing so, they consciously challenged the claims of the masters that they were still slaves and unconsciously turned their backs on some of the most progressive of the abolitionists who saw the abolition of the slave trade as a step in the direction of eventual emancipation. Objectively, however, whatever side one took the abolition of the slave trade was the beginning of the end for the slave institution in the Anglophone Caribbean. Within three decades, slavery became insupportable, and emancipation became real.

A perusal of the introduction of the first edition emphasises the fact that this effort is beholden to a large number of people, beginning with the members of the National Committee for the Commemoration of the 150th Anniversary of the Abolition of Slavery in the early 1980s.

Unfortunately, some of the members of that distinguished group of individuals are now deceased. Special recognition of their contribution is here acknowledged.

I am also beholden to the Department of History of the University of the West Indies St Augustine which organised the public lecture series that commemorated the Bicentenary of the Abolition of the Trans Atlantic Trade in Enslaved Africans. The decision to describe the series as the "Freedom Road Lecture Series – Culture and Emancipation" was challenging to say the least. The decision to expedite the reissue of *Freedom Road* was my response to that challenge. The honour of an invitation to present the closing lecture in the series was inspirational to put it moderately. Inspirational, too, was the selection of Heather Cateau to preside over the arrangements associated with my participation in the series. I thank her warmly for answering all of my many questions and for providing the information and leadership that helped to make the series a success and to make my participation a reality.

Circumstances dictate the recognition of the passing of Dr Fitz Baptiste, a longstanding member of the Department of History at St Augustine, who died unexpectedly before the series came to an end. Fitz was a passionate and tireless researcher, teacher and writer on all the issues associated with the development of the Black diaspora worldwide and will be greatly missed.

Our gratitude is also recorded to the José Martí publishing house in Cuba, which made the first edition possible. Some of the circumstances which impeded the fullest publication of that edition have also undermined the survival of the house itself which no longer exists in the form and with the vigour with which it operated in those days.

As is to be expected, a lot of other obligations have accrued in the interim. These obligations are principally to students and staff at Oberlin College where all of the preparation work of the second edition took place.

To the College itself, I owe the experience of enhanced computer

Introduction

literacy, with all its complexities, and material support from time to time with respect to different aspects of the preparation of the material. Among the individuals who helped with the scanning and the typing were Gretchen Higgins, Dolorus Nevels, Rejoice Acolatse, Corrinne Millette, Lorraine Leete, and Nicole Davis, Letitia Mosby and Natasha Zamor, students in the Mellon and McNair summer programmes who helped with the difficult task of ensuring the survival of the manuscript by typing and retyping sections of it, in changing word processing formats, from time to time.

I also have to thank Sandra Hardie who inspired this final push to completion by the timely and insistent reminder that if I did not do it, then it probably won't ever get done. And I have to thank my wider family – Mildred, Suzanne, Corrinne, Kimberlee and Melissa – who sustained and distracted me by turns as the work proceeded over the years.

In the final days of preparation, exactly the time when so many unexpected tasks emerge, like Internet pop-ups, all over the place I was fortunate to have the pleasant, constant and efficient assistance of Ramaesh Bhagirat who was in at the close and made it possible to bring the long task finally to an end.

As usual, and I say it not only because it is usual, the participation of others in the publication of this work in no way diminishes my responsibility for the deficiencies that have survived.

> James Millette
> Oberlin College
> Oberlin Ohio
> *August 1st, 2007*

Introduction

TO THE FIRST (1988) EDITION

On August 1st, 1834 slavery was abolished in the West Indian territories of the British Empire. On that day, the dread gilpin that had been hanging over the heads of the regional plantocracy finally dropped. An institution that originated in the fifteenth century and had come to maturity in the two hundred years following the establishment of the West Indian sugar plantations came to an end legally but not (except for Antigua and Bermuda) immediately. From that date onwards, no new slaves could be made; thenceforth, it was only a matter of time before all existing slaves were freed. A socio-economic system that had long survived the denunciation of numberless critics was finally being discarded.

While the arrangements envisaged under the Abolition Act anticipated full freedom for all by 1840 and for non-praedials two years earlier, such were the dynamics of the situation that after four years – on August 1st, 1838 – Emancipation Day had arrived; the system of slavery, the physical possession and exploitation of man by man was utterly destroyed, consigned in the archipelago of English-speaking territories, from Bermuda and the Bahamas in the north to Guiana in the south, to the historical scrap heap.

Before emancipation arrived, however, a period known as apprenticeship was instituted, its announced objectives being to prepare the slaves for freedom and to accustom the slave-owners to the dire prospect of managing without slave labour. This was a clever piece of imperialist rationalisation which failed completely in its objectives if only because the slaves had been anticipating freedom for years and were only too eager to embark upon it, while nothing could accustom the planters to the reality of an existence without slaves. The unannounced and still more significant effect of apprenticeship was to slow down and modify the process of liberation, to dampen the impact of what was by any calculation a major turning point in contemporary Caribbean history and to give imperialism the opportunity to ensure that the drastic changes which were taking place

Introduction

would not result in any radical overturning of the status quo.

Within the two hundred years or so spanning the era of the West Indian plantations, roughly from the 1620s to the 1830s, West Indian slavery had acquired an international prominence which largely eclipsed the significance of slavery as an institution known to classical Greece and Rome, known to the city kingdoms and empires of Africa, the Middle East and Asia and known within the Caribbean itself before the period of the sugar plantations. In its effects on the modern world, West Indian slavery was to have an influence out of all proportion to the size and population of the areas concerned; an impact that can only be understood in terms of the socio-economic and geo-political framework within which the system of slavery was located.

In the first place, the West Indian slave system was from its inception an international phenomenon, unique to no single country nor any single continent though visited with disastrously baleful effects upon a single people. At its height it commanded the attention, the enterprise and the management of all the European powers and only the most efficient of them were able to sustain a successful involvement with it. At its height it also integrated international intercourse between three continents, namely, Europe, Africa and America and facilitated productive activity in the other two. For the period of its existence until its liabilities began to outweigh its positive contributions, West Indian slavery was the strongest link in the chain of European imperialism.

It was international in other senses as well. Demographically, it was part of that dramatic explosion of the world's peoples, in particular the people of Africa, into areas of the world far beyond which they were born and raised, and made the diaspora of African peoples one of the most prominent features of demographic dispersal over the last five hundred years. Ships' captains set sail from London and Liverpool, Nantes and Bordeaux, Lisbon and Oporto – to name only a few – carrying merchandise of assorted manufacture, fetched up thousands of miles down the Atlantic seaboard of Africa on a curve stretching from Gorée to Luanda, and around the Cape into Mozambique plucked their live cargo from any of a thousand possible places, beat westwards to trade their precious shipload of human beings, or those of them left alive after the arduous Middle Passage, in places as far apart as Brazil, Barbados, Martinique, St Domingue, Jamaica, Central and South America, the Thirteen Colonies and British North America. In an age of relatively primitive transport millions of African men, women and children traversed thousands and thousands of miles, distances that are enormous even in the perspective of the age of jet travel. To destinations unknown, in conditions empathically not of their own choosing and for purposes only ultimately and horrifically disclosed, they headed. Their baggage was body and soul, brain and brawn but, particularly, brawn: muscles and labour power. Their mission was to work "from day clean to first dark", in crop time at breakneck speed for months on end, averaging as in Trinidad eighteen hours per day on the very eve of Emancipation: hard toilsome labour without reward and often unto death.

With respect to the British islands with whose systems we are primarily concerned, it is true that they were only a part of a wider New World system of slavery. But they were at the hub of that system. At its greatest extent and at its zenith, New World slavery embraced the British, French, Spanish, Dutch and Danish West Indian territories, the vast expanse of the Spanish mainland colonies, the Portuguese colonies in what is today Brazil, and the United States of America. But as far and as wide as the system ranged, it was here in the British West Indian islands that it came to rest. From time to time, the bountiful plantations of a St Domingue or a Cuba might dwarf all else with their fabled wealth sweated out of the labour of countless hordes of slaves but it was the British West Indian islands which, in long term effect, etched the name Caribbean on the word sugar and the word sugar on the African slave.

The reason lay in the strength and durability of British imperial power. Where St Domingue and Cuba had natural gifts which no British sugar island could match, France and Spain had fatal flaws which British imperialism never possessed. With the French and Spanish empires, the weakness was at the centre; at the British centre only strength resided. British imperial power, and in particular, its dominant connection with sea transport, ideally fitted it for the task of imperial exploitation of overseas colonies. Sea transport, the most advanced and cosmopolitan instrument of international communication in the two or three centuries that mattered, was the peculiar British forte. What air travel is in the twentieth century, seagoing was in the fifteenth to the nineteenth century and, for most of this period, certainly from the late seventeenth to the late nineteenth century, Great Britain either had its fair share of that traffic or dominated it. At the height of the slave system, Britain's ascendancy as a seagoing power grew side by side with her involvement in the slave trade and slavery. And when the time came to attack both, it was Britain's control of sea power that enabled her to internationalise abolition with more than usual effect. But sea power was the symptom not the substance of imperial strength. The sinews of the British imperial system lay in industry, small but growing in the fifteenth, sixteenth and seventeenth centuries, powerful and dominant in the mid eighteenth and nineteenth centuries and, in that significant period of imperial conflict with France (1713-1815), all the more crucial because of its interconnection with the slave trade and slavery. The basic argument, first advanced by Eric Williams, that fortunes made in West Indian sugar sweated out of the labour of slaves accelerated the process of capital accumulation in Great Britain and stoked the fires of the Industrial Revolution, has remained unshaken in the face of incessant, revisionist, historiographical assault and only because it was and remains true.

Both the slave trade and slavery represented the epitome of unequal exchange at all levels and in that sense symbolised the earliest modern example of the inseparable connection between development and underdevelopment on a global scale. It was not only that bodies were exchanged for baubles; it was that baubles and such like impedimenta came to be regarded as fair exchange in the trade. Whether in cash or in kind, the standard of exchange was always the same: something for nothing. Indeed, the slave coasts over time established their own standards and values but they were standards and values which involved, on the one hand, the purchase of labour power without which the sugar plantations could not be sustained and, on the other hand, the sale of trifles and commodities without which Africans would very often have been far better off.

In all these senses, the slave trade and slavery were an integral part of the process by which a genuinely modern international system of trade, commerce and exchange came into being and was maintained. This is another way of saying that the development of the international capitalist economy was ineluctably connected to the trade in slaves and the profitable exploitation of slave labour on the plantations. It is for this reason that New World, and in particular British West Indian slavery, achieved significance and a distinction far beyond the intrinsic importance of the areas within which the slave system flourished.

The ironies of history are legion in recorded time. But what could be more ironical than the fact that in the seventeenth and eighteenth centuries Caribbean islands which not too long ago were contemptuously referred to by an elder European statesman as "specks of dust" were more highly preferred than vast expanses of territory that have evolved into some of the more prestigious countries in today's world?

The evaluation of those "specks of dust" was based not on size but on the contribution which they could and did make to the creation of wealth, the generation of surplus, the realisation of competitive advantage and, not infrequently, the outcome of rivalries, confrontations and wars in Europe and elsewhere in the world.

In every aspect considered to be significant, even fundamental, in the growth of the international economy up to 1917 (after which socialism made a distinct and unique contribution to its modification) the slave trade, slavery and their consequences made a decisive input. The overseas discoveries, the price revolution consequent on the inflow of mineral wealth from the New World, the rise and consolidation of nation states, industrialisation, international transport, the accumulation, concentration and centralisation of capital, free trade which in its more dynamic aspects was nothing less than the forcible opening up of non-European countries to the trade and influences of Europe, and finally the so-called new imperialism which marked the final, relentless division of the world between so many competing 'cut throat' empires: all of these stemmed from the dichotomies created by the economic, social and political systems which evolved and took shape in the heyday of slavery and the slave trade.

In a phrase, they stemmed from the internationalisation of inequality among people which was at the core of the master-slave relationship. When all is said and done the most remarkable thing about slavery was "the world that the slaveholders made". For themselves, there was one world; for everybody else, there was another. In the colonies there was, on the one hand, a white entrepreneurial or planter class always inhabiting the positions of dominance, oriented to the metropolis and tending in some colonies, notably the British, towards an exaggerated absenteeism and for that reason looking on the colonies as places of sojourn rather than of residence. On the other hand, there came into being large black or coloured slave or otherwise dependent populations, living under conditions of coercion, deprivation and want, barely subsisting under the enervating conditions of near slavery or slavery *durante vita* or else succumbing to it.

Out of this clash of race and class and culture there developed the basic premises of racial antagonism and discrimination born of the historical relationship which came to exist between white and black in this period. Where, for example, the European adventurers left Europe in the fifteenth century in part to find the legendary African king, Prester John, Christian by repute and a potential ally against the Moors, perhaps more powerful than any king in Europe, by 1763

Introduction

Europeans had long outgrown such beliefs. By that time nothing was more prominent in the European mind than the ascendancy of European persons and things over all that was non-European. With specific reference to slavery, the European experience of mastership over millions and millions of African slaves, whether at the moment of capture in Africa, or on the overstuffed slave ships, or again on the overstocked plantations of the New World, bred an abiding contempt for black people as well as the belief that servility, docility and stupidity were attributes springing naturally from the "inherent inferiority" of black, particularly, African people.

As history has shown, the "inherent inferiority" of the African led in due course to other presumptions of "inherent inferiority" affecting Indians, Chinese, Latin Americans, Arabs and all others who did not fit the narrow notions of racial superiority held in Europe and afterwards in America and other countries of European settlement and exploitation. But it is not in its social as much as in its economic and political aspects that slavery has left its indelible imprint on the modern world. The racial pre-suppositions upon which slavery was once based have been largely discarded, except among those lunatic fringes incapable of keeping up with the times. Intelligent racists have conceded the dysfunctionality of racism. But "the world that the slaveholders made" is still perpetuated in the economic and political systems that they created. In the mercantilist scheme of things slavery had an honoured place not because the slave was a black man or came from Africa but because slavery facilitated the ultimate rationalisation of an international economy which had two clear poles, one metropolitan and temperate, the other colonial and tropical.

It was the mercantilist desire to integrate colonial and metropolitan production and to appropriate the surplus wealth created in the process that strengthened the need for slavery and for the slave trade, its inseparable handmaiden. In a non-machine age, the slave system facilitated the application of a machine-like, factory-type aggregation of labour power to the exploitation of tropical agricultural resources. There was no other system of production that could, within the prevailing social, economic and political conditions, organise production for profit in the New World with so much efficiency and with so much effectiveness. It was only later, when direct competition for capital developed between slave supported enterprise and manufacturing industry that the consciousness of slavery as an inefficient system of production came to the forefront. Even so, it was not that slavery was inefficient in itself; it was that it was inefficient by comparison with the sophisticated new industries which were then becoming more and more prevalent in England and in relation to which new class and production relationships were quickly developing.

In the mercantilist age, the most persuasive analyses relating to the economic development of colonies emphasised two things: first, the absolute necessity of subordinating the colonial to the metropolitan economy; and secondly, the clearly unrivalled superiority of the slave system of production within the colonies. Simply to mention these two factors provokes the recollection that in today's world the multinational corporations, the International Monetary Fund and the leading centres of imperialist power are working ceaselessly to perpetuate precisely the same ends.

To the original protagonists of these views it did not matter that one of the first fruits of the introduction of slavery into the West Indies was the displacement of the white indentured, or small-holding labouring population, by a black population. It did not matter one bit that such a displacement sent thousands of ordinary people packing with their dreams of 'El Dorado' unfulfilled, or that resident planters in the West Indies were becoming increasingly alarmed by the growing deficiency in numbers of the white population compared with the burgeoning black population. The fact was that the African slave helped to produce precisely what England and France needed from the tropics and also to consume British exports of coarse cloth, linen and wool. Production for the West Indian slave economy enlivened the industry in England and diminished unemployment. As Josiah Child put it: "One Englishman with the ten blacks that work for him, counting what they eat, use and wear, would make employment for four men in England." In the mercantilist understanding there was no sane argument against that.

Nor is there in the neo-mercantilist international environment of modern capitalism. Of course, there are differences. Under developed capitalism, it is the multinational corporation not the state that makes the rules of commercial intercourse. Under developed capitalism, too, the multinational corporation has no particular concern about diminishing unemployment at home any more than it is concerned about reducing it abroad. But if it is cheaper to make, say, textiles or calculators in a 'Third World' country than it is to make it in the metropolis that is where it will be made. Of course, what makes it cheaper are the labour costs payable to textile or assembly line workers. And, what makes those labour costs lower can run all the way from foreign exchange equivalents to an underdeveloped sense of the real value of labour; more often than not, however, the real reason has to do with the backward social and economic conditions forcibly

Introduction

imposed by illiberal political structures on neo-colonised peoples.

"The world the slaveholders made" is still too much with us. It is the reality of that world and the continuing struggles against it by those who are oppressed that give point to the celebration of the 150th anniversary of the abolition of slavery which this book is intended to celebrate. In its emergence it has had to contend with the views of those who proclaim the futility of commemorating the abolition of slavery, either because it took place too long ago or because it brings up the unpleasant past. These selfsame critics have no problem celebrating the 200th anniversary of the declaration of US independence or Bastille Day both of which are, admittedly, occasions for joy; or in commemorating the death of their chosen prophet on a yearly basis which, if they are to be believed, must surely be the most unpleasant event ever to have occurred.

Nor do we have any problem in celebrating the abolition of slavery. The end of slavery was the beginning of a new society in the West Indies. It made possible all that is positive in the growth and development of the West Indies and, properly considered, is a decisive stage in the upbringing of the West Indian peoples, their societies and their institutions. Needless to say, that process is far from finished. The slaveholders have made their world. We must now make ours.

The stimulus for this publication was provided by the National Committtee for the Commemoration of the 150th Anniversary of the Abolition of Slavery chaired by Max Ifill and, comprising at its most active stage, Esmond Ramesar, Ralph Henry, James Millette, Claudia Harvey, George Sammy, Margaret Rouse-Jones, Clifford Sealy, Marina Maxwell, Pat Bishop, Marjorie Thorpe, Clifford Payne, Bridget Brereton, Joanne Darcheville, Peggy Boissiere and Gordon Rohlehr.

Once the idea for the book had been conceived a committee convened by myself and comprising colleagues in the History Department at the University of the West Indies, St Augustine, drew up a list of contents and began to solicit contributions. Several members of that committee themselves contributed chapters to the book. To them as authors, and to all other contributors, much thanks is due.

With very slender resources at its disposal the committee instituted a search for a publishing house willing and able to produce the book. The new José Martí Publishing House from Cuba agreed on being approached to publish the book as a contribution to the commemoration effort.

Even so, we were unable for many reasons to achieve our original goal of publishing on or before August 1st, 1984. A number of factors made it impossible to achieve this objective but then 1984 is but the beginning of four years of commemoration ending on August 1, 1988. Late though we are for Abolition we are in good time for Emancipation.

Thanks are also due of course to the secretaries in the Faculty of Arts and General Studies, and particularly to Elizabeth Marcano, Elaine Gordon, Chandra Bhaggan and Corinne Flores for the lion's share of the typing.

Substantial effort has been made to give the book a wider Caribbean perspective. The essays are varied not only in time and place but also in theme, the reason being that the abolition of slavery was but an episode, albeit a most important one, in the growth and development of the Caribbean people. It was an episode which occurred in 1834 in the English-speaking territories and it was a process which, while freeing the slave, opened up the prospect for the coercion of other, mainly East Indian, indentured labourers. Accordingly, we have been concerned with the non-English-speaking territories and we have been concerned with indentureship.

Notwithstanding these efforts there is a sense in which the book is dominated by the national preoccupations of its mainly Trinidadian authorship. In the circumstances, that was unavoidable.

James Millette
University of the West
Indies, St Augustine,
September 1st, 1984

CHAPTER ONE

Labour and Capital under Slavery: Trinidad, 1783-1838

James Millette

In 1783 full slavery was introduced into Trinidad; it was to be fifty-five years before full freedom would be achieved. In the scale of West Indian slavery this seems like a very brief span of time and for this reason two very inaccurate conclusions are often drawn about slavery in Trinidad: first, that it was underdeveloped and, for that reason, relatively mild; secondly, that it was of little, if any, long run significance in the ultimate development of the society. Both conclusions are grossly inaccurate yet they are persuasive and influential specifically in that they have been incorporated into the ruling ideas of a society which has been made to thrive on a platform of historical half-truths and misrepresentations which have produced a national psyche that is truly a wonder to behold.

Among the most powerful of these misrepresentations is the endless empty repetition that slavery is of absolutely no significance in explaining present day realities whether those are expressed in an intolerable work ethic, in a gross and growing inequality between the races and the classes, or else in an indeterminate and confused sense of national identity. It is the perspective of this writer that a proper understanding of these things – what they are and why they are not what they should be – is impossible without a proper understanding of the critical role that slavery has played in shaping the essential foundations of this society. At the same time, slavery was only a specific form of exploitation which existed in maturity between 1783 and 1838. Its essence was perpetuated into the period of indentureship when East Indian labour largely replaced African slave labour on the plantations and to a lesser extent in other sectors of the society. The exploitations which that took place under indentureship also explain the position of the East Indian in contemporary Trinidad.

The continuation, since the end of indentureship, of the essential exploitation of the African and Indian masses speaks directly to the point of class antagonism and the growing significance of class in explaining the subordinate status of both groups. What follows is a contribution to the proper understanding of these realities.

When in 1783 the social and economic foundations of modern Trinidad were laid as a result of the promulgation of the *cédula* and the consequences which followed therefrom, a specific socio-economic formation was at the same time introduced. That socio-economic formation was slavery, a form of society long known to man but existing in institutionalised form in the Caribbean since the sixteenth and early seventeenth centuries. This system of slavery was quite unlike any that had previously been known and was characterised by several important features.

First of all, it was inseparably associated with sugar plantation agriculture, a development which took place in the Caribbean in the first half of the seventeenth century. Sugar displaced tobacco which had been up until then the main crop and which was based on small-holding – the typical labour force being the white family and/or the white indentured worker. The change to sugar led to the dispossession of large numbers of smallholders, the eventual disappearance of smallholding and the extinction of white servile labour. Thereafter the sugar plantation – comprising extensive fields of sugar cane, a sugar factory, a few white supervisory staff usually responsible to a manager or overseer, himself more often than not beholden to an absentee proprietor, and large gangs of field slaves as well as a few domestics – had emerged as the typical economic unit. And though plantations devoted to the cultivation of other crops – cocoa, coffee, cotton, dyestuffs – were in existence, it was the sugar plantation that was dominant, it was the sugar plantation that was typical.

Secondly, a system of slave supply predominantly from the coast of West Africa had developed to meet the needs of the West Indian plantations. For the next two hundred years this trade in slaves was to become an end in itself, a source of great wealth and power to its participants in Europe, Africa, America and the West Indies, giving rise to a quadrangular traffic which was the outstanding manifestation in its time of large scale international trading. Most importantly, the steady supply of slaves conferred on the slave system itself a unique character, the essence of which was that the life of the slave, however valuable he might be, was a thing of little value. He could be easily replaced and the conventional wisdom, supported by all the calculations and racial prejudices which had sprung up, decreed

1 Labour and capital under slavery: Trinidad 1783-1838

that it was better to work the slave to death than to cherish him.

Thirdly, slavery itself came to be associated with black men and women, with Africans and 'creole' blacks. It was New World slavery, the replacement of the native Indian labourer and later, the white own-account and indentured worker by African slaves, that fixed on the black man an indelible association with slavery. Before New World slavery spawned that association, Africans were regarded as at least equal and sometimes superior to Europeans. After that association developed, Africans were regarded as inferior, black men and women, 'creole' or African, as fitted only to be slaves. This perception had fateful consequences for all persons "tainted with black blood" in the New World as the free coloureds in particular bore evidence. But it was also important in colouring for all time the relations existing between Europeans and Africans in Africa as well as between Europeans and other coloured races throughout the world.

Fourthly, the slave came to be regarded as property, losing in the process all those rights and entitlements which would have attached to him were he to be regarded as a person. Thus, Marx wrote that: "The slave-owner buys his labourer as he buys his horse. If he loses his slave, he loses capital that can... be restored by new outlay in the slave-mart."[1] As capital, the slave had no civic rights: no right to family, no right to comfort, to food, to raiment and shelter, no right to protection, no right to be heard, no right to protest, ultimately no right to life itself. A slave had no wife or husband, no children, no territory. The children of a slave belonged to the master, to be sold, kept or otherwise done with as he in his sole discretion determined. This condition continued for as long as the slave was a slave and the slave was a slave for life, *durante vita*.

Lastly, and most importantly, the system of plantation slavery fixed upon the slave the duty of continuous labour without reward. When the slave was captured or sold into slavery he was sold bag and baggage in the fullest and deepest meaning of that phrase.

> The slave, together with his labour power, is sold once and for all to his owner. He is a commodity that can pass from the hand of one owner to that of another. He is *himself* a commodity, but (his) labour power is not *his* commodity.[2]

When he got up in the morning and went to work he did so knowing full well that the product of his labour for that day was not his but his master's and this sentiment was reinforced by the surest knowledge that for as many days as he would work, for as long as he was a slave, the product of his labour would never be his. At best the master would return to him only so much of the product as was necessary for keeping him alive; the remainder, the overwhelming balance, he would retain for himself. But the decision was not the slave's. It was his master's and his master's alone. If he wished, the master could simply let him starve. If he was a good worker the master benefited, if he was a bad worker the master suffered. For him there was no social mobility except it was the modest ascent from the field to the master's dwelling, but the rules remained the same. In any case, the trip from field to house was one that only an infinitesimal number of slaves, usually the comeliest and the shapeliest of women, could make.

It was into this socio-economic formation, guided by these precepts, that the slave population coming to Trinidad in the period after 1783 moved. The essential perquisites of the system were not all evident in Trinidad before 1783 but they were all immediately evident afterwards. The reason lies in the fact that even though Trinidad was in a manner of speaking a *tabula rasa*, it was not a clean slate upon which anything could be written. In the West Indies of that era, modernisation, economic reorganisation, 'development' – call it what you will – meant one thing and one thing only, sugar; and the sugar plantation meant slavery. In the logic of events, that slavery did not move by gradations upwards through varied patriarchal forms until it attained the maturity of the West Indian stereotype. Rather, that stereotype was introduced in all its maturer aspects into Trinidad from the inception.

Some, but not much mitigation of the system occurred in the period 1783 to 1797 when the island developed under Spanish auspices. To begin with, the Spanish conception of slavery was different from that of the British. That conception harked back all the way to the thirteenth century when Spain made contact with slavery in a European setting long before plantation slavery had been established in the New World. This pre-plantation variant of slavery had been regulated by strict moralistic codes drawing heavily on the Christian religious tradition and enshrined in the *Siete Partidas*. The laws remained the formal basis of Spanish regulation of New World slavery, barely surviving the opportunistic temptation to rewrite the moral code to suit the new convenience. Instead, from time to time modified versions of the basic laws were put out; but increasingly these proved difficult to implement principally because plantation slavery was impatient of the restraints the law sought to impose.

Thus, it was that E.L. Joseph could describe the slave code "introduced" into the island in 1789 as

1 Labour and capital under slavery: Trinidad 1783-1838

the most liberal and humane law, for the government of slaves, that ever was enacted by any legislature in ancient or modern times... its humanity and liberality can only be appreciated by those who are acquainted with the wretched regulations and mockery of justice which in English, French, Portuguese, Danish and Dutch colonies were called slave laws.[3]

And a perusal of the provisions of that code does indeed disclose the influence of several principles of which, for example, Picton's slave code of 1800 was completely innocent.

Baptism was prescribed for the slaves; so too was religious instruction.[4] And the master was put under obligation to provide them. Rations were fixed as to quantity and quality, and a protector of slaves identified to enforce the relevant regulations.[5] Slaves under 17 and over 60 could not be forced to work. Able-bodied slaves were to be paid two dollars per year, and the amount of work to be required of them was fixed by law.[6] Slaves were to be given the days off on the occasion of named religious holidays, be sent to mass and allowed to enjoy themselves thereafter.[7] The condition of the slave dwellings was also regulated.[8] The aged and the sick were to be treated with humanity and compassion. Slaves who were ill or otherwise unfit for work could not be set free. They remained the responsibility of their master.[9] Pre-marital sex was forbidden; marriage was not only permitted but encouraged.[10] Rules were established for facilitating slaves from different plantations living together as man and wife on being married.[11]

Ill-treatment of slaves was punishable under law.[12] To some extent the slave was made equal under law.[13] A registry of slaves was to be kept in every district in order to better keep an account of the slave population and to protect the slaves.[14] The priests were enjoined to inform themselves, and not by reference to masters alone, about the condition of the slaves and to bring cases deserving of investigation to the attention of the public authorities.[15]

All of this was, of course, excellent on paper. It even anticipated some of the ameliorations for which British humanitarians later had to struggle in Britain. But in actual fact most of it was a dead letter. Joseph himself deserves to write the epitaph of this "most liberal and humane law":

... it was so opposed in the Spanish colonies and the government of Spain had become so feeble that it was in but few places, if any, ever enforced, and omitted in the *Recopilación* of the laws of the Indies, consequently it soon fell into disuse. It is doubted if ever this law was legally confirmed by the *audiencia* of Caracas.

At the same time it must be admitted that so much of this law was enforced in the Spanish colonies it rendered the slaves the least oppressed of any in the New World; after all, this certainly is saying little in praise of their treatment.[16]

The fact was that in the late eighteenth century it was easier for Spain to treat the slave kindly in word than it was in deed. Over the preceding years the perspectives of colonial economy had changed and with it the prospects; but the Spanish monarchy had not changed. Only a violent upheaval in Spanish society itself, such as the period of Napoleonic expansion, could achieve that. Accordingly, the Spanish monarchy continued to proclaim what was essentially an outworn and obsolescent programme of slave regulation after it had become no longer possible to apply it. In an age when the Spanish colonies were beginning to blossom as plantation economies, the enfeebled Spanish monarchy was still trying to implement an essentially patriarchal regime of slavery in the vain hope that it would thus be able to serve god and man at the same time.

But neither in Trinidad nor in Cuba, nor for that matter in St Domingue before the revolution was the Spanish or the French monarchy able to enforce the prescriptions of essentially moralistic codes which in theory differed from those of the British islands by recognising the personality of the slave. As one French official said: "Reality is sometimes far from corresponding to moral prescriptions."[17] In 1771, as Elsa Goveia has shown, the Crown recognised the reality by instructing its officials in St Domingue accordingly:

> It is only by leaving to the masters a power that is nearly absolute, that it will be possible to keep so large a number of men in that state of submission which is made necessary to their numerical superiority over the whites. If some masters abuse their power, they must be reproved in secret, so that the slaves may always be kept in the belief that the master can do no wrong in his dealing with them.

And she concludes:

> All the evidence points to one conclusion. As they were actually administered during the eighteenth century, the French slave laws differed far less from their English counterparts than might be imagined... the provisions safeguarding the slave as 'persona' were either laxly enforced or neglected.[18]

In Cuba, where the great transformation in that island's agriculture took place shortly before Trinidad's, from the early 1760s onwards, the same conclusion is valid. From being "an underpopulated, underdeveloped settlement of small towns, cattle ranches, and

1 Labour and capital under slavery: Trinidad 1783-1838

tobacco farms" Cuba was transformed in a short space of time, almost exactly contemporaneous with Trinidad, into a "community of large sugar and coffee plantations".[19] As the sugar revolution took hold and Cuba emerged as a major sugar producer and exporter, the system of slavery underwent perceptible changes. Manumission, for example, became less frequent. A Yankee traveller in Cuba in 1853 reported, perhaps cynically, that "emancipation of slaves very seldom occurs in Cuba, where they publicly shout that abolitionists are those who have no slaves."[20] Further, as Franklin Knight has pointed out, apropos the view purveyed most notably by Tannenbaum, that cultural and religious traditions made Spanish slavery a different institution from British slavery:

> The economic basis of Negro slavery greatly modified the inheritance of culture or the intervention of any religious denomination. Roman Catholicism and the Iberian heritage played no significant role in the variations which developed in the institutions of slavery and race relations in Cuba and Puerto Rico during the nineteenth century.[21]

Discerning contemporaries were not unconscious of the fact that slavery was slavery. When, for example, the sustained attempt to hold Trinidad up as a 'model slave colony' ran into heavy waters in the 1820s and 1830s, it was in part because men like Wilberforce had been driven to the conclusion that African slavery on the plantations, despite the auspices under which it was administered, was

> in its leading characteristics and more prominent tendencies and effects, when uncontrolled by some powerful external influence which shall make the emancipation of the slave the ultimate end of its regulations, is the same revolting institution, whether it be administered by Spaniards or Portuguese, Frenchmen or Dutchmen, Englishmen or Americans.[22]

Under similar persuasions George Smith, chief justice of Trinidad, in 1810, argued that the protection of the slave against injustice "can only be afforded by an authority over which the master of the slave has no control and to which he must submit".[23] Accordingly, he came out firmly in support of authoritarian, 'Crown colony' rule as opposed to the old representative system for which the white colonists were then petitioning.[24]

In actuality, the large scale migration of slaves into Trinidad after 1783 took place from its inception under conditions of duress which feelingly attest to the plight of the slave in that period. The recruitment of slaves evoked all the memories of 'crimping' and

'Barbadoeing' which had featured the recruitment of indentured servants from Europe in the early seventeenth century. Free persons of black or brown complexion were forcibly taken up in the neighbouring islands and landed as slaves in Trinidad.[25]

The *cédula* itself made it clear that only free black and coloured persons being "planters and heads of families" were entitled to receive land;[26] the corollary was that the individual free black or coloured migrant was more likely than not to be claimed as someone's slave and forced into bondage.[27] On the other hand, since the flight to Trinidad offered some prospect of freedom, many slaves fled from the islands and tried to, and sometimes did, pass themselves off as free men in Trinidad.

As for the slaves themselves, those who came fell into three main categories each of which conditioned the colonists to establish the most exacting regime over them. First, there were those who were relegated in their own island to the ranks of the criminally discontented or condemned, and for whom shipment to Trinidad as the property of immigrant planters desperate for as much land as they could claim was regarded as a fitting punishment.[28] Associated with these were the stolen slaves, the luckless individuals 'press ganged' into slavery usually in the keeping of traffickers or desperate, notorious individuals fleeing from debt and other demands in their own country and seeking refuge and a new start in Trinidad.[29] The activities of such individuals caused such havoc in Grenada that a law was passed imposing a bond of £1000 sterling on all persons arriving from Trinidad as a guarantee of good behaviour, the alternative being to be declared vagabonds and committed to jail.[30] Slaves taken up under these auspices were regarded, to an extent even greater than usual, as property, commodities to be sold to the highest bidder and tools to be used in the most arduous occupations associated with clearing and bringing new lands into cultivation.

Secondly, there were the direct imports from Africa and other New World colonies. With specific reference to these, their hardships began even before they landed in the island. Many of those newly arrived from Africa died before they could be inured to local conditions while many of the New World slaves were poor, worked out, diseased specimens brought to Trinidad in the hope of realising higher values than were possible in their colonies of origin. By 1795, according to Joseph, out of every 40 to 50 such slaves only one-eighth remained alive for more than a few days after being landed.[31] Once purchased, the survivors were subjected to the harsh regimen of opening up new plantations, always the hardest job for a slave

1 Labour and capital under slavery: Trinidad 1783-1838

population even a 'creole' slave population. What is more, these imports were not long attached to the planters who purchased them and were quite unable to extract, and certainly did not receive, the consideration which planters sometimes extended to slaves who had been in their possession for a long time.[32]

Thirdly, there were the slave migrations which began after the French revolutionary outbreak and its Caribbean consequences. Thousands of slaves came with their masters in flight from the upheavals which convulsed the region. The cumulative result of those events was to put the entire slave population under the most searching scrutiny, a scrutiny that extended to the free coloured population as well, and which grew in intensity after the British took control of the island. Already, under Spanish rule, the master had enjoyed substantial discretion in the treatment of his slaves not only because the Spanish code remained inoperative but also because Article 25 of the *cédula* of 1783 had specifically conferred such an initiative.[33] With reference to this personal initiative in the regulation of the slaves, Joseph balked at reckoning the number of "deaths of the newly-imported African slaves... occasioned by inhumanity or neglect".[34] But he was sure that the "humane disposition" of Governor Chacon was insufficient protection against the rapacity of the planters. Still less were the slaves protected after the conquest when the new government showed itself exceedingly sensitive to questions of security and saw the slave population as constantly bordering on revolt In addition, oppressors of the slave population were now stiffened in their resolve to oppress the slaves by the experiences acquired in the islands from which they had fled.[35]

Trinidad slave society, therefore, was unique only in that unlike most other slave societies in the West Indies it developed late in the day, but it developed quickly. And it was like any other slave society in that it reflected to the fullest extent the principal characteristics, antagonisms and contradictions common to such societies modified by some peculiarities which were specifically Trinidadian. Among these peculiarities was the fact that for several reasons Trinidad was a critical factor in the rising polemic over the future of plantation slavery in the West Indies. As a prospective slave colony the island's cession to Spain in 1802 was significant enough to threaten the campaign at that time aimed at diminishing the spread of the slave institution, though not yet at abolishing it. As an underdeveloped slave colony with only a fraction of available land under cultivation, the island was sure to give a strong stimulation to the slave traffic if plantations were established and cultivated principally, more likely exclusively, by slave labour. Current estimates suggested that the island could absorb one million slaves if brought to full cultivation.[36]

Moreover, given the stage of the debate between the anti-slavery movement and the slave apologists, such a development was bound to lead to a disastrous decline in the momentum of attack against slavery. The abolitionists who at this stage were the most consistent advocates of the anti-slavery cause, viewed with alarm the possibility that slavery should be seen as of necessity to be the only method of agricultural enterprise in an island like Trinidad. It was vital that that view should not prevail unchallenged particularly because, as important as the island was in its own right, it was only one of several territories being acquired by Britain (Guyana and St Lucia were others) which were likely to go the same route. It was essential, therefore, that the new lands being acquired should not automatically lead to the extension of slavery and the slave trade beyond their existing limits.[37]

In the event, that struggle was lost. Slavery did become the principal method of cultivation in Trinidad after the cession of the island in 1802, as it did in British Guiana and St Lucia. But the struggle was not completely lost. The transformation of British society and economy, which was already reflecting the impact of bourgeois influence in several spheres, identified the slave trade for extinction and by 1807 its demise was legally accomplished. In Trinidad as elsewhere in and out of the British empire, legal prohibition of the trade did not, however, mean its abrupt cessation. The trade continued to exist openly and secretly and thus generated the first real clash between the contending forces over the slave question.[38]

In this context it must be understood that the British government never intended to abolish slavery by abolishing the slave trade. At best it hoped to ameliorate it, and by so doing, even to prolong its existence. The abolition of the slave trade, whatever the abolitionists and other interested parties might have hoped, was part and parcel of the British government's attempt to forestall attacks on slavery by claiming to have devised a method for gradually abolishing it. The British government was, of course, representative of the aristocratic classes who were still politically powerful and who were tied by several connections to the slave holders and their allies. At home, the political rulers could not and did not wish to abandon with unseemly precipitation their class allies who still possessed West Indian plantation property and who were committed to exploiting that property by the use of slave labour. In the West Indies, the last thing they wished to see was the sudden, irreversible decline of the planter class

1 Labour and capital under slavery: Trinidad 1783-1838

which would certainly follow if their helot labour force were unceremoniously snatched away.

Accordingly, the abolition of the slave trade was, in essence, a device for prolonging slavery, preparing the way for its quick and orderly disappearance and for maintaining planter social and political hegemony after the traditional economic foundations of planter power were removed. Understandably it was only one of several devices used for this purpose. Others included, significantly, the demarcation of constitutional boundaries between the newly acquired territories whose ruling classes were weak and infirm and the older settled colonies where the long established traditions of assembly government had created more confident, powerful ruling classes who could be entrusted with the task of themselves ameliorating slavery out of existence.[39] Time was to prove the difficulties involved in implementing this manoeuvre. In the newer colonies where the ruling classes needed imperial support in order to survive, imperial supervision became a cloak under which slavery continued to flourish, even if under slightly modified auspices. In the older colonies, where the assemblies possessed and were allowed to exercise their abundant facilities for impeding imperial authority, the invitation to participate in the process of amelioration provided an opportunity to frustrate amelioration completely. In the end the British government itself, more alive to the contradictions and the perils of planter intransigence, had perforce to sweep slavery away literally over the protests of a still determined and avaricious planter establishment. And yet that, too, was not a complete sweeping away, as we shall see. *Plus ça change, plus c'est la même chose.*

Against this background, it is not difficult to understand the battle lines between labour and capital in the first decades of the nineteenth century. The abolition of the slave trade did nothing to stem the flow of slave labourers into the island. Between 1807 and 1812 slave imports continued virtually unabated, to such an extent that serious measures had to be considered for stemming the flow of the traffic.[40] The means adopted was the Registry Act which was proclaimed into law in the colony on August 31st, 1812.[41] Its objectives were firstly to stop the illegal importations of slaves by putting into practice a system of regularised enumeration of the slave population; and, secondly, to impose on the slave-owning population some measure of accountability for the slaves under their charge.

If ever there was an ineffective piece of legislation designed to secure worthwhile objectives, it was the Registry Act. In the eight years following its proclamation 3,329 slaves, many of them disguised as domestics, were illegally imported from virtually every island of the Caribbean: from Antigua (99), Barbados (237), Bermuda (118), Dominica (1,079), Grenada (1,173), Guadeloupe (226), Martinique (110), Bahamas (296), St Vincent (196), St Lucia (130). And even after steps were taken to procure the more vigorous enforcement of the registration process – the most telling of these being to refuse to recognise as property and to treat as collateral all slaves not duly registered according to law – the system continued to exercise a far from effective influence on the depredations of the planters in the colonies, Trinidad included.

By 1823 all the available evidence amounted to this: despite the abolition of the slave trade, despite the efforts to make abolition more effective and despite the registration system, slavery was not being ameliorated and nothing was further from the minds of the planters than that they should become collectively engaged in ameliorating the institution. In those islands possessing legislative assemblies, the planters used every resource available to them to interfere with, delay and frustrate any attempt to improve the lot of the slave. Even in the Crown colonies like Trinidad, the path of amelioration was not an easy one. The process of registration even when directly administered by the Crown became a casualty to conflicts of interest, nepotism, irregularity, connivance and administrative neglect.[42] Accordingly, the slave population throughout the West Indies stood in urgent need of official protection.

The main disabilities under which the slave population laboured were the following:

I. That slaves were not tied to the soil, that is, to the estates on which they lived or worked, nor or even to the territory in which they resided and could be removed at any time from the environment in which they had been born and raised and transferred elsewhere at the whim or requirement of their masters;

II. That slaves were not regarded as persons but solely as things, as objects, as property of greater or lesser value, or of no value at all;

III. That they had no recourse to the courts of law, could neither complain of ill-treatment, seek redress or even give evidence in their behalf or on behalf of any other slave or disadvantaged person in those courts;

IV. That all blacks were regarded as slaves unless they could prove otherwise; the onus of proof was not on the person claiming to

1 Labour and capital under slavery: Trinidad 1783-1838

own a slave to prove that the slave was his, but rather on the black to prove that he was not a slave;

V. That the prospects for manumission were not only bleak but often deliberately restricted;

VI. That the slave who wished to obtain manumission had no option but to do so by paying the full price of freedom, all at once, before obtaining it; there was most notably, no privilege of *coartación* or partial purchase as existed in the Spanish system;

VII. That very often the same officials to whom the slave was constrained to look for protection, officials like the governor, attorney general, judge, registrar or else were themselves slave-owners and so possessed of a natural bias against the slave;

VIII. That no facilities were available for the regular education of the slave even if that education was solely and completely religious;

IX. That family units among slaves were not legally recognised and often not respected in practice;

X. That insufficient time was allowed for the slave's own business, in particular for tending to his provision ground if he had one, and for rest, relaxation and repose; and

XI. That the slave was subject to constant and brutal punishment and to be driven like a beast when in the field at work.[43]

If these disabilities were to be reviewed the most forthright and determined plan of action, rigorously enforced, was required. From the very beginning, however, the prospects for such a plan and for such a procedure were vitiated by a continuous process of interaction between the imperial government of the day and the principal representative organisation of the planter interest in London, the West India Committee of Planters and Merchants. As soon as the government was informed of the intentions of the abolitionists in mid-April 1823 to move for the radical reform of slave system in the West Indies it contacted the West India Committee and sought out its opinion and response. In the period April to June of that year continuous negotiations between the government and the Committee resulted in a substantially watered down set of proposals which recommended:

I. That greater facilities for religious instruction be established;

II. That Sunday markets be abolished to provide more opportunity for attending church and generally for observing the Sabbath;

III. That the flogging of females be abolished;

IV. That the use of the driving whip in the field as a symbol of authority be prohibited;

V. That punishment be supervised and recorded;

VI. That slaves be permitted to make complaints against their masters and be protected while doing so;

V1. That slave property be secured under law;

VIII. That slave evidence be admitted under certain conditions; and

IX. That manumission be facilitated.[44]

In other words, notwithstanding the substantial modifications of the new proposals slaves were:

(a) continuously to be regarded as property;
(b) to be movable at will by their owners;
(c) to be burdened with supplying proof of manumission if freed and subsequently challenged;
(d) to benefit from no legal recognition of the marriage bond;
(e) to continue to be subjects to the authority of officials who were slaveowners;
(f) to have no particular allotment of time for their own business;
(g) to remain subject to brutal, but supervised and recorded, punishment.[45]

In recommending the proposals to the resident plantocracy in the West Indies, the West India Committee of Planters and Merchants voiced its anxiety to have them adopted as speedily as possible since it viewed "with the greatest alarm, the effect which may be produced on the minds of the negroes by the reports which will reach them – liable to be both misinterpreted and misunderstood – of the discussion of such a question in Parliament".[46] Additionally, they specifically proposed that the measures should be implemented by recourse to a two-tiered approach within the colonies.[47]

In the Crown colonies the imperial executive should itself undertake a specific plan for achieving the amelioration of the condition of the slaves. In those territories possessing legislative assemblies, proposals similar to those introduced by executive fiat in the Crown colonies should be introduced by specific enactments of those legislatures.

Furthermore, in a report written to alert the colonial sugar interests about the state of metropolitan opinion, the Committee informed its West Indian associates that

1 Labour and capital under slavery: Trinidad 1783-1838

a deep and general, though undoubtedly most unjust and unmerited, impression has been created that the colonial legislatures have been hitherto very remiss and that what they have done, has been done rather with the hope of temporizing them with the intention of realizing the expectation of the British public, and of raising the negro in the scale of society... [everything should be done] to remove such a prejudice against the West Indian local governments.[48]

In other words, a programme of amelioration must be speedily adopted; otherwise, it might be forced upon the planters "by some decided act of interference by the British Parliament".[49]

These were prophetic words. In due course, given the stubborn resistance of the West Indian plantocracy, this is precisely what would have to be done. For the time being, however, the Committee emphasised that stubbornness on the part of the West Indian assemblies might result in an accelerated movement towards the equalisation of sugar duties, a measure which the colonial interest feared more than the devil himself; and counselled that the best method of dealing with the amelioration question was not to oppose it but to take control of the programme and to implement it themselves – the operative principle being that the slaves "should look up to those who have immediate authority over them, and not to the British Parliament, British Government or British public – as their protectors – and as the authors of any indulgence or benefit which can be extended to them... "[50] Nor, least of all, to themselves!

All of this is supremely instructive, the more so since the amelioration programme that emerged was quite clearly a negotiated arrangement between the government and the West India Committee accepted by the abolitionists as better than nothing but far less than that for which they had hoped. What it shows is that official policy was very much the outcome of backstair dealing between the government and the representatives of the planting interest. But, even more importantly, it unveils the tactics of the planting interest whose every move was inspired by the apprehension that the planters in the colonies would fail to recognise the importance of publicly associating themselves with what was an inevitable development in the slave issue. Metropolitan opinion interested in the perpetuation of planter hegemony in the West Indies recognised the great benefit to be gained, in terms of the future development of the society and of the planter's position in it, by avoiding an open break between planter and slave; rather, the latter should be encouraged to believe that any improvement in his social position derived from the goodwill of the former. To have the slave believe that such improvement occurred *despite* his master's opposition was to weaken the bond of authority and dependence unfavourably to the master's position.[51]

Ultimately, this tactic was to be the inspiration of all major acts of executive intervention on the slave question, as amelioration, apprenticeship, emancipation and the policies of the post-emancipation period amply testify. For the time being, however, these pleadings fell on deaf ears. Angered by the proposals and provoked beyond restraint, the West Indian assemblies responded as they were accustomed. In the Jamaica Assembly calls were made for the dismissal of Earl Bathurst, the Secretary of State, and for the secession of Jamaica from the British Empire.[52] In Barbados, the passions of the planters were visited on the head of William Shrewsbury, a dissenting missionary, and he was forced to flee the island for fear of his life.[53] In Demerara, where the slaves actually revolted in the belief that their masters were depriving them of the freedom which the King had given them, another missionary John Smith ended up in jail where he died.[54] Ultimately, years were to pass before any serious measures were adopted by some of the assemblies and then only after incessant prodding and pleading by the British government.

But it was not only in the colonies possessing legislative assemblies that the amelioration programme ran into trouble. Even in the Crown colonies it was stoutly resisted; and it was only the overwhelming authority residing in the hands of the Crown and its officials that prevented an open and reckless rebellion against the amelioration proposals. In Trinidad, for example, the promulgation of the Order in Council giving effect to the measures triggered off a series of protest meetings which in late 1823 and early 1824 provided an opportunity for trenchant criticism and recrimination.

At Arima, on September 29th, resolutions were passed declaring that interference with the 'right' to inflict punishment was subversive of discipline on the estates. It was also argued that to force planters to punish on the day after that on which an offence was committed was to imply that planters usually punished their slaves under the influence of uncontrolled passion, which they declared they were not in the habit of doing.[55]

At Naparima, on October 16th, a meeting of proprietors declared that, contrary to what the government might have thought, to have witnesses at the place of punishment was not an amelioration but a burden and an added aggravation of the punishment inflicted on offenders. Four days later, at Pointe a Pierre, the proprietors swore that "flogging is the most *humane*, prompt and efficacious mode to

1 Labour and capital under slavery: Trinidad 1783-1838

crush disorderly behaviour".⁵⁶ William Burnley, the largest planter in the island, was incensed by the prohibition of female flogging and declared that

> the idea appears to me so monstrous and extraordinary that I hardly know how to approach the subject... Strange deed, it appears to be to bestow on our female slaves prerogatives never to be aspired to or enjoyed by their free sisters in Africa and to attempt to arrest an immutable law of nature by a British Order in Council.⁵⁷

In the Council of Advice, efforts were made to have the amelioration order suspended on the grounds of hardship and the subversion of good order and discipline. Such efforts failed, but the governors were more often than not anxious advocates of planter protest constantly explaining away abuse on the ground of human frailty, arguing the difficulties of implementing the law as written and even proposing, as Woodford did, that "some boon in the shape of special bounty to the produce of the colony" be given so as to encourage the planters "to cheerfully cooperate in a measure which they now feel exposes to danger and to risk the property of themselves and their children".⁵⁸

It is not too much to say, in the light of the evidence, that the response of the planters in the Crown colonies foreshadowed, even though in lesser degree, the ultimate failure of amelioration. Even in these territories where, owing to the power of the Crown, slavery arguably existed in its mildest form, the tally of punishments was a standing rebuke to the inefficiency of the amelioration system. According to a return of the Protector of Slaves in Trinidad submitted by Woodford to the secretary of state on February 26th, 1827, punishments administered totalled 11,131; punishments administered in jail totalled 865: 11,996 punishments in all, visited on an adult slave population numbering 16,298.⁵⁹ Woodford himself was embarrassed by the statistics and could only offer the lamest of explanations:

> Although the proportion of offenders of 11 to 16 may appear large, yet your Lordship will see that serious offences such as would subject the perpetrators to loss of liberty at least in Europe, appear here expiated by the domestic correction of the Proprietor, who too often prefers to pass over the crime than surrender his slave to justice.⁶⁰

True; but not out of consideration for the slave! The fact was simply that the slave as property was far more productive on the estate where he could be returned to the field after punishment than cooling his heels in jail at an economic cost to the planter. In other words, he was 'better off' than his European counterpart not because he was of higher social status but because he had none at all. He was, as property, a mere thing.

It was not only in Trinidad that this predilection for frequent, if regulated, punishment was manifested. In British Guiana, in 1828, 10,054 punishments were inflicted in one six-month period on a population of 62,352 slaves.[61] As James Stephen pointed out:

> This is at the rate of 20,000 and upwards per annum, so that every third slave in Demerara receives a punishment once a year. No less than 4,265 were punished under the heads of 'neglect of duty' and 'not doing a day's work'. If in this country the labouring classes had been punished in the same proportion there would have been in the United Kingdom between six and seven millions of punishments in the last year. This, it must also be observed, is the *improved* condition of society. What it must have been before the necessity of making these matters known was established by law, it would be difficult to imagine.

And he continued, not unreasonably:

> While such is the number of punishments which have befallen the slaves, the Protector has not found occasion to commence a single prosecution against any owner, manager, or overseer in the colony during the last half year..."[62]

If prosecutions of the master were rare, punishments of the slave were the exact opposite. In the former Crown colonies it was estimated that 68,921 punishments were registered in the two-year period 1828-29. Of these, notwithstanding what the law said, 25,094 were inflicted on women. Very often as well the legal limit of 25 lashes was executed. The abolitionists estimated that at a nominal average of 20 lashes for each punishment, the number of strokes delivered would have been more than 1,350,000. What was more, as Buxton was to argue in the House of Commons on April 15th, 1831, the slave population had annually decreased in the period 1807-1830 despite substantial importations. In the 23-year period, the West Indian slave population had dropped by 100,000 from 800,000 to 700,000. In the decade 1821-31, in the midst of amelioration, the slave population had decreased by 45,800. Obviously, the lash of the whip was taking its toll.[63]

Added to the whip, however, was hard work – a factor which, no matter how abundantly contributed, is never deemed to be sufficient by critics of the labouring poor who, more often than not, ascribe their poverty to an aversion to 'hard work'. "The whip," Buxton remarked, "is not the cause of mortality. It is extreme toil." And so it

1 Labour and capital under slavery: Trinidad 1783-1838

was indeed. Already the planters were engaged in extracting the last ounce of labour power in what in their bones they felt to be the last years of slavery. In Trinidad, the apprehensions occasioned by the amelioration order added to the opening up of the largely uncultivated virgin soils of the island, resulted in the stepped up expansion of productive output and consequently the stepped up exploitation of labour.

In Trinidad in the years between 1812 and 1827-28, that is, from the Registry Act to the later years of the decade in which amelioration was introduced, the production figures for the island's two main commodities reflected the galloping acceleration of output stimulated by the planters' response to registration and amelioration. In tonnage produced, sugar nearly doubled between 1812 (6,800 tons) and 1827 (11,979 tons). Cocoa increased nearly sixfold: from 640,732 lbs in 1811 to 3,695,144 lbs in 1827.[64] When one considers that the slave population increased between December 1811 and December 1827 from 21,143 to only 23,164 despite importations, the conclusion to be drawn from the greatly increased output by a marginally greater slave stock can be expressed in two phrases: extreme hard work and high mortality. And neither manumissions (totalling 2,279 between 1811 and 1828) nor the presence of a significant free labouring element in cocoa growing, estimated at 5,720 'free proprietors' in 1828, significantly detracts from this conclusion. The production figures speak for themselves and so does the mortality rate. Between 1813 and 1828, total recorded slave deaths amounted to 11,473; births totalled 7,477, giving rise to a net natural decline of 3,996.[65]

The fact was that all the measures taken by the British government beginning with the Registry Act stimulated in the minds of the planter a serious concern for his property rights in the slave. Registration, amelioration, apprenticeship and emancipation, as far as the planter was concerned, transgressed the planter's claim, largely recognised up to that point, to do with the slave as he wished subject only to such public and other considerations that might from time to time apply. In fact, the British government itself had long ago conceded the right of the planter to treat the slave largely as he wished by putting the initiative for regulating slavery by law in the hands of the planters. It was only because it had chosen to interpret the slave trade as an issue of imperial regulation, being international, that the traffic was abolished. Planter property in slaves was a different matter, not to be brushed away lightly by a stroke of the pen or by Act of Parliament.

As the contradictions within slavery and between the supporters of slavery and their opponents developed, however, this Chinese wall limiting the jurisdiction of the imperial power over slavery slowly collapsed even though successive British governments tried hard to maintain it. As for the planters, it is arguable that by spurning the advice of their more sophisticated allies in Britain and by refusing to adopt the government's policy as their own and to temporise, procrastinate and dally along the way while pretending to cooperate, they hastened the complete collapse which they hoped to avoid by intransigence and confrontation.

As time went on even the figures of production began to reflect the impact of the strongly developing race and class struggles between the planters and the slaves. With the onset of the 1830s, an irresistible decline overtook the main crops, particularly sugar and cocoa, in respect of both of which production decreased markedly. Sugar production peaked at 16,980 tons in 1834, declined to 14,312 tons in 1838 and bottomed out at 12,288 in 1840. Cocoa fell from 3,695,144 lbs in 1827 to 1,417,047 lbs in 1831, climbing again in 1838 to 2,212,486 lbs.[66]

All of this was, to say the least, not unexpected. By 1830, the writing was clearly on the wall for all who wished to read it. Even the most moderate of the abolitionists were beginning to be converted to the prospect of immediate abolition. And their leader, Buxton, averred that "all attempts at gradual evolution [towards emancipation] are wild and visionary". In May, he proposed "at the earliest period the entire abolition of slavery throughout the British dominions". By July of the same year he was able to boast with conscious irony born of the fruit of planter intransigence:

> Our slavery concerns go on well: the religious public has at least taken the field. The West Indians have done us good service. They have of late flogged slaves in Jamaica for praying and imprisoned the missionaries and they have given the nation to understand that preaching and praying are offences not to be tolerated in a slave colony. That is right – it exhibits slavery in its true colours – it enforces your doctrine, that, if you wish to teach religion to slaves, the first thing is, to put down slavery.[67]

Goaded by the abolitionists but confronted more than anything else with the clearest proofs of planter resistance to the amelioration programme, the British government introduced a new 'stiffened' Order in Council on November 2nd, 1831 which

(a) limited the hours of slave labour;

(b) regulated the issue of food rations and clothing; and

1 Labour and capital under slavery: Trinidad 1783-1838

(c) empowered the Protectors of Slaves (dubbed by the planters as 'salaried informers') to enter estates and slave huts on suspicion of an offence committed against a slave or slaves.[68]

In a circular despatch communicating the provisions of the Order to the islands possessing legislative assemblies, the Secretary of State, Lord Goderich, himself read the requiem for the British tactics pursued thus far: "The cause of authoritative admonition has been pursued for eight years and has been. . . utterly unsuccessful."[69]

It had not only been unsuccessful, it was to continue to be unsuccessful. All the legislatures scorned the new Bill and none of them saw fit to adopt it, not even in face of the fact that the British government indicated that it was willing to ease the passage of the measure by providing for the economic relief of the colonies. In particular, it was offered, the lowering of duties on West Indian sugar would be promptly and urgently conceded.

The new Bill survived a storm of protest. Jamaica declared that any measures for the amelioration of the slave population must proceed from its own initiative and no one else's, overlooking completely that that was precisely the plan which the imperial government wished it to follow. In addition, they proposed that a standing army be raised for the island's defence and, once again, proposed annexation to the United States of America. Antigua described the measures as "ruinous in their effects, being compatible neither with the safety of the Colony, nor with a fair and equitable consideration of the rights of property". In St Lucia storekeepers closed their shops for a week with less effect than was achieved one hundred-and-fifty-odd years later when their descendants did the same with more effect, and thus removed a beleaguered Labour Party government from power.

The Tobago Assembly rebuffed the imperial government with the retort that:

> The direction of His Majesty's Government to pass a law in the very words of the Order in Council, without allowing the Legislature to alter its language, or to adapt it to local circumstances, is a species of distortion before unheard of, and appears to be a first step towards depriving the Colony of its Charter and Constitution, and the Legislature of the deliberative power of enacting laws for the internal government of the island.
>
> The House will always be ready and willing, as occasion may require, to enact any further measure that may be necessary for the improvement of the Slave Population; but they must protest in the most solemn manner against the endeavour to enforce the Order in Council and without particularly setting themselves up in opposition to the wishes of His Majesty's Government, this House

is determined to oppose by every legal and constitutional means the attempt thus made to legislate for the Colony, and therefore will take no further notice of same.[70]

In Trinidad, the Order in Council, proclaimed into law on January 7th, 1832, was promptly dubbed the 'Code Noir' and roundly denounced. Every species of mischief and bad consequence was laid at the door of the Order. Joseph Marryat, the island's Agent in London, described the Order as one of the major factors militating against the success of the sugar industry.[71] For three years previously the weather had been bad and sugar prices had been falling. The price of £1 4s 11d per hundred weight for sugar was less than half as much the £3 9s 9d that prevailed in 1814. Cocoa was in the toils and sugar and cocoa estates were threatened with ruin on all sides. The Order in Council provided just that element needed to focus planter hostility on a single object, and it did. The 'Code Noir' consolidated the anger of the planting community, particularly, by reference to those of its provisions which prescribed criminal prosecution for any master ill-treating his slave, even to the point of terminating the owner's property rights in the slave on grounds of cruelty. Accordingly, what can only be described as a judge's strike ensued with the result that the *alcaldes* refused to prosecute offenders brought up before them.[72]

It was not long before the turmoil raging among the official and propertied classes percolated down to the slaves and stimulated a significant response. On several estates unrest, sabotage and arson broke out, and some strikes took place. At Palmiste Estate in Carapichaima, at Felicity Hall, Cascade and elsewhere there were clear signs of turmoil. The slave population was agitated and expectant. And with St Domingue clearly in the minds of the planters in several areas, particularly in North and South Naparima, and in Port of Spain and the estates surrounding it, precautionary measures were taken. In the city, the *Cabildo* organised a Committee of Safety of 200 men to patrol and keep the peace.[73] After a few estates had been burnt, the *Port of Spain Gazette* voiced the planters' apprehensions as follows:

> A few days will, we fear, prove beyond a doubt that they [the fires] are only more of the workings of the villainous Order in Council of the 2nd November – that prolonged scourge invented by the 'Saints' of Downing Street to goad to madness the oppressed, insulted and bitterly persecuted West Indian planters. The die had at last been thrown – the work of devastation had been commenced – Heaven only knows where it will stop.[74]

1 Labour and capital under slavery: Trinidad 1783-1838

The events of this period are correctly to be perceived as the result of the sharply increasing tensions between masters and slaves in what was clearly becoming the terminal period of the slave era. In all the islands, in greater or lesser degree, these tensions were being felt and in some notable instances they were productive of great violence. In Jamaica, for example, in the period December 1831-January 1832 a formidable rebellion broke out affecting large numbers of slaves and bringing to the fore the rabidly anti-democratic spirit of the planters. Not only did they put down the rebellion with the expected ferocity, but organised bands of them, operating under the nomenclature of the Colonial Church Union, turned upon the missionaries who ministered to the slaves, destroyed their chapels, abused them and embarked on an orgy of vengeance and bloodletting which only closed when the state, taking the initiative, allowed the law "to take its course". Consequentially several of the black leaders were executed, some of the missionaries were brought to trial and the unsuccessful prosecution of Edward Jordan, a prominent free coloured editor and newspaper proprietor, was undertaken.[75]

Ultimately it was this incidence of resistance, rebellion, arson, sabotage and strike action that precipitated the final collapse of slavery. On May 24th, 1832 the reformed British parliament, itself the product of the new economic and political forces presaging the rise of European and British liberalism, appointed a Committee

> to consider and report upon the measures which it may be expedient to adopt for the purpose of effecting the extinction of slavery throughout the British Dominions, at the earliest period compatible with the safety of all classes in the Colonies, and in conformity with the Resolutions of this House on the 15th day of May, 1823.[76]

History is proud to record that before the Committee could finish its investigations, circumstances had again moved so far forward as to force the government to bring forward on May 14th, 1833 a plan for the immediate abolition of slavery.[77]

Thereafter, apprenticeship prevailed. In the chronicle of the emancipation process there is a continuing counterpoint between gradual and immediate emancipation. Apprenticeship was another surrender to the gradualistic idea. It demonstrated above all the imperialist determination that if emancipation had to be accomplished it was better that it was not accomplished quickly. Ostensibly, apprenticeship had two principal objectives: one, to prepare the slaves for freedom; and two, to provide the planters with a period of adjustment to the reality of having to make do without slave labour. In reality, however, its objective was simply and baldly to ensure the survival of the old positions of power and privilege accorded to the white plantocracy even after the economic props upon which that position had been based were demolished.

In any significant meaning of the event, the emancipation of the slaves ought to and would indeed have destroyed planter ascendancy if possessed of two complementary characteristics: one, that it was immediate; and two, that it was unaccompanied by unusual initiatives aimed at perpetuating in essence the economic and social domination of ex-master over ex-slave.

But it was precisely these two factors which the British government was unwilling to allow to emerge. This was why, for example, in the final analysis emancipation became a political match sprint between the administration and the slaves (to ensure that the slaves did not free themselves) and a devil-take-the-hindmost between the administration and the planters (to ensure that emancipation did not come until it could absolutely no longer be prevented). There is a time element to revolutionary change which qualitatively determines the character of the transformation that ensues. Given time, even the most worn out, discredited and incompetent order can so adjust itself as to become part of the solution to the problem which it has itself created. As worn out and discredited as the old plantocracy was, Britain was determined that it should be provided with sufficient time to make the necessary adjustments. On the eve of emancipation, apprenticeship was the instrument selected to achieve that objective; and the struggles waged over its duration were a foreshadowing of the post-emancipation conflicts that raged around the issue of making freedom meaningful.

In the four years that ensued before slavery finally and irrevocably gave way to a new order, the contradictions between capital and labour were expressed in sharply different responses to the crises which wracked the old order. The actual events taking place within the period of apprenticeship revealed the utter bankruptcy of gradualist approaches to emancipation and the failure of apprenticeship to achieve the objectives which the British government had identified.

As before, and notwithstanding the establishment of the system of stipendiary magistrates, flogging and undue punishment continued to be the bane and burden of the slave population. In fact, this was partly the result of the failure to establish the stipendiary system in any meaningful way. It was officially proclaimed in eleven districts on October 19th, 1835 but none of the two magistrates appointed had arrived in the island by emancipation day. As a result local officials

1 Labour and capital under slavery: Trinidad 1783-1838

such as commandants, assistant commandants, selected individuals in the various quarters – in a word, the plantocracy – were pressed into service. It was not to be wondered at, therefore, that the previously high incidence of punishments was maintained.[78]

In the period August 1834 to June 1835 in four districts – Port of Spain and Western, St Joseph, Tacarigua, and Eastern – 1,601 punishments were inflicted on a total adult apprenticed population of 8,079, a ratio of 1 to 5. Of these 48.5 per cent were whipped and placed in stocks; 23.2 per cent were subjected to hard labour; and 28.4 per cent were subjected to extra labour. What is more, the figures showed only a slightly appreciable distinction between punishments visited on men or women: 951 males as against 750 females.[79] When one considers that these figures relate to recorded punishments for a period of eleven months in one section of the island, one is impressed by the continuingly high incidence of punishments.

Indeed, figures for North and South Naparima, Carapichaima, and Southern Districts for the quarterly period April 1st to June 30th, 1835 reveal an incidence of 771 punishments (353 males, 418 females) in a population of 8,510 persons; or, at a yearly rate, 3,084 punishments affecting 36.2 per cent of the population. Even in respect of punishments administered under the authority of the special (stipendiary) magistrates in the period November 1st, 1835 to May 31st, 1836 a total of 1,370 punishments were inflicted, the enormity of which the Colonial Office statistician tried to mask by rendering per centages against the total population on a month by month basis: in the event, the proportions varied between 1 and 3/5 per cent per month. More to the point, on an annual rate, the punishments numbered 2,349 or 14.65 per cent of the apprenticed population at a ratio of 1 to 7 of that population at its greatest extent (16,030) in that year.[80]

What was also extraordinary was that punishment by whipping, confinement, stocks, etc. alternated with the frequent sentence to 'hard' or 'extra' labour. Sometimes these sentences ran for quite long periods, in several cases amounting to one to three months and at least in three recorded cases of punishment administered on the authority of the special magistrates amounting to 230 days, 17 months and 3 years respectively. Already constrained to provide labour to their masters for 45 hours per week according to the terms of the Abolition Act, the apprentices also became subject to the determination of planters to make the terminal period of slavery, in effect, as remunerative a period as possible in terms of the extraction of surplus labour. A whole range of penalties aimed at making additional labour available to the planters was introduced for a wide variety of offences.

On being absent for more than 7½ hours in any week, the apprentice was deemed to have deserted his job and became subject to a penalty of 1 week at hard labour. Absence for 2 days earned him the description of vagabond and the penalty of 2 weeks at hard labour; absence for 6 days attracted the title of runaway and the penalty of 4 weeks hard labour, plus a flogging of up to 30 lashes. For being indolent, careless or negligent in his work, the apprentice would be punished with extra work to a maximum of 15 hours or, in the case of non-praedial labourers, 15 lashes. What is more, this regime of hard and unusual punishment was supported by an increased vigilance and policing of the apprenticed population under a system of pass laws and other restrictions which had the effect of severely curtailing the freedom which the apprentice had a right to feel he had already earned. Squatting, for example, was made an offence punishable by 3 months imprisonment, as was fishing without a license. And boats could only be kept on license granted by the governor. One cannot help but feel that the range of offences declared and the punishments imposed were all part of a system aimed at providing the plantocracy with free "hard and extra labour".[81]

Another major area of conflict, as was well known, was over the length of the working day. In respect of the 45 hours which the apprentice was forced to give freely to his master, an immediate and fundamental conflict developed. From the point of view of the apprentice, if the hours had to be worked then the sooner they were worked the better. For him the most efficacious arrangement would have been a mix of the fewest number of days and the longest hours: 4 days of 11¼ hours or 4 days at 10½ hours followed by a period of 3 hours on the fifth day, or 5 days at 9 hours. Not so for the master: for him the best equation was one which tied up the apprentice for as long as possible in estate employment and reduced his capacity to increase his level of independence by being about his own business for as much of his time as he could. Accordingly, in a feigned excess of zeal for the apprentice's well-being, the master often opted for one of the following formulae: five days of 8 hours, followed by one half day of 5 hours; or at best 4 days of 10 hours followed by one half day of 5 hours.[82]

All of this speaks directly to the point of the single-mindedness with which planters pursued the goal of securing a hard, extra and inordinate labour contribution from the apprenticed population. As planters felt the bonds of authority over the apprentice loosening as a result of the provisions of the Abolition Act, they responded by attacking and attempting to undermine the status of free labourers

1 Labour and capital under slavery: Trinidad 1783-1838

as well as slaves. Within the Legislative Council itself, it was argued that it was necessary not only "to convert the coerced labour of the slave into the voluntary exertions of a hired labourer" but also "to reduce other classes of society not possessing property or other means of support to the same habits of regular industry".[83] In other words, if there were to be apprentices then the description should be extended to include not only the existing slave population but also those categories of persons who could be regarded as impoverished, vagabond and generally nondescript. Such groups, it was suggested, should include:

1. Slaves manumitted under the Abolition Act;
2. Children apprenticed under the Act;
3. Persons entering into voluntary contractual apprenticeship;
4. Vagrants or persons who, though free, were without visible means of support;
5. Free persons condemned to hard labour;
6. Slaves forfeited to the Crown in the Vice Admiralty Court;
7. Fugitive slaves from other colonies;
8. Apprentices sent out from Europe.[84]

If the system had been introduced, apprenticeship would have become a status visited on slave and free persons alike. It was not the first time that efforts had been made to draw the free labouring population into the scale of reckoning in the war against slave emancipation. In 1832 planters at Savanna Grande had argued that since the effect of the 'Code Noir' would reduce their income from the slaves by an estimated two-fifths, the rates applicable to free labour, in particular blacksmiths, carpenters, masons, coopers, etc. should similarly be reduced. It was also suggested that medical facilities such as they were on the estates should be reduced.[85]

In essence, all of these manoeuvres on the part of the plantocracy make the point more sharply than words can, that in the labour of the apprenticed and ex-slave population lay all the hopes of the planters for making a profitable return on their investments. As such, the planters could not regard with equanimity a situation in which increasing degrees of control were forfeited, bit by bit, over the slave. Every act, every desire, every species of intervention was tried in order to prolong and perpetuate the master's control over his slave and so to ensure to the former the fruits of the latter's labour. In fact, the planters resorted to psychological assault as well the vain attempt to enlist the slave himself in the campaign against abolition.

Thus spake the *Port of Spain Gazette* of July 18th, 1834 to the slave population:

> As from August 1st you will no longer be slaves but free men. You will be punishable only by the magistrates after a trial. You only have to work six more crops for your master, after which you may leave the estate or even the island. But when your masters are unable to make you work for them, you cannot compel them to give you your allowance of clothing; to care for you when you are sick or aged; or to provide you with house or garden. These things you must do for yourselves.[86]

In other words, the apprentices were better off as slaves! History is again proud to record that the apprentices were singularly unimpressed and continued to struggle with might and main to enlarge the boundaries of their freedom. History also needs to record that the text and tone of this statement foreshadowed the struggles which ensued after emancipation in the course of which imperialism secured for the plantocracy a victory which otherwise it would have been completely denied.

1 Labour and capital under slavery: Trinidad 1783-1838

Notes

1. Karl Marx, *Capital*, 3 vols (Moscow, 1978 edition), vol. 1, p.253.
2. Karl Marx, "Wage Labour and Capital," in Marx and Engels, *Selected Works*, vol. 1 (Moscow, 1977 edn), p.74.
3. E. L Joseph, *History of Trinidad* (Trinidad, 1837), p. 174. For summary of slave code see pp.174-75.
4. Slave code, clause 13.
5. Joseph, op. cit., p.176.
6. Elsa Goveia, *The West Indian Slave Laws of the 18th Century* (St Lawrence, Barbados, 1970), pp. 44, 48.
7. Franklin Knight, *Slave Society in Cuba during the Nineteenth Century* (Madison, Wisconsin, 1970), p.191.
8. William Wilberforce, *Negro Slavery* (London, 1823); reprinted in *Slavery in the West Indies* (New York, 1969), p.33.
9. Also, James Millette, *The Genesis of Crown Colony Government, 1783-1810* (Trinidad, 1970), pp.242ff.
10. Ibid., pp.17-18; and note 76, p.17.
11. Joseph, op. cit., pp.166-67.
12. Ibid., p.166; also p.206.
13. Ibid., p.166.
14. Ibid., p.167.
15. Ibid., p.169.
16. Ibid., p.169.
17. Elsa Goveia, op. cit., p.48. Quoted.
18. Ibid., pp.44, 48.
19. Knight, op. cit., p.3.
20. Ibid., p.93.
21. Ibid., p.191.
22. Wilberforce, op. cit.
23. Millette, op. cit., pp.246-47.
24. Ibid.
25. Ibid., pp.17-18; Joseph, op. cit., pp.166-67.
26. "The Royal Cedula of Population of 20 November, 1783", Article 4. See L.M. Fraser, *History of Trinidad, 1781-1839*, 2 vols (Trinidad, 1891-1896), vol. 1, Appendix, pp.i-v (abridged).
27. Joseph, op. cit., pp.106-107.
28. Ibid., p.167.
29. Ibid.
30. Ibid.
31. Ibid., p.169.
32. Ibid., pp.166-67, 169.
33. The *cédula* permitted "the old and new settlers to propose... through the Governor, such Ordinances as shall be most proper for regulating the treatment of their slaves and preventing their flight".
34. Joseph, op. cit., p.169.
35. See Millette, op. cit., pp.61-65.
36. Ibid., pp.79-80.
37. *Parliamentary Register*, Lords and Commons, Vol.18, 1802, pp.535-65, and passim.
38. See Eric Williams, "The International Slave Trade after its Abolition in 1807," *Journal of Negro History*, Vol.XXVII (April 1942).
39. See, for example, R.L. Schuyler, *Parliament and the British Empire* (Columbia, 1929), ch. IV; and D.J. Murray, *The West Indies and the Development of Colonial Government* (London, 1965).
40. Williams, op. cit.; also see his *Documents on British West Indian History, 1807-1833* (Trinidad, 1952), p.385, table 6.
41. C.O. 295/28, pp.250-64: "Order-in-Council for the Registration of Slaves in Trinidad," March 26, 1812; C.O. 298/5, "Minutes of the Board of Cabildo," August 31, 1812.
42. See British *Parliamentary Papers (PP)*, 1824, XXIV, 427, Schedule 3, pp.141-58.
43. See Vincent Harlow and Frederick Madden (eds.), *British Colonial Developments: Select Documents, 1774-1834* (Oxford, 1953), pp.556-57 for a statement of what really was the maximum programme of the abolitionists at this time.
44. Ibid., p.558.
45. Ibid., pp.558-59.
46. Ibid., p.559.

45

47 See Schuyler, op. cit., chap. IV; also, W.L. Mathieson, *British Slavery and Its Abolition, 1823-1838* (London, 1926); and F.J. Klingberg, *The Anti-Slavery Movement in England* (Oxford, 1926).
48 Harlow and Madden, op. cit., p.558.
49 Ibid., p.559.
50 Ibid., p.559.
51 Ibid., pp.558-59.
52 Mathieson, op. cit., pp.133-34.
53 Ibid., pp.161-63; also, see Stiv Jakobson, *Am I Not a Man and a Brother?* (Uppsala, 1972), pp.374-91.
54 Mathieson, op. cit., pp.148-49.
55 Williams, *Documents* ...; Resolutions of the General Meeting, Arima (September 29, 1823).
56 Ibid., Meeting at Pointe-a-Pierre (October 20, 1823).
57 Ibid., Opinion of Mr. Burnley on 1823 Resolutions.
58 Ibid., Woodford to Bathurst, May 7, 1824.
59 C.O. 295/74, Woodford to Bathurst, February 26, 1827.
60 Ibid.
61 Williams, *Documents*..., Governor D'Urban's despatch of December 5, 1828. Quoted, p.149.
62 Ibid.
63 John Harris, *A Century of Emancipation* (London, 1933), pp.43-44.
64 Williams, *Docments*..., p.387, Table 8.
65 Ibid., p.384, Table 4.
66 L.M. Fraser, op. cit., vol.II, pp.302, 370.
67 Harris, op. cit., p.41. Quoted.
68 Harlow and Madden, op.cit., pp.579ff; 581-82.
69 *PP*, 1831-32, XLVI, "Slave Melioration Papers", p.9.
70 Schuyler, op. cit., p.174. Quoted.
71 *PP*, 1831-32, XX, "Minutes of Evidence before Select Committee on the Commercial State of the West Indies", p.148. Q. 121.
72 L.M. Fraser, op. cit., vol.II, pp.276ff.
73 Noel Titus, "Amelioration and Emancipation in Trinidad, 1812-1834," MA thesis, UWI (1974), pp.233-34, chs 8 and 9, passim.
74 *Port of Spain Gazette* (March 25, 1832).
75 See Mavis C. Campbell, *The Dynamics of Change in a Slave Society* (New Jersey, 1976), chs 4 & 5.
76 Harlow and Madden, op. cit., p.587.
77 *PP*, 1836 (166), Vol. XLIX, "Papers in Explanation of Measures Adopted for Giving Effect to the Abolition of Slavery".
78 Ibid. See also, Raphael Sebastien, "Pre-capitalist Relations of Production in Trinidad from the Pre-Columbian Era to the End of Apprenticeship," UWI, St Augustine (1982), typescript, pp.117ff.
79 Sebastien, op. cit., table no.2, p.124; and *PP*, 1836, (166), No. XLIX.
80 Sebastien, op. cit., Table No. 3, Returns... of Punishments Received by Lieutenant Governor of Trinidad, from the Special Magistrates, from 1 November 1835 to 31 May 1836; *PP*,1836, (166), No. XLIV.
81 Ordinance of June 1834, Cap. 5, Sections 4-6. See also Titus, op. cit., pp.264-66.
82 See W.E. Riviere, "The Emergence of a Free Labour Economy in the British West Indies, 1800–1850," PhD thesis, Glasgow (1968); also, "The Apprenticeship System in the Colonies", *PP*, 1836 (560), XV ; and 1837(510), Vol. VII.
83 Titus, op. cit., p.263.
84 Ibid., p.264.
85 C.O. 295/101, "Proposed Report on the System of Apprentice Laws"; also, Titus, op. cit., p.264.
86 *Port of Spain Gazette* (July 18, 1834).

CHAPTER TWO

Freedom before Emancipation: Manumission in Trinidad, 1808-1830[1]

Margaret D. Rouse-Jones

Manumission[2] was infrequent in the British West Indian sugar-producing islands during the late seventeenth and first three quarters of the eighteenth centuries.[3] Sugar production was on the increase and planters were not inclined to free slaves. In Barbados, as early as 1692 and 1707, laws existed which outlined the conditions under which freedom could be granted, but relatively few slaves were manumitted as a result Manumission by self-purchase was not in fact specified by law, and although custom permitted the practice, it rarely occurred. Manumission only became more frequent in Barbados and Jamaica during the later years of slavery.[4]

The increase in the numbers of slaves manumitted in the early nineteenth century has been linked to the decline in sugar production. When there was economic depression such as occurred towards the end of the eighteenth century, manumission was more frequent, as it was uneconomical for a planter to keep and maintain a large contingent of slaves who were not producing. Also during a period of economic decline, it was likely that a planter would offer manumission at a lower price than usual.[5] Thus manumission was more likely to occur in a slave society in economic decline rather than one where sugar production was on the increase or at its peak.[6]

During the early nineteenth century, Trinidad was at the same stage of development as Jamaica, Barbados and the other Leeward Islands had been during the late seventeenth and first half of the eighteenth centuries: large scale settlement and development had only recently taken place and the production of sugar and other crops was on the increase. In 1783, the Spanish *cédula* provided incentives for settlers to come to Trinidad and the population, which had been a mere 2,763 then, had risen to 17,712 in 1797 at the time of its capture by the British.[7] In 1808, the total population had almost doubled to 32,478 of which 21,895 were slaves (see Table 1).[8] Many of the new

47

settlers, landed proprietors from other West Indian islands, had been attracted to Trinidad by the reputed potential of the land and the generous provisions of the *cédula*, and they replicated the patterns of economic activity they had known in their earlier homes, concentrating on sugar and other types of agricultural production. In March 1797 there were only 238 landed proprietors in the island[9] but, within a decade, their number had increased considerably to at least 517.[10]

Table 1
Slave Population in Trinidad, 1808-1828

Year	Males	Females	Children	Total
1808	12,357	9,416	-	21,895
1809	12,104	9,439	-	21,475
1810	11,605	9,023	-	20,729
1811	11,827	9,316	-	21,288
1812	-	-	-	-
1813	10,917	8,206	6,594	25,717
1814	10,018	7,944	6,367	24,329
1815	10,110	7,983	7,778	25,871
1816	-	-	-	24,846
1817	-	-	-	23,828
1818	-	-	-	21,310
1819	9,419	7,868	6,402	23,039
1820	-	-	-	24,868
1821	-	-	-	21,719
1822	9,017	7,732	6,478	23,227
1823	12,144	11,101	-	23,245
1824	11,908	11,209	-	23,117
1825	13,062	11,465	-	23,227
1826	12,008	11,115	-	23,123
1827	11,772	11,292	-	23,064
1828	11,528	10,908	-	22,436

Source: Figures for 1808-1821 are taken from Eric Williams, *Documents on British West Indian History, 1807-1833* (Select documents from the Public Record Office London, England relating to the Colonies of Barbados, British Guiana, Jamaica, and Trinidad) (Port of Spain, 1952), Appendix III, Tables 1 & 2, pp.380-84; British Sessional Papers, House of Commons (hereafter *BSPHC*), Vol. XXI, 1830.

In 1808, therefore, sugar production was still a relatively recent phenomenon in Trinidad. The year 1787 is generally accepted as the date of the establishment of the first sugar mill. However, even before its capture by the British diversified agricultural production was evident. In 1797 there were 159 sugar plantations, 130 devoted to coffee, 100 to cotton, and 60 cocoa farms.[11] The list of Crown lands still available for settlement in 1797 detailed 420,160 acres suitable for sugar production, 302,400 acres for coffee, 50,560 acres for cotton

2 Manumission in Trinidad, 1808-1830

and 97,280 acres for cocoa.[12] For this reason, Trinidad probably did not qualify as a sugar plantation society at the beginning of the nineteenth century in the same sense as did Jamaica, Barbados and the Leeward islands, where there was much heavier emphasis on sugar production. Eric Williams has stated that in 1833 Trinidad was not a plantation society but "a society of small estates operated by a few slaves", with the average owner possessing about seven slaves.[13] Moreover, large-scale sugar production had only been introduced after 1783.

At the same time however, Trinidad, compared with the other islands, had great potential, which if exploited could lead to significant progress which was obviously vital at this stage of its development. In a report to the Secretary of State concerning the affairs of the colony, Governor Sir Thomas Picton wrote that planters who had had experience with Trinidad's soil found it more conducive to the growing of sugar cane than that of any other West Indian island. He added that with much less "art and intelligence" in methods of sugar manufacture, a far finer quality of sugar could be produced in much larger quantities.[14] Several years later, Joseph Marryat, former agent to the island, wrote that the soil of Trinidad was "very fertile and very rich".[15]

In addition to the fertility of the soil itself, the cultivable land area was underutilised on account of the shortage of labour. In 1797 only about four per cent of the land was under cultivation. There were some 10,000 slaves at that time and by one estimate it would have required some 250,000 slaves to exploit the island's land potential.[16] In 1808, the slave population was only 21,895, clearly insufficient for expansion.

The demand for slaves was further emphasised by the fact that the more slaves a settler had, the better able he would have been to take advantage of incentives offered. In 1815 a proclamation by Governor Sir Ralph Woodford declared that the government would only grant Crown lands to those persons who could first show that they had the means to cultivate the land and render it valuable. Furthermore, grants of land were given on the condition that one quarter of the land had to be cultivated within a period of five years from the date of the grant. Failure to meet this requirement resulted in the land being reclaimed by the Crown.[17] Thus without sufficient labour, planters on Crown lands were in danger of losing their means of livelihood.

The labour situation in the West Indies was completely different in 1808 from what it had been at the time of the growth and development of the older West Indian sugar islands. Britain had abolished the slave trade in 1807, thus cutting Trinidad off from the main source of slave supply. Settlers who came to the island did bring their slaves with them and some 3,600 slaves were introduced into Trinidad between 1813 and 1821. But the supply clearly was insufficient to solve the labour shortage, and the problem remained.[18]

In the period under discussion, sugar production increased very rapidly. Evidence presented in Table 2 shows that between 1811 and 1827 the island's output of coffee and cotton declined and that of cocoa and sugar increased respectively by factors of 5 and 2.5.[19] But the degree of concentration on sugar far exceeded that for cocoa.

Table 2

Economic Production in Trinidad, 1811-1827

Year	Cocoa (lbs)	Coffee (lbs)	Sugar (lbs)	Cotton (lbs)
1811	640,732	276,243	18,513,302	159,136
1813	1,029,512	540,716	22,288,145	184,400
1815	1,065,808	262,289	25,075,281	115,160
1816	1,056,662	119,974	24,122,415	93,710
1817	1,341,461	215,190	22,784,767	65,951
1819	1,506,445	258,220	30,205,731	131,990
1821	1,684,114	222,890	31,127,803	52,871
1822	1,809,720	205,586	35,595,932	64,300
1823	1,892,195	245,567	37.032,618	91,550
1824	2,433,388	245,592	36,855,946	45,750
1825	2,835,935	274,735	36,280,347	58,189
1826	2,640,989	275,196	43,154,460	58,030
1827	3,229,474	248,380	44,471,619	45,630

Source: Williams, *Documents*, Appendix III, Table 6, p.385

Yet, in spite of the severe labour shortage and the increase in sugar production, manumission of slaves occurred to an extent comparable with that which was occurring in the older sugar islands (see Table 3).

Table 3

Some Manumission Returns for Antigua, Barbados, Jamaica, Trinidad, within the 1808-1830 Period

	Year	Numbers in the Registry	Decrease by manumission
Antigua	1817	32,269	not given
	1821	30,895	208
	1824	30,314	218
	1827	29,839	228
Barbados	1817	77,493	not given
	1820	78,493	250

2 Manumission in Trinidad, 1808-1830

	Year	Numbers in the Registry	Decrease by manumission
	1823	78,813	297
	1826	80,551	322
	1829	81,902	670
Jamaica	1817	346,150	not given
	1820	324,382	1,016
	1823	336,253	921
	1826	331,119	957
	1829	321,421	1,117
Trinidad	1816	25,544	not given
	1819	23,537	
	1822	23,388	467
	1825	24,452	441
	1828	23,776	418

Source: Extracted from Returns of the Numbers of the slaves in each of the West India Colonies, as they stood at the Original and each of the subsequent registrations; stating the date of Registration, and distinguishing the sexes; and also the Numbers, distinguishing the sexes which at each registration have been added on account of birth or have been taken off on account of death or manumission, BSPH, Vol. XXVI, 1833. pp.474-77

Figures listed in Table 4 show that a total of 2,439 slaves were manumitted between 1808 and 1830 (October 29th).[20]

Table 4
Slaves Manumitted in Trinidad, 1808-1830

Year	Males	Females	Total
1808	21	35	56
1809	13	23	36
1810	8	23	31
1811	22	45	67
1812	38	63	101
1813	44	59	103
1814	31	51	82
1815	45	57	102
1816	61	85	146
1817	35	87	122
1818	45	85	130
1819	46	78	124
1820	47	80	127
1821	22	61	83
1822	33	58	91
1823	31	54	85
1824	50	91	141
1825	66	109	175
1826	64	103	167
1827	67	100	167
1828	36	92	128
1829	32	55	87
1830	11	21	32
(to Oct. 29)			

Source: Williams, Documents, Appendix III, Table 17, p.390; BSPHC Vol. XXII, 1826-27, p.90. 56 slaves manumitted by will over the period 1821-25 are not included in the figures for these years

Two avenues of manumission were open to the slaves. They could purchase their freedom or they could be freed voluntarily by their masters, either during the master's lifetime or as a bequest in his will – sometimes for faithful service or for other reasons. The process of manumission in Trinidad, a new plantation society with great potential for expansion in the period following the abolition of the slave trade, may be especially revealing of the factors which did in fact make for the accessibility of freedom to slaves as compared with the other West Indian islands in their early stage of development. How was it that manumission was available in the first instance? Why was it allowed to continue even in spite of the labour shortage? Were there other social or economic forces on the island which would encourage manumission?

There seems to be some ambiguity as to precisely which laws were in operation for the governance of the slaves on the particular question of manumission. Generally, the changeover from Spanish to British law was slow.[21] In 1810, when the subject was being discussed, Secretary of State Lord Liverpool in a dispatch to Governor Sir Thomas Hislop reported that the Government was still considering the question: the issue was "necessarily extensive and complicated" and he could not give a decided opinion.[22] In 1813, when Sir Ralph Woodford became governor, his commission stated that as far as possible Spanish law was to remain in force in the island.[23] Some writers believe that Spanish law relating to manumission was more favourable than British law.[24] However, on the specific question of the laws relating to the slaves, Franklin Knight points out that the 1789 Spanish slave code which aimed at ameliorating the condition of the slaves was never promulgated in the colonies and was never actually in force.[25]

Governor Picton's slave code of 1800 was probably the law under which Trinidad slaves were governed until 1824. Although it had been described as 'generous and humane', it made no provision for manumission.[26] An Order in Council of 1812 which modified Picton's code had as its main objective the establishment of a Registry of slaves. Although there were no specific provisions made for manumission as such, slaves who were not registered could not be held as slaves and were, therefore, free in the eyes of the law.[27]

It was not until 1824 that conditions for manumission were provided for by law. An 1824 Order in Council[28] introduced for the reform and amelioration of slavery included, in certain circumstances, the means for the slave to leave the state of slavery and attain the rights and privileges of a free man.[29] However, although manu-

2 Manumission in Trinidad, 1808-1830

mission was not provided for by law prior to 1824, it is clear from the data in Table 4 that it did occur before that date. Thus it is reasonable to assume that before 1824 the traditional laws for the governance of slaves in the Spanish colonies were in fact in operation to some extent in Trinidad.[30] Under this code, masters were required to maintain the sick or aged and children. They could only grant a slave his freedom if they first gave him sufficient stock to maintain himself without assistance. The manumission then had to be approved by the Justice and the Syndic.[31] Slaves could also free themselves by purchase or compulsory manumission.[32] Prices varied according to skills, ability or age. The price at which a slave could be purchased was used to regulate the value of the slaves in cases of manumission.[33]

The 1824 Order stipulated that no duty or tax was to be payable on manumission except the 20 shillings fee to be paid to the Registrar of Deeds by the Protector of Slaves. Any slave who was desirous of purchasing his freedom or that of his spouse (lawful or unlawful), sibling or offspring was permitted to do so. If the slave wishing to be manumitted was involved in any legal matters, then the issue was to be reported to the Chief Judge by the Protector of Slaves. In issues involving the value of the slave, if owner and slave could not agree, three persons were to be appointed to make the final decision. In cases where the slave was to be manumitted gratuitously, he/she had to appear before the Protector of Slaves. For any slave under the age of 6 or over 50, or who was sick in mind or body, the owner had to pay a bond of £200 ensuring the care of the slave until he reached the age of 14 in the case of infants, or until his death in other circumstances. Gratuitous manumissions were not valid until such bonds were executed and deposited.[34] This obligation did not apply to manumissions by will.[35]

The new Order in Council did not in fact introduce any drastic innovations but merely embodied traditional principles of Spanish law and, as in the case of compulsory manumission, confirmed Spanish usage.[36] Thus it would seem that in Trinidad, from the very early stages, two variables exogenous to the pressures and mores of sugar culture contributed to make manumission legally available: its Spanish heritage, and the efforts of the anti-slavery lobby.

It is now important to consider whether and to what extent the attitudes of slave-owners coincided with the permissiveness of the law. Surviving evidence clearly reveals that the vast majority of landowners in Trinidad were opposed to Spanish law. In 1810 Governor Hislop collected the sentiments of the white landed proprietors on the issue of the law, and his return shows that out of a total of 517 proprietors, 438 favoured British law, 26 favoured Spanish law, 51 were neutral, while 2 did not commit themselves in any way.[37] As we have seen, prior to 1824 British law did not favour manumission. There is also much further evidence that the general attitude of the planters towards the new manumission regulations, in particular, were hostile. There were petitions against the Orders in Council, as well as expressions of opposition in first-hand accounts, and evidence given before a committee appointed by the local council in 1824 to enquire into the 'Negro character' in Trinidad. In the petitions against the Orders in Council, slave-owners who objected fell into two categories: those who considered, or seemed to consider the welfare of the slaves, and those who were obviously motivated by self-interest.

Objecting to the Order in Council of March 26th, 1812, slave-owners gave reasons which appeared to have the physical and moral welfare of the slaves at heart. They felt that the Order did not make provisions for sick, poor, aged or infirm slaves and that it was necessary to guard against the "destitution continually experienced after emancipation". Slave-owners also showed concern for the slaves' moral state, pointing out that the Order, by promising protection to slaves who became informers against their owners in issues pertaining to their freedom and by declaring their evidence as acceptable would encourage the slaves to commit perjury.[38] The Alcaldes in Ordinary and Regidors of the Cabildo[39] expressed the sentiment that the Order in Council of 1824 would be "injurious to the well-being of the slaves themselves".[40] Members of the Council also petitioned that there would be "great loss and injury" among the slaves as a result of this 1824 Order.[41] Some planters also expressed concern that the slave should have every possible opportunity for manumission, and felt that the clause imposing the bond would discourage those who gave manumission to infant slaves at baptism.[42]

More fundamentally, of course, the slave-owners were concerned for their own interests. The objections to the 1812 Order in Council were based on the view that it turned the attention of the slaves toward emancipation and, by imposing freedom of the slave as a penalty on proprietors in some cases, endangered the safety of the white population.[43] Concerning the 1824 Order in Council, slave-owners felt that some provision should be made to compensate them for loss of valuable time from estate duties, not only of the slaves themselves but of the proprietors and/or managers, when they were involved in cases before the Protector of Slaves or Court of Justice. They feared that an old, infirm, or crippled slave would have the

2 Manumission in Trinidad, 1808-1830

option to purchase the freedom of a younger member of his family and himself remain to be supported by his master. They felt, too, that because the clause requiring a £200 bond for the maintenance of young, diseased, or old slaves applied only to those who were manumitted gratuitously, the public needed some kind of safeguard that would prevent slaves who bought their freedom from becoming a public nuisance.[44]

Notwithstanding the moral issue surrounding the whole question of slavery, the planters' desire to safeguard their own interests is understandable. The large majority of them had only come to Trinidad a few years before and their fortunes were at stake. The maintenance or further acquisition of property depended upon a supply of labour. As L.M. Fraser has pointed out:

> ... what they dreaded was not the order itself, but that of which it was but only too manifestly the precursor. Behind the stalking horse of a law to ameliorate the condition of the slaves lurked, what to them meant ruin – Emancipation.[45]

Further evidence seems to suggest that the slave-owners' opposition to manumission was partly justified by what they claimed happened to the slave after he was given his freedom. Of the 25 persons who gave evidence before the Committee to enquire into the 'Negro character', seven made reference to manumission in their testimony. Five of those seven were of the opinion that manumission was the beginning of the road to deterioration for the freed slave. One witness knew a slave who had purchased his freedom for 500 dollars – indicating that he was industrious – but who never worked after he had been freed and died after weeks in want, misery and debt.[46] Another reported having known slaves who were healthy while in slavery but who became sickly "from their excesses" after they had been freed.[47] Joseph Peschier, planter and Commandant of one of the quarters, found that the manumitted slaves in his district lived in homes which looked better than those of Negro slaves in outward appearance but were actually the same in comfort. The slaves ate and dressed better than those who had been manumitted and the latter were in no respect equal to the best slaves. The manumitted slaves occasionally worked for neighbouring planters but it was very difficult to get them to rear poultry and they inevitably ended up being dismissed.[48] A planter's wife, in explaining a slave's alleged unwillingness to work after he had been manumitted, suggested that it could be attributed to the fact that the slave had a different conception of what it meant to be free; that freedom to him meant not working at all: "Freedom is prized by them, not for the sake of personal liberty in the British sense of the word, but as they have invariably told me, 'to sit down softly'."[49]

But the evidence of these witnesses cannot always be taken too seriously because their experiences were with isolated individual cases (two of them even based their opinions on experiences with slaves in Tortola and the Bahamas[50]), and because it was so clearly self-interested. As will be argued later, manumitted slaves, as a group, seem to have been relatively self-sufficient in Trinidad.

The data given in Table 4 clearly show that despite the generally hostile attitude toward manumission on the part of slave-owners, slaves were able to take advantage of the opportunity to acquire their freedom. A close analysis of the available figures allows for some speculation as to what other factors influenced the occurrence of manumission. The slave population over the period was fairly constant, ranging from a low of 20,729 in 1810 to a high of 25,871 in 1815 (see Table 1). Thus significant changes in the extent of manumission such as occurred in 1809-1810 and during the 1824-1830 period do not merely reflect changes in size of the slave population. The decrease in numbers manumitted in 1809 and 1810 seems to have been a direct consequence of the recently abolished slave trade, while the increases of the later period can be attributed to the new enactments of the home government.

This can be seen clearly by an examination of manumission data for the period 1821-1831 as presented in Table 5.

Table 5

Slaves Manumitted in Trinidad, 1821-1830

Year	Gratuitous	Purchased	Testamentary	Total
1821	33	50	-	83
1822	49	42	-	91
1823	52	33	-	85
1824	47	94	-	141
1825	68	107	-	175
1821-25	-	-	56	56
1826	53	108	6	167
1827	32	129	6	167
1828	28	84	16	128
1829	44	41	2	87
1830 (Oct. 29)	9	22	1	32

Source: CO 295/72: also BSPHC, Vol. XIII, 1826-27, p.90; CO 295/85 in Williams, Documents..., Appendix III, Table 17, p.390

With the exception of the years 1822, 1823 and 1829, purchased manumissions always exceeded gratuitous ones, a fact which indicated that the slave had a greater chance of attaining his freedom by

2 Manumission in Trinidad, 1808-1830

purchase than by voluntary gift from his owner and that his desire to acquire freedom was greater than the slave-owner's inclination to give it. There was also a marked increase in the numbers manumitted between 1823 and 1827, mainly through purchased manumissions which continued to rise. The increase in purchased manumissions at this time was clearly the direct result of the 1824 Order in Council, which facilitated purchased manumission by preventing planters from standing in the way of slaves who wanted to buy their freedom. The clause which dealt with gratuitous manumissions, it will be recalled, required that slave-owners pay a bond of £200 when the slaves were under 6 or over 50 years of age or diseased in body or mind. The decrease in gratuitous manumissions suggests that many of the slaves previously manumitted gratuitously probably fell into those categories. This is not surprising because the increases in sugar production and the perpetual labour shortage made it unlikely that planters would voluntarily free the most productive of their slaves under normal circumstances.

Problems of enforcement and administration led to a decrease in purchased manumissions after 1827. One problem that arose was disagreements over a slave's worth. The average price of a slave for a three-year period immediately after the Order of 1824 was issued was £62 but the Consolidation Act of 1825, which prevented the importation of plantation slaves from the old colonies, had forced the price of slaves to rise to £100[51] with the result that slave-owners sometimes requested more from a slave who was about to purchase his freedom.[52] This development was quite likely the source of most of the increase in disagreements and litigation between master and slave over the value of the slave at manumission.[53] Other problems arose from charges that the sworn appraisers had pronounced an unjust decision favouring the slave-owners.[54] Much higher prices were also reported: £162.10 and £169 were paid for a personal and plantation slave respectively in 1825. Moreover, the Protector of Slaves was not totally clear as to what his duties and obligations were, and disagreements between him and other officials on the subject prevented the manumission process from running smoothly.[55] Finally, slaves experienced delays in obtaining their freedom because of the requirement imposed on masters to insert a notice in the *Gazette* during three successive publications.[56]

These problems in the actual enforcement of the law on manumission occurred in the post-1824 period when the Order in Council was in operation and when slave-owners could not legally stand in the way of the slave who wanted to buy his freedom. One would tend to suspect that before 1824 planters' attitudes made it much more difficult for a slave to purchase his manumission. The fact that there were so many manumissions, especially by purchase, indicates that the desire for freedom among the slaves was strong.

The slaves' occupation and consequent ability to earn money were important factors in determining who had easiest access to manumission. Slaves were provided with as much ground as they could cultivate to supply themselves with food. They were allowed every Sunday, half a day extra in every week of the out-of-crop season, four public holidays, and mealtimes to themselves. Slave-owners sometimes purchased the provision and stock produced by their own slaves. The proceeds from the sale of surplus produce of his provision ground were the plantation slave's chief means of earning money. A slave from St Vincent who had visited Trinidad with his owner reported on the fertility of the soil in Trinidad adding that, "Trinidad Negroes had it in their power to get on fast in money making."[57] Slaves could also hire themselves out for task-work on Sundays at the rate of 2 shillings for any time not exceeding 4 hours or for 4 shillings per day.

They could also be employed as tradesmen or domestics or hired out by overseers as servants for carrying goods about the country for sale.[58] A return for the period between June 24th, 1824 and December 24th, 1827 shows that of 409 purchased manumissions, 137 were by plantation slaves and 272 by personal slaves.[59] Personal slaves obviously had more opportunity to earn money than plantation slaves and, as the breakdown in figures for the period above shows, more personal slaves bought their freedom than plantation slaves.[60]

The tendency, too, was for female slaves to attain their freedom in greater numbers than males. There is also a high correlation between the increases and decreases in the numbers of males and females manumitted (see Table 4). Not only were more women manumitted than men overall, but women dominated each mode of manumission. This can be seen from the figures for the period 1821-1825, as set out in Table 6.

Table 6
Manumissions in the Period, 1821-1825

	Voluntary		Purchased		Testamentary	
	M	F	M	F	M	F
Total	76	173	126	200	13	43
%	30.5	69.5	38.6	61.4	23.2	76.8

Source: *BSPHC*, Vol. XXIII, 1826-27, p.90; see also CO 295/72 *in* Williams, *Documents...*, Appendix III, Table 17, p.390

Lack of evidence prevents any conclusive explanation of why more women than men were manumitted in Trinidad. As has been suggested in studies of free coloured groups throughout the hemisphere, however, it might have been the result of a general tendency to manumit female infants in greater numbers than males.[61] The tendency for more women to be freed by purchased manumissions seems to have been unusual. The female slave may have had as many opportunities to earn money as the male; but there was a substantial free coloured population in Trinidad and it is perhaps conceivable that some of the males might have been buying wives.

The slave's desire for freedom could also be conditioned by the life that awaited him or her as a freed man or woman: the prospect of a reasonable, respectable life can be assumed to have served as an incentive for the slave to strive for manumission. Patterson, for example, notes that, "The Jamaican slave was, rightly, quite cynical about the whole idea of manumission. It was easy for him to see that the free Negroes about him possessed little more than a beggar's freedom."[62] Two first-hand accounts present conflicting pictures of the freedman's prospects in Trinidad. Henry Coleridge, a visitor to the island in 1825, wrote that by giving slaves an opportunity to save their money and purchase their freedom, one had not in fact done anything for their benefit:

> ...all you have done is this, that whereas as a slave he was compelled to labour and thereby kept within certain bounds of sobriety, as a freedman he becomes in the first week a vagabond, the second a grinder of corn by the sweat of his legs in the jail of Port of Spain.[63]

M. Dauxion-Lavayasse, a landed proprietor in Trinidad wrote on the other hand that:

> ...when the Negroes succeed in obtaining their liberty they are generally found to form new plantations, and some of them by dint of hard labour and economy, become great proprietors in the end. Others act as extensive traders, and as such are seen in all the

colonies, especially at Trinidad, where they become considerable merchants.[64]

A return containing two 1824 accounts, one of the labourers born free and the other of the manumitted slaves resident in the island,[65] permits us to have a fair idea of what occupational opportunities were available to freed men and thus, to attempt some evaluation of this contradictory testimony. Although the return for the manumitted slaves does not consistently give precise figures, it does allow us to have an idea of occupational distribution (see Table 7).

Table 7
Occupations of Manumitted Slaves Domiciled in Trinidad in 1824

District	No. of slaves			Occupations
	M	F	T	
Arima	22	20	42	Cocoa planters; provision planters (mostly)
Arima (village)	9	14	23	Carpenters (some); chairmaker (1); labourers; hucksters
Aricagua	14	6	20	Labourers; landowners (2); some old and infirm cotton planters; fishermen (principally)
Bocas	14	-	14	
Carenage & Chaguaramas	?	?	31	Fishermen (few); woodcutters
Caroni	3	2	5	Labourers (2); huntsman (1)
Cedros	7	4	11	Carpenter (1); landowner (1); cooper (1); sawyers (2); labourers
Chaguanas	5	4	9	Carpenter (1); tailor (1); labourers (the rest)
Cimaronero	10	6	16	Landowners (5); labourers (6)
Couva/Savoneta	10	25	35	Labourers; servants
Diego Martin	33	18	51	Labourers (majority); tradesmen (very few); shopkeepers
Gunapo	23	9	32	Carpenter (1); shoemaker; (1); servants (a few); labourers (the rest)
Hicacos	1	8	9	Seamstresses; washerwomen
Irois	3	1	4	These did not work and lived with their masters
La Brea & Gunapo	5	23	28	Provision planters; servants; shoemakers; seamstresses
Laventille	60	48	108	Cultivate provisions for their own subsistence and for sale in Port-of-Spain

2 Manumission in Trinidad, 1808-1830

District	No. of slaves			Occupations
	M	F	T	
Maraval	33	51	84	Provision planters; coffee planters owning land 931); labourers (the rest)
Maracas Valley	17	-	17	Chairmakers (3); provision planters; cocoa planters
Mayaro	1	1	2	Sugar boiler
Mucurapo	6	6	12	Wheelwright (1); hired labourers (others)
North Naparima	75	55	130	Landowners; labourers (50%); hucksters (women); lived with masters (several)
Oropouche	4	4	8	Lived with masters; worked out for hire
Pointe-a-Pierre	21	7	28	Carpenters (2); overseers (2); fishermen (some); some lived with masters
St Anns	30	38	68	Landowner (1); servants & seamstresses (women); coffee planters (4); provision planters (others)
Santa Cruz	21	1	22	Cocoa planters (18); hired labourers
St Joseph	2	1	3	Labourer (1); sugar boiler (1); cook (1)
St Joseph (town of)	13	2	15	Carpenters; carter (1); indentured servant (1); tradesmen (majority)
St Juan (town of)	11	23	34	Hired labourers (when work was available)
Savanna Grande	5	7	12	Provision planters; carpenter (1)
South Naparima	10	-	10	Carpenters (2); coopers (2); masons (2); labourers (4)
Tacarigua & Arouca	26	17	43	Carpenters; servants; sugar boiler; cook; millwright; masons; brickmaker (most live with their masters)
Toco & Cumana	2	1	3	Provision planters; fishermen
Valley of Caura	4	3	7	Provision planters; carpenters (1); labourers (2); unemployed (others); 2 live with masters

Source: Return prepared by Mr. Hodgkinson, Commissary of Population, Trinidad, transmitted to the Colonial Dept. in December 1824, by Sir Ralph Woodford, containing accounts of the labourers born free, and of the manumitted slaves with an account of their property and character, presented to the House of Commons on June 3, 1829, *BSHPC*, XXV, 1829, pp.42-45

The occupations in which the manumitted slaves found themselves fall into two main categories – land (or sea) labourers and tradesmen. In the first category, a few were land-owners. Those who worked the land were engaged in cultivation of cocoa, coffee, cotton or provisions for sale or for their own consumption. Fishing was done on the coastal areas. Among the tradesmen class were carpenters, chairmakers, bakers, hucksters, coopers, sawyers, tailors, a sugarboiler, wheelwright, millwright, carter and brickmaker. Generally, the women were hucksters, servants, washerwomen, or cooks. One individual in the Savonetta district owned a slave; two others in San Juan and La Brea owned 3 slaves and 1 slave respectively. A brickmaker in the Tacarigua-Arouca district owned 15 slaves. The tradesmen earned from $3 to $16 per week while the labourers earned between $2 and $4 per week. Some were also given food as part of their wages. In some instances, they lived with their former masters. The description of the manumitted slaves in 1824 tends to give a more favourable picture than is expressed in the first of the two views given above: that the manumitted slaves, as a group, were relatively self-sufficient and independent.

The presence of a group of free born small farmers and labourers in occupations in which a slave could envisage himself may have also made the state of freedom attractive to the slave. There was in 1824 a fairly large class of free born labourers: 1,579 heads of families, about two-thirds of whom were not born in Trinidad but who had come there mainly from other West Indian islands and South America. About half of these cultivated lands for themselves, one-fifth cultivated land for others, one-fifth were tradesmen or merchants. A few on the coastal areas also worked as fishermen. These prospects would have served as an incentive for the slave to work and accumulate money, especially since he had a greater chance of earning his freedom through purchase.

Thus, a series of external and internal factors contributed to stimulate manumission in Trinidad even though the society was at a stage of development which did not favour it. There is some ambiguity as to which laws actually governed the slaves but it would seem that, in so far as manumission was concerned, Spanish slave laws were in operation in the period immediately after the British takeover. Later, British law, as set out in the 1824 Order in Council, confirmed Spanish usage. The slave-owner, however, remained opposed to manumission and a slave was more likely to gain his freedom by purchase rather than by a gratuitous act on the part of his master. The slave's means of income was the proceeds from the sale of his surplus produce. The personal and skilled slaves had a better chance of earning money and more of those did acquire freedom. But on the whole it must have taken the slave a number of years to accumulate

2 Manumission in Trinidad, 1808-1830

enough money to buy his freedom. The fact that the freeborn labourers and freedmen could have lived off the land or as tradesmen or merchants would have made freedom attractive to the slaves and served as an incentive to strive after the only sure way of earning their freedom.

One can say then that the island's Spanish heritage combined with the efforts of the anti-slavery party made freedom legally possible for the slaves in Trinidad. The economic opportunities available to them, together with the social situation of the free coloureds and blacks, provided an added stimulus.

Notes

[1] An earlier version of this paper was presented to the Atlantic History and Culture Seminar (1974) at the Johns Hopkins University, Baltimore. The author wishes to thank Jack P. Greene, D. Barry Gaspar, Edward Cox, other members of that seminar and also Bridget Brereton of the University of the West Indies, St Augustine for useful comments.

[2] The term 'manumission' is used to refer to the formal release of slaves from servitude while slavery was still in force. It is distinct from 'emancipation' which generally refers to the freeing of all slaves when slavery was abolished. *Trinidad and Tobago, Map Collectors Series*, no. 10 (London, 1963), pp.11-15.

[3] Richard Dunn, *Sugar and Slaves: the Rise of the Planter Class in the English West Indies, 1624-1713* (Chapel Hill, 1972), p.255; Frank W. Pitman, "Slavery on the West India plantations in the eighteenth century," *Journal of Negro History*, Vol. 11, no. 4 (1926), pp. 615-16; Orlando Patterson, *The Sociology of Slavery* (New Jersey, 1967), pp. 90-91.

[4] Jerome S. Handler and Arnold A. Sio, "Barbados," in David W. Cohen, and Jack P. Greene, eds., *Neither Slave nor Free* (Baltimore, 1972), pp.224-26, passim; Patterson op. cit., p.90.

[5] See for example Charles Wagley and Marvin Harris, *Minorities in the New World: Six Case Studies* (New York, 1968), p.91; Michael Craton and James Walvin, *A Jamaican Plantation: the History of Worthy Park, 1670-1970* (Toronto, 1971), p.191; Magnus Morner, *Race Mixture in the History of Latin America* (Boston, 1967), pp.117-24, passim.

[6] See Franklin Knight, *Slave Society in Cuba during the Nineteenth Century* (Madison, 1970), p.191, where he states that "the practice of manumission declined as the demand for labour increased".

[7] Martin R. Montgomery, *History of the West Indies Comprising Jamaica, Honduras, Trinidad, Tobago, the Bahamas and the Virgin Islands*, (London, 1836), pp.214-15.

[8] Lionel M. Fraser, *History of Trinidad* (Port-of-Spain, 1891), Vol. 1, p.275. Slave population statistics are given in table 1.

[9] F. Mallet, "Descriptive Account of the Island of Trinidad" (London, 1802), in Map Collectors Circle, *Some Early Printed Maps of Trinidad*

and *Tobago*, Map Collectors Series, no. 10 (London, 1964), pp.11-15.

10 517 proprietors are accounted for in a "Copy of returns made to Governor Thomas Hislop of the sentiments of the white landed proprietors on the question of a change of laws," *British Sessional Papers, House of Commons* (hereafter *BSPHC*), 1810-1811, Vol. XI, return no. 5, p.338.

11 Jean Dauxion-Lavayasse, *A Statistical, Commercial and Political Description of Venezuela, Trinidad, Margarita and Tobago* (London, 1821), pp.330-35, passim.

12 Mallet, op. cit., foldout facing page 15.

13 Eric Williams, *History of the People of Trinidad and Tobago* (Port-of-Spain, 1962), p.85.

14 Governor Picton to Secretary of State, quoted in Gertrude Carmichael, *History of the West Indian Islands of Trinidad and Tobago, 1498-1900* (London, 1961), p.53.

15 CO 295/75 Marryat to Murray, August 19th, 1828 *in* Williams, Eric, *Documents on British West Indian History, 1807-1833*. Select documents from the Public Record Office, London, England, relating to the colonies of Barbados, British Guiana, Jamaica and Trinidad (Port-of-Spain, 1952), Document no. 136.

16 Williams, *History*, op. cit., p.67.

17 Proclamation of Ralph James Woodford, Port-of-Spain, Trinidad, December 5th, 1815 – Clauses first, fourth and ninth, *in* Carmichael, *History...* Appendix III, pp.393-94.

18 Williams, *Documents...*, Appendix III, table 8, p.387; Williams, *History of the People of Trinidad and Tobago*, p.75.

19 Williams, *Documents...*, Appendix III, table 6, p.385.

20 CO 295/94 Return of manumissions granted in the island of Trinidad Jan. 1817-Dec. 31st, 1830. Enclosure in Major-General Lewis Grant to Viscount Goderich, Nov. 1st, 1832, Dispatch no. 82 gives some slightly different totals but the figures are not sufficiently different to prevent them from serving as a guide to how manumission was occurring. Manumission figures after 1830 are not available.

21 John L. Mahar, "Trinidad under British Rule, 1797-1950," PhD dissertation, University of Wisconsin (1955), p.20.

22 Earl of Liverpool to Hislop, *BSPHC*, Vol. XI, 1810-1011, p.355.

23 Carmichael, *History*, op. cit., p.105.

24 Frank Tannenbaum, *Slave and Citizen: the Negro in the Americas* (New York, 1946), p.68-69; Herbert Klein, *Slavery in the Americas: A Comparative Study of Virginia and Cuba* (Chicago, 1967), p.121-22; see also Patterson, op. cit., p.90.

25 Knight, *Slave Society*, op. cit., p.125.

26 James Millette, *The Genesis of Crown Colony Government, Trinidad, 1783-1810* (Trinidad, 1970), pp.64-65.

27 Extract in F.R. Augier and S.C. Gordon, *Sources of West Indian History* (London, 1962), p.128. See also "Reasons assigned in the petition of Proprietors of Slaves in Trinidad to General Munro against enforcing the Order in Council of 1812" in Williams, *Documents*, op. cit., Document no. 215; Bridget Brereton, *A History of Trinidad 1783-1962* (London, 1981), pp.52-53.

28 For background to the 1824 Order in Council see William Law Mathieson, *British Slavery and its Abolition, 1823-1838* (London, 1926), pp.115-29; see also Eric Williams, *Capitalism and Slavery* (New York, 1944), pp.178-96.

29 Hansard, *Parliamentary Debates*, Vol. 10, second series, p.1104.

30 See Evidence of Chief Justice, "Report of His Majesty's Commissioners of Legal Inquiry on the Colony of Trinidad 1824", *BSPHC*, Vol. XXIII, 1826-1827,

p.312 (hereafter Report... Legal Inquiry).
31. Translation of the Royal Ordinance or *Cédula*, for the Government and Protection of slaves in the Spanish Colonies, *BSPHC*, Vol. XI, 1810-1811, p.348.
32. Evidence of Judge of Criminal Inquiry, Report... Legal Inquiry, *BSPHC*, Vol. XXIII, 826-827, p.312.
33. Evidence of R. Garcia – Extracts from the Committee of the Council of Trinidad, appointed on the 4th day of November 1824, for the purpose of obtaining a more correct knowledge of the Negro Character, as exhibited in this colony, in the state both of slavery and of freedom (hereafter Committee... Negro Character), *BSPHC*, 1826-1827, Vol. XXIII, p.54. Several public officers and prominent planters resident on the island for varying periods gave evidence to the Committee.
34. *BSPHC*, Vol. XXV, 1825, p.398.
35. CO 295/63 Governor Woodford to Commandants, August 21, 1824, in Williams, *Documents*, op. cit., Document No. 21.
36. Mathieson, op. cit., p.49.
37. Copy of returns made to Governor Hislop by the Commandants of Quarters and *Alcaldes del Barrio*, transmitted in July last, of the sentiments of white landed proprietors of Trinidad, to a change of laws, *BSPHC*, Col. XI, 1810-1811, p.338
38. CO 295/31 Petition of Proprietors... in Williams, *Documents*, op. cit., Document No. 215.
39. These were magistrates and were "Spanish only in their titles", Mathieson, op. cit., p.149.
40. Petition to Sir R. Woodford from the Alcaldes in Ordinary and the Regidors of the Illustrious Cabildo, *BSPHC*, Vol. XXXVI, 1825, p.370.
41. William H. Burnley, Alexander Duncasson, Francis Peschier to Woodford, 20th May 1824, *BSPHC*, Vol. XXVI, 1825, p.375.
42. Woodford to Earl Bathurst, 26th May 1824, *BSPHC*, Vol. XXVI, 1825, p.366. After the Order was sent to the island, the free inhabitants met and appointed a Committee through which their petitions against the Order were forwarded to the Governor and later passed to the Secretary of State.
43. CO 295/31 Petition of Proprietors... in Williams, *Documents*, op. cit., Document No. 215.
44. Petition to Sir Ralph Woodford, 17th May 1824, *BSPHC*, Vol. XXVI, 1825, pp.388-89.
45. Fraser, op. cit., p.173.
46. Evidence of Dr James Lynch O'Connor, Committee... Negro Character, *BSPHC*, Vol. XXIII, 1826-27, p.23.
47. Evidence of Dr Alexander Williams, Committee... Negro Character, ibid., p.20.
48. Evidence of Joseph Peschier, Committee... Negro Character, ibid, p.15. See also evidence of Antione St Bresson and Robert Mitchell for further unfavourable reports of manumitted slaves, pp.16 & 37.
49. A.C. Carmichael (Mrs.), *Domestic Manners and Social Conditions of the White, Coloured and Negro Population of the West Indies*, 2 vols (New York, 1969; originally published 1833), vol. 2, p.194. The Carmichaels came to Trinidad with slaves in 1820 from St Vincent, having considered the island to be a land of opportunity; See Donald Wood, Trinidad in transition: the years after slavery (London, 1968), p.34.
50. Evidence of Joseph Harrigan and Burton Williams, Committee... Negro Character, *BSPHC*, Vol. XXIII, 1826-1827, pp.10-24.
51. CO 295/77 Woodford to Huskisson, March 7th, 1828; Woodford to Bathhurst, Rec. 1826.
52. Much higher prices were also reported on occasions: see discussion in Noel Titus, "Amelioration

and Emancipation in Trinidad 1812 to 1834", MA Thesis, University of the West Indies (1974), pp.192-96.
53 For example 25% of the slaves manumitted for the period June to December 1827 were done through suits of the Chief Judge, CO 295/77 Protector of Slaves Report to Dec. 31st, 1827, Appendix C, No. 1 and Appendix F. See also Williams, *Capitalism and Slavery*, op. cit., p.199.
54 CO 295/73 Stephen to Horton, Oct. 5th, 1826 in Williams, *Documents*, op. cit., Document No. 222.
55 See correspondence between Attorney and Protector of Slaves, Dec. 12, 1824 – April 3, 1826, *BSPHC*, Vol. XXVI, 1826-1827, p.67.
56 Remarks upon the Order by the Protector of Slaves, *BSPHC*, Vol. XXVI, 1826-27, p.67.
57 Evidence of James Lamont, Committee... Negro Character, *BSPHC*, Vol. XXIII, 1826-27, pp.49-50; Dispatch from Bathurst to Sir Ralph Woodford, 11 Sep. 1824, *BSPHC*, Vol. XXV 1826, p.398; see also, "A Return of wages fixed by the Protector of Slaves for Sunday labour of slaves," 26 Feb. 1827, *BSPHC*, Vol. XXIII, 1826-27, p.3.
58 Carmichael, *Domestic Manners*, op. cit., vol. 1: pp.36, 82-83.
59 CO 295/77 Statement of the Protector of Slaves of the number of slaves manumitted in the island of Trinidad, from the 24th day of June to the 24th day of Dec. 1827 inclusive, exhibiting the number of those who obtained their freedom gratuitously, by bequest, and for a valuable consideration, distinguishing the plantation from the personal.
60 CO 295/77 Returns of monies paid for the manumission of slaves in Trinidad from 24th June 1824 – 3rd March 1828.
61 Cohen & Greene, op. cit., p.7.
62 Patterson, op. cit., p.91.
63 Henry Nelson Coleridge, *Six months in the West Indies in 1825* (London, 1832), p.90.
64 Dauxion-Lavayasse, op. cit., p.394.
65 Return to and address of the House of Commons dated 3rd June 1829 for a Copy of the Returns prepared by Mr Hodgkinson, Commissary of Population, and transmitted to the Colonial Dept. in Dec. 1824 by Sir R. Woodford, containing accounts of the labourers born free, and of the manumitted slaves with an account of their property and character, *BSPHC*, Vol. XXV, 1829, pp.42-45. It was an order of Government that free labourers of every description report themselves to the Commandant on entering the quarter. In addition, every proprietor, in the month of December, was supposed to report every free person fixed upon or working the time on his estate. Returns were accumulated and sent to the Office of the Commissary of Population. Evidence of John Lamont, Committee... Negro Character, *BSPHC*, Vol. XXIII, 1826-27, p.49.

CHAPTER THREE

The Struggle of Blacks and Free Coloureds for Freedom in Barbados, 1800-1833

Hilary M. Beckles

Black people in the British West Indies did not win their freedom by armed revolution. It was Parliamentary legislation in 1833 and 1838 that ended some two hundred years of slavery in the region. These imperial legislative interventions, however, took place within the context of a persistent and intensive struggle on the part of slaves to free themselves. At the turn of the nineteenth century, while other planters within the region were concerned most with the impact of the abolition of the slave trade upon their slave-based economies, their Barbados counterparts were involved primarily in discussing the constitutional and military aspects of controlling the black and free coloured population. In the first half of Governor Seaforth's administration (1801-3), they debated at length whether the murder of a black by a white person should be made a capital felony and were finally persuaded that it should be so in 1805 only after the imperial government had intervened in favour of the legislation. At the same time, they also debated whether the legal civil rights of the free coloureds should be reduced or extended. They were aware that effective control and manipulation of these free people required a different set of techniques to the slaves but also saw that their respective struggles for socio-legal reform and full emancipation were intricately linked. In both Haiti and Grenada during the rebellious 1790s, it was a military coalition of slaves and free coloureds, which crippled critical areas of the different planters defence system. In awareness of these developments, most planters in Barbados conceived that the struggles of both groups were segments of the same wider political movement, in spite of the pro-slavery socio-economic interest of the propertied free coloured elite.[1]

By 1800, the free coloured people, a small and oppressed minority, were not legally the most disadvantaged of their kind in the British West Indies. As in Jamaica where the largest numbers existed, they had no franchise, could not testify in courts against whites and could not hold office in the legal or administrative structures of the colony. They were, therefore, legally debarred from any such posts, which carried significant respectability and authority. Unlike in Jamaica, however, the Barbados free coloureds were not subjected to legal limitations upon the amount of property which they could buy or sell, inherit or bequeath.[2] Consequently, a number of them had grown considerably wealthy by West Indian standards and were recognised as 'propertied gentlemen' within local society.

As a result of their inability to testify in courts, however, the free coloureds were not legally positioned to protect their properties and persons with ease within a society which was structured and animated by deep-rooted prejudices against most things and persons 'non-European' in origin. In Barbados, according to Handler, whites could therefore ignore debt, rob, cheat, falsely accuse and even assault them "with relative impunity".[3] Here, the poorest illiterate whites were fond of offending them – knowing that they could not be legally persecuted upon their evidence. The wealthiest members of the free coloured community therefore had to suffer these hostile acts from their class inferiors without legal redress. The ability to give testament in courts against whites was, therefore, the most important civil right being pursued by the free coloured community during this time.[4]

Between 1801 and 1805, a debate charged with intense emotions developed in Barbados between the articulate spokesmen for the free coloured community and the white planter elite (plus its political and intellectual representatives) concerning the need to legally reform the social conditions of the free coloured peoples. The debate had resulted from the attempts of Governor Seaforth (newly appointed, and a liberal man within the ideological parameters) to ameliorate the condition of both the slaves and free coloureds.[5] His specific concerns with the free coloureds emerged almost wholly from what he recognised to be a contradiction within the society resulting from their unchecked ability to acquire property and their legal inability to protect and fully enjoy such property. He summed up this situation in Barbados in a letter to the Earl of Camden as follows:

> By our present system we compel a considerable part of our population to become our enemies, who are desirous of being our friends... so blind are we that while we oppress this free part of the king's subjects in defiance of every principle of either policy

3 The struggle for freedom in Barbados, 1800-1833

or justice, we let them acquire unlimited real property as if it was possible to separate the possession of property from the enjoyment of influence.[6]

Governor Seaforth believed that such a situation was sociopolitically disequilibrating and suggested that unless flexibility was exercised in the legal management of the free coloured community, the whites would drive them away from their traditional politics of moderation and into the ambit of slave radicalism. Most assemblymen were aware of the possibility of such an ideological shift among the free coloureds but believed that it should be mitigated, not by the granting of legal concessions, but by drastically limiting their demographic rate of growth. In 1801, before Governor Seaforth's amelioration drive had gained momentum, the legislative council passed a manumission act, which raised the fee to £300 and £200 for females and males respectively. This measure, it was hoped, would ensure the reduction of the rate of growth of the free coloured community and, therefore, make insignificant their numerical contribution to any future slave rebellion.[7]

John Poyer, white Creole intellectual, historian by profession, and leading ideologue for the dominant conservative wing of the planter elite, considered this measure insufficient and began a campaign calling for clearly defined and strictly implemented legal limits upon the ability of the free coloureds to accumulate wealth. Rather than reforming the legal system to make their social standing consistent with their economic value, Poyer proposed that their economic worth be reduced to make it correspond with existing legal and social provisions. In response to Governor Seaforth's reforming initiative, Poyer's letter addressed to him stated:

> In every well constituted society, a state of subordination necessarily arises from the nature of civil government. Without this no political union can long subsist. To maintain this fundamental principle, it becomes necessary to preserve the distinction which naturally exist or are accidentally introduced into the community. With us, two grand distinctions exist resulting from the nature of our society. First, between the white inhabitants and free people of colour, and secondly, between masters and slaves. Nature has strongly defined the differences [not] only in complexion, but in the mental, intellectual and corporal faculties of the different species. Our colonial code has acknowledged and adopted the distinction.[8]

This conception of social structure and race relations was popular among whites of all classes who objected to free coloureds accumulating property beyond a level consistent with their social status. In 1801, John Allyene, absentee planter, in a letter to his estate manager expressed what seemed to have been the popular opinion as follows:

> I am very sorry to hear of the large purchases made by the coloured people in our country of land and slaves: if it is permitted to go on without some check, we shall perhaps in no great distance of time find ourselves in the same situation that the neighbouring island of Grenada was in not long since. I am astonished that we are so blind to our own interest and safety.[9]

The dominant opinion of most assemblymen, therefore, was that the free coloureds were more of a threat than an ally and should therefore be the victims of further legal restrictions. Within a year of Poyer's address to the Governor, a bill based upon his views was brought before the Assembly by Robert Haynes, a General in the island's militia and prominent speaker of the planter elite, which called for the placing of significant property limitations upon the free coloureds. It gained almost full support in the House but was sent back by Governor Seaforth's Council on the grounds that it needed moderation and refinement.[10]

While the Assembly was preparing changes to the bill, the free coloureds took the opportunity to address the Council on the matter, emphasising the seriousness of the proposed legislation. Their letter stated that should such a bill become law it would "remove the best security of our loyalty and fidelity", and in a society structured upon possession of property, "death would be preferable to such a situation"[11] of being propertyless. It was the first occasion that the free coloureds had addressed the Council on the subject of their loyalty to whites, but the letter nonetheless effused more a state of desperation than a tone of aggression. It was a subtle attempt to play upon the fears of white society by implying that the option of placing themselves in the vanguard of the anti-slavery movement was also open to them.

In response to the letter, John Alleyne Beckles took up the free coloureds' case in November sitting of the legislative council in 1803 and became the leading opponent of the Assembly's bill. Beckles, suspecting that the free coloureds were running out of moderation in their civil rights demands, linked his rejection of the bill with the issue of their loyalty to whites in the event of slave rebellion. He won his battle – the bill was abandoned. He concluded his speech, which carried the Council into opposing the bill, by stating:

3 The struggle for freedom in Barbados, 1800-1833

I am inclined to think that it will be political to allow [the free coloured] to possess property. It will keep them at a greater distance from the slave and will keep up that jealousy which seems naturally to exist between them and the slaves; it will tend to our security, for should the slaves at any time attempt to revolt, the free coloured persons for their own safety and the security of their property, must join the whites and resist them. But if we reduce the free coloured people to a level with the slaves, they must unite with them, and will take every occasion of promoting and encouraging a revolt.[12]

On Easter night, 14th April 1816, the slaves revolted and Beckles' perception of the free coloureds and their political analysis was put to the test.

The rebellion was the first of the three slave uprisings that took place in the British West Indies between the abolition of the slave trade in 1807 and general emancipation in 1838, the other two rebellions occurring in Demerara in 1823 and Jamaica in 1831. It began about 8.30 p.m. in the south-eastern parish of St Philip. A local newspaper, attempting to illustrate the topographical unsuitability of the area for such an occurrence, stated that this parish was "the most level and fertile and least laborious where many of the plantations were so fully stocked with slaves, that (they) had not sufficient work to keep them constantly employed".[13] The African Institute, a pro-abolitionist London based organisation, conducted an investigation of the revolt and supported this view. In its report, the Institute stated that in the first instance, "Barbados was the very worst field for such an experiment, since in no British colony was success in an attempt to obtain even a short lived freedom by insurrection so hopeless".[14] In relation to the St Philip and neighbouring parishes, the report stated: "There are no mountains, no fastnesses, no forest. European foot, and even horse, can traverse it in all directions, hence, the obvious military advantage of the planters' armed forces in the field."[15]

Regional topography, however, while being a most important factor in the dynamics of armed rebellion, was overridden according to the Institute by social forces specific to Barbadian society during this period of legislative reform to West Indian master-slave relations. The Institute noted that the Barbadian planters for over two decades "sullenly refused to accept legislative reforms, and their 17th century slave code remained unaltered".[16] In addition, the Institute noted, "in no part of the British dominions did this unhappy state of society exist in a more unmitigated form than in this island".[17] The rebellion, therefore, according to the Institute was directly related to the planters' refusal, unlike those in Jamaica, the Windward and

Leeward Islands, to take meaningful legislative action ameliorative of the slaves' conditions. In this sense, it was the planters' socio-political rigidity and conservatism in their slave management which resulted in the general rebellious attitudes among the slaves.

From St Philip, the rebellion quickly spread throughout most of the southern and central parishes of Christ Church, St John, St Thomas, St George and parts of St Michael. Minor outbreaks of arson (but no skirmishes with the militia) also occurred in the northernmost parish of St Lucy. No fighting between rebel slaves and the militia forces was reported for the eastern and western parishes of St Andrew, St James and St Peter. In geopolitical terms, more than half of the island was engulfed by the insurrection.[18] The rebellion was short-lived. Within three days it was effectively squashed by a joint offensive of the local militia and imperial troops garrisoned on the island; included among the latter were the black/slave soldiers of the left wing of the 1st West Indian Regiment.[19] Mopping up operations continued during May and June, and martial law which was imposed about 2.00 a.m. on Monday, April 15th, was lifted 89 days later on July 12th.

The death toll by the end of September, when the militia believed that the rebellious slaves were finally eradicated, was very unevenly balanced between blacks and whites. Governor Leith's report of April 30th stated in relation to the rebels:

> It is at present impossible with any certainty to state the numbers who have fallen; about 50 however are at present conjectured to be the amount. The number executed under martial law have been about 70, also many prisoners have been tried and still continue to be judged; there being no other mode of ascertaining the nature and extent of the conspiracy and the guilt of the individuals.[20]

By the 21st of September he had revised his figures to 144 executed under martial law, 70 sentenced to death and 123 sentenced to transportation.[21] The anonymous author of an account of the insurrection (written most probably in September that year) suggests that the Governor's figures represent a gross underestimation of the total fatalities. The author stated that "a little short of 1,000" slaves were killed in battle and executed at Law.[22] Colonel Best, commander of the Christ Church parish militia, stated that his men alone killed 40 rebels in battles during Monday, April 15th and the following Tuesday morning. The reason, according to Colonel Best, why many more had to be executed in the field was because "the numbers not only implicated but actively employed" were great.[23] In addition, Colonel Best stated, many of those tried

3 The struggle for freedom in Barbados, 1800-1833

had to be executed because "they were all ringleaders".[24]

Only one white militiaman was killed in battle, one Brewster, a private of the St Philip parish militia.[25] Several, however, were seriously injured in combat and many elderly white people died of what Mrs Fenwick, a resident English woman, described as "fatigue" caused by the rebellion.[26] In addition, during the clashes between slaves and the imperial troops at Bayleys and Golden Grove plantations on the Monday evening, two of the 150 men of the West India Regiment were killed while forming their line to attack.[27] Damage to the property was estimated by the Assembly's investigative committee at £175,000. Twenty-five per cent of the year's sugar crop was burnt, as arson was used extensively by the rebels both as an instrument to undermine the economic base of the planters as well as logistical signals to their scattered contingents.[28]

The rebellion did not proceed according to plan. It broke out three days prematurely. Unlike the 1675 and 1692 aborted rebellion attempts, however, it was not deliberately betrayed from within the ranks of the slave community. The premature rising was an accident caused, according to the Governor, "by the intoxication of one of the revolters".[29] This statement was also supported by Colonel Best of the Christ Church militia. No details, however, were given as to how this development occurred. It is not known whether the drunken rebel, either by his direct actions or through incorrect information relayed to other rebels, initiated the uprising. The Governor, however, concluded his assertion by noting that: "There is every reason to believe that the premature bursting out of the insurrection on the night of the 14th instance… instead of the 17th instance, made it more partial than would have been otherwise the case."[30]

The rebels had organised what seemed to be an islandwide conspiracy to overthrow the planter class and to obtain their freedom; the Governor, the Colonels of the militia and the Commandant of the imperial troops were all convinced that this was the case. They denied that the rebellion was intended to be limited in nature or directed specifically against a section of the island's planter class. Neither was it intended to be simply a collective protest by slaves against the planters demanding the amelioration of their social and work conditions. Colonel Best noted that the rebels had intended the Monday night to be the time for the beginning of an arsonist attack upon the white communities; canes and buildings were to be burnt to the ground. During the confusion caused by this action, the Tuesday and/or Wednesday was for the "murder of the white man" across the island.[31] One captured rebel who was tried by a court martial confessed that they had intended the whites to cry "water" on Monday night and "blood" on subsequent nights.[32] It was this sequential mixture of arson and warfare that lay at the base of the rebels' military strategy.

Whites generally believed that their slaves, not having attempted any insurrections since the minor aborted Bridgetown affair in 1701, were more prone to running away, withholding their labour in protest, petitioning estate owners, attorneys and managers concerning conditions of work and leisure, than to armed insurrection. Slaveowners boasted about the subduing effects upon the slaves of the ameliorations to their social conditions implemented continuously since the mid-eighteenth century. They claimed that their slaves were given "liberties" which planters in other islands could not dare to even consider.[33] The ability of most slaves to travel the island extensively in pursuit of social and economic activity was held up by the planters as proof of the long-standing mildness of race relations and planter management on the island.[34] John Beckles, Speaker of the Assembly at the time of the insurrection, confessed that the slave laws did "wear a most sanguinary complexion" and were a "disgrace" to the island; but he affirmed that they were rarely applied, and in this sense they were largely "dead letters". Furthermore, he argued, the slaves had "comfortable houses", were "well-fed and clothed," and were "well-taken care of both in sickness and in health," and were "not overworked".[35]

The planters on the eve on the revolt, while recognising a significantly increased level in slave unrest, seemed to have possessed an unspoken confidence in the strength and security of their regime. Robert Haynes, planter-assemblyman, stated his position in a letter dated September 1816, as follows: "The night of the insurrection I would and did sleep with my chamber door open and if I had possessed ten thousand pounds in my house I should not have had any more precaution, so well convinced I was of their [slaves] attachment..."[36]

This attitude seemed to have been general throughout the white community. Governor Leith, in awareness of this long held complacency which he had never shared, informed the Secretary of State for the Colonies at the end of April:

> The planters of Barbados who have flattered themselves that the general good treatment of the slaves would have prevented them from resorting to violence to establish an elusion of material right, which by long custom sanctioned by law has been hitherto refused to be acknowledged, had not any apprehension of such a convulsion.[37]

3 The struggle for freedom in Barbados, 1800-1833

The slaves had been planning the rebellion soon after the House of Assembly discussed and rejected the imperial Registry Bill in November 1815. Watson noted that the decision was made by the rebels in February 1816 that the rising should take place in April of that year.[38] The alleged primary leader, though this was not stated by the Assembly's investigative committee, was a slave by the name of Bussa (or Bussoe), an African born man, chief driver at Bayleys plantation in St Philip.[39] As yet, no specific evidence was found to attribute that status to Bussa, though he has remained so identified within the island's folk tradition. Biographical data on Bussa are also unavailable but certain inductive points may be raised. First, it is of much significance that an African born man should be the prime leader of a predominantly creole rebellion. In 1816, at least 92 per cent of the slave population was creole and the other leaders of the rebel contingent were creole.[40] Secondly, that an African should have achieved the status of chief driver suggests that he most probably was not a young man in 1816, since the slave trade was abolished in 1807, and in general it took at least ten years for Africans to acquire the language and managerial skills, plus their masters' confidence, in order to become chief slave personnel on estates.

Data supplied by rebels who confessed during their trials suggest a decentralised form of leadership. Each plantation actively involved in the insurrection threw up a rebel group which had one dominant leader. These leaders, all male slaves, met frequently to discuss logistics and strategy. Jackey, a creole slave and head driver at Simmons plantation in St Philip, was chiefly responsible for the overall coordination of these groups and convened the meetings – most of which took place on his plantation. The Assembly's report stated that he frequently invited the leaders of the rebel contingents from plantations in St Philip, such as Gittens, Byde Mill, Nightengale and Congor Road to support the insurrection. John, a slave and ranger at Simmons plantation, was Jackey's chief messenger.

According to the report, John frequently took messages to rebel groups throughout the southern and central parts of the island and also kept Bussa at Bayleys plantation informed.[41] James Bowland, a literate slave belonging to the River plantation in St Philip, confessed that John had been in frequent contact with Bussa since March and that he often took instructions to rebel groups in all the "different parishes."[42] John seemed to have believed that some measure of force was necessary in recruitment. During one of his visits to Bayleys plantation he threatened the slaves there that if they did not join in setting fire to the estate they (the other leaders) were determined to

75

burn down all their houses as well as the houses of those slaves on plantations that did not join in the rebellion.[43]

At Bayleys plantation, the chief organisers were Bussa, King Wiltshire, Dick Baileys, Johnny the Standard Bearer and Johnny Cooper. At Simmons plantation, they were Jackey, John and Nanny Grigg. In addition to these individuals, the politicisation of the field slaves and the general spreading of insurrectionist propaganda were done by three literate free coloured men, Cain Davis, Roach and Richard Sarjeant. Davis held meetings with slaves on several plantations such as Rivers and Bayleys in St Philip and Sturges in St Thomas. He propagated the view among slaves in these southern and central parishes that local planters were opposing metropolitan efforts to have them freed and that if they wanted freedom "they must fight for it".[44] Sarjeant was also reported to have mobilised slaves in the central parishes using the same kind of information and techniques as Davis.

A small number of literate slaves was also reported to have recruited many slaves in a similar manner, stating that they had obtained their information from English newspapers. The most prominent of these literate slaves was Ben James, who belonged to Ayshford plantation in St Thomas. Evidence of James' political activities are to be found in the Assembly's report. William, a slave, and chief driver at Sturges plantation in St Thomas and Jack Groom, a slave, and driver at Haynesfield in St John both confessed to being drawn into the rebellion after discussions with James, who frequently visited Bridgetown on Saturdays returning with the latest information on the progress of the abolitionist movement in England.[45] These politicising agents had established by 1816 a network of committed slaves, mostly plantation officers such as drivers and tradesmen, throughout the southern and central parishes of the island. The critical role of this small number of literate slaves and free coloured men who fomented anti-slavery sentiment was recognised by the militia. Conrad Adams Howell, Lt Colonel of the St Michael Royal Regiment of Militia, after presiding over court martial for seven weeks, trying 150 slaves and 4 free coloured men, concluded his analysis of the rebellion by stating that it was the critical activity of these "better informed"[46] individuals which accounted for the extensive nature of the rebellion.

These men were not acting independently but were in consultation with Jackey through messages taken by John. For example, in early April, Jackey sent a message to one of these freemen "who could read and write" to let the slaves on his plantation know what

3 The struggle for freedom in Barbados, 1800-1833

assistance they were to give in effecting the rebellion.[47] This particular freeman lived at River plantation. In the Assembly report it is noted that he held frequent talks with Jackey. While these men were laying groundwork for rebellion under Jackey's coordination, groups of rebels were also being organised into plantation contingents for the defeat of the local militia.

The final planning of the rebellion took place at the River plantation on Good Friday night, April 12th, under the cover of a dance.[48] At this dance were Jackey, Bussa, Davis, Johnny Cooper and many of the other organisers.[49] One of the decisions taken was that Joseph Pitt Washington Francklyn, a free coloured man, the illegitimate mulatto son of Joseph Bayley Francklyn, small planter and J.P. (owner of the small plantation by the name of Vinyard in St Philip) was to be made Governor of the island in the revolutionary government.[50] At birth in 1789, Francklyn took the status of his slave mother, Leah, according to law, and was enslaved on his father's estate. In 1804, he was manumitted by his father. In that same year, the last of his father's wills, which provided handsomely for him, was declared invalid by the courts. The reason given was that it was written while Francklyn was "inflamed with passion and liquor and not of a sound and disposing mind".[51] This statement made by whites could not be contested in the courts by young Francklyn, who being a coloured man, was legally unable to give evidence in court cases involving whites. This event seemed to have hardened Francklyn's attitudes against white society. In 1807, he was tried and sentenced to six months closed imprisonment by the Court of Grand Session for threatening to flog a white man.

In 1811, however, when propertied elite among the free coloureds petitioned the Assembly in vain for the right to give testament in courts against whites, Francklyn's name appears on the petition next to those of the respected free coloured gentlemen such as John Montefiore, Jacob Belgrave, the Collymores and the Bournes.[52] The petition was read and quickly passed over. The political climate was not conducive to an extension of the rights of the free coloureds, particularly, in the apparently conservative parish of St Philip, where Francklyn lived. At the next general election, Thomas Briggs, senior member of the House for the parish, lost his seat for proposing to the constituents that the free coloureds be enfranchised.[53]

The strategy of the rebel leaders was to integrate most slaves with authority on their estate into the rebellion. These plantation officers (drivers, tradesmen and other artisans) were to spearhead the attack upon the planters. In other words, these slaves who were entrusted with authority and status by their masters were to use it against them. Theoretically, this meant self-rejection of their role as 'middle-management' since they were the ones most responsible for keeping the field slaves productive and subordinated. In association with the four free coloured men and the few free blacks, these officers were the vanguard of the armed struggle for general emancipation. It was primarily an elitist rebellion in terms of leadership.

Unlike the rebellions, which took place in Demerara and Jamaica in 1823 and 1831 respectively, organised religion did not play an important role. None of the rebels were identified as priests or magicians and the church was not used in order to foster rebelliousness. The role of black Baptists was prominent in the Jamaica rebellion; Sam Sharpe, the primary leader, was a Baptist preacher. The Demerara rebellion also partially revolved around the missionary activities of John Smith. Though the Barbados Assembly passed an anti-obeah law shortly after the rebellion and suggested in the preamble that some slaves were using black magic and witchcraft to encourage insurrectionist attitudes, none of the leaders tried and executed or killed in combat were identified as obeah men. It was also essentially a secular rebellion.[54]

On the morning of Easter Sunday, Jackey had instructed Mingo, the ranger at Byde Mill plantation, to assemble his men and to rendezvous at Simmons for instructions. Mingo was also instructed to take a message to John Barnes, driver at Gittens plantation, also in St Philip, to meet him with his contingent below his garden at Byde Mill before proceeding to Simmons.[55] By 8.30 p.m. that day, the rebellion broke out.

Table 1
Principal Slave Organisers of the 1816 Barbados Rebellion

Name	Origins	Sex	Plantation	Occupation
Bussa	African	Male	Bayleys	Ranger
King Wiltshire	Creole (C)	M	Bayleys	Carpenter
Dick Bailey	C	M	Bayleys	Mason
Johnny	C	M	Bayleys	Standard Bearer
Johnny Cooper	C	M	Bayleys	Cooper
John Ranger	C	M	Bayleys	Ranger
Charles	C	M	Sandfords	Driver
Dainty	C	M	Mapps	?
Davy	C	M	Palmers	?
William	C	M	Sturges	Driver
Sandy Waterman	C	M	Fisherpond	Driver
Nanny Grigg	C	Female	Simmons	Domestic

3 The struggle for freedom in Barbados, 1800-1833

Table 1 cont'd

Name	Origins	Sex	Plantation	Occupation
Jackey	C	M	Simmons	Driver
John	C	M	Simmons	Ranger
Mingo	C	M	Byde Mill	Ranger
Will	C	M	Nightengale	Ranger
John Barnes	C	M	Gittens	Driver
King William	C	M	Sunberry	Driver
Will Green	C	M	Congor Road	Driver
Prince William	C	M	Grove	Driver
Toby	C		Chapel	Driver
Little Sambo	C	M	Adventure	?

Canes were being burnt throughout most of St Philip, signalling prematurely to rebels in the central and southern parishes that the rebellion had begun.

The image that emerges from the nature of troops and militia mobilisaton is not supportive of the planters' assertion that their internal defence system was very efficient. News of the rebellion did not reach Bridgetown and the St Anns Garrison, fifteen miles away, until 1.30 to 2.00 a.m. Monday. Colonel J.P. Mayers had travelled from Christ Church to inform Colonel Codd, commandant of the imperial troops at the St Anns Garrison, of the developments. Governor Leith was off the island and President Spooner was responsible for calling out the troops and the militia as well as the declaration of martial law. Colonel Codd was informed that

> a perfidious league of slaves in the parishes of St Philip, Christ Church, St John and St George in their mad career were setting fire to canes as well as pillaging and destroying the buildings on many estates and otherwise pursuing a system of devastation which has seldom been equalled.[56]

In spite of this information it was not until minutes before 10.00 a.m. that parties of the imperial troops moved out of the garrison. The mobilisation of the militia, though slow, was somewhat more efficient than the muster of the imperial troops. Though one cannot argue firmly that the white imperial soldiers, probably still recovering from the war against the French, were not fully convinced that this was primarily their battle as their movements during the entirety of the rebellion showed a certain lack of enthusiasm for combat.

The St Philip and Christ Church militia was fully mustered by 5.00 a.m. About 6.00 a.m., the Life Guard, part of the militia force, was prepared to convey intelligence to the field officers concerning the spread of the insurrection. According to Colonel Eversley of the St Philip and Christ Church Regiments, the first detachment moved out at 5.00 a.m., the second about 7.00 a.m. and the third, under his command, about 9.00 a.m.[57] By 9.30 a.m., the imperial troops had not been fully mustered.[58] The battalions of St Philip and Christ Church militia, once in the field, moved quickly and with great confidence. The second detachment under the command of Colonel Best, one of the largest planters in the parish of Christ Church, was subsequently highly praised by the Assembly for the efficiency of its performance.[59] In addition, it was noted that throughout the rebellion the speedy manoeuvring of Colonel Best's detachment was matched only by the left wing of the 1st West Indian (Black) Regiment under the command of Major Cassidy.[60]

The core parishes of the rebellion, St Philip and Christ Church, while being topographically unsuited to the 'hit and run' methods of warfare used by rebel slaves in the New World, were the two most densely populated – outside of St Michael where Bridgetown, the capital, was located. The islandwide census for 1817 (see table below) showed Christ Church with a slave total population of 9,915, the largest after St Michael. Next was St Philip with 9,475. Other parishes had slave populations of between 3,000 and 6,000. Outside of St Michael, or more precisely, Bridgetown and its environs, these two parishes also contained the largest white population. St Philip had a total white population of 1,393 and Christ Church, 1,618.[61] These two parishes had the largest proportions of the island's white males who were able to bear arms and consequently, at least numerically, had the strongest militia. In April 1816, the total black population of the island was approximately 77,000. The free coloured population, which under the 1812 Militia Act was required to contribute to militia service, was 3,007. By this time the size of the militia force was between 3,200 and 3,350 men.[62]

When the parishes of St John, St Thomas and St George are included as the outer circle of the rebellion then the estimated total slave population exposed directly to the rebellion would be about 36,700. In 1816, the sexual structure of the slave population was approximately 54 per cent female and 46 per cent male. Of the same 16,982 males, about 30 per cent were aged (over 60 years) and juvenile (under 16 years).[63] This meant that only about 12,887 male slaves in these parishes were able to bear arms. By piecing together the data on the rebellion it is possible to state, though tentatively, that no more than 30 per cent of these men took up arms and engaged the militia and imperial troops. Therefore, based upon this calculation, about 3,900 male slaves were involved in armed combat with the militia and regular soldiers, who totalled about 4,000 men. Watson,

3 The struggle for freedom in Barbados, 1800-1833

without giving any calculation, suggested that no more than 5,000 slaves were involved.[64]

No known evidence exists to suggest that women, though they were involved in the organisation of the rebellion, for which some of them were executed, took part in the armed clashes. Taking into consideration that a small proportion of the island's total militia forces were deployed in St Lucy, St Peter and St James and that a detachment of the imperial troops was sent to guard Bridgetown, it is possible to suggest that the number of slaves involved in armed combat probably did not exceed the number of militiamen and imperial soldiers deployed.

Table 2

Size and Distribution of the Barbados Population, 1816-1817[65]

Parish	Free Coloured 1816	Slaves 1817	Whites 1817	Blacks to Whites 1817
St John	100	5,469	1,246	4.3:1
St Joseph	89	3,466	1,124	3.0:1
Christ Church	82	9,915	1,618	6.0:1
St Michael	1,933	18,193	5,038	3.6:1
St Thomas	76	5,173	835	6.2:1
St George	94	6,762	945	7.1:1
St Andrew	178	3,394	630	5.3:1
St Lucy	35	5,466	1,058	5.1:1
St Philip	147	9,475	1,393	6.8:1
St Peter	240	6,230	1,379	4.5:1
St James	33	3,950	755	5.2:1
Total	3,007	77,493	16,021	4.8:1

The first major battle between the militia and the rebel army took place on Lowthers plantation at noon on Monday. Colonel Eversley noted that the three detachments of the Christ Church and St Philip militia were instructed before leaving Oistin Bay in Christ Church to rendezvous at Fairy Valley, immediately south of Coverley plantation in the parish. He stated:

> It was about twelve o'clock that we met with a large body of the insurgent slaves in the yard of Lowthers plantation [1½ mile north of Fairy Valley], several of whom were armed with muskets, who displayed the Colours of the St Philip Battalion, which they had stolen, and who, upon seeing the division, cheered and cried out to us, 'come on!' but were quickly dispersed upon being fired on.[66]

Colonel Best was accredited by the Assembly for engineering the defeat of the rebels at Lowthers – the battle which is said to have undermined the morale of the rebels and illustrated their military weakness.[67] His account of the battle represents to date the most detailed report on an encounter between militia forces and the rebel forces.

Colonel Best stated that on arrival at Lowthers with the 2nd detachment, they encountered a rebel contingent which outnumbered his men by a ratio of four to one. The militiamen, nonetheless, were confident that they could defeat the slaves and drew great psychological strength from the realisation that, in the words on Colonel Best, "defeat would have been worst than death".[68] The militiamen fought as if the entire existence of white civilisation was at stake. Reports of the rebel massacre of white soldiers and civilians in Haiti were common topics of discussion among Barbadian whites and Colonel Best had no difficulty generating a high level of courage and enthusiasm among his men. He noted that the rebels had consolidated their position at Lowthers, "joined by every Negro belonging to the plantation".[69] For no other plantation is there evidence that all the slaves joined the rebel forces. On seeing the militia approach the estate they formed what Colonel Best describes as an "irregular line" before commencing their attack. The formation of lines was a common strategic technique in European military culture and its adoption by the Lowthers' slaves reflects either their military confidence or the extreme degree of creolisation experienced by the island's slave community. Ambush and surprise attacks, the common military techniques used by the West Indian slaves and maroons in their battle with white and militiamen, were initially abandoned at Lowthers, though employed in other battles later that day. The militiamen also formed their line, no doubt a more regular one and the battle was commenced. Best noted:

> My lads were too anxious and began to fire while I was leading them close up... One Negro was brandishing his sword, which my soldiers could not witness without endeavouring to knock him over. Others were arm'd with pitchforks, which on seeing the militia commenced firing... They gave way immediately.[70]

Under pressure from the militia's superior firepower, the rebel army fled in different directions but to reassemble later for the counter-attack. Many fled north through Woodbourne and some east into Searles. The largest group, however, fled south through Coverley, the direction which the militia took to Lowthers after it had assembled at Fairy Valley. Best continued:

> We pursued and killed some; their rapid flight, however, saved numbers. We had to march from estate to estate to quell the

3 The struggle for freedom in Barbados, 1800-1833

insurgents for they all set to plunder and destroy the dwelling houses. We killed about 30 men... [and] had not even a man wounded. Yes! One slightly by a shot from a pistol. The villain was shot down immediately.[71]

While the Christ Church militia was pursuing the rebels, one group, which had reassembled on the periphery of Lowthers, doubled back and proceeded to finish the destruction of the estate.[72] At Coverley, just south of Lowthers, the slaves did not assist the fleeing rebels in combat with the militia. When Colonel Best took a unit of his men through the estate in search of the fleeing Lowthers rebels, the slaves merely observed them passively. Colonel Best was not convinced, however, that this meant their non-commitment to the rebellion. He noted that the following day these Coverley slaves went on strike. Their refusal to work, Best believed, was the result "either of fear of the rebels or from being too deeply implicated in their plans".[73] He offered no specific explanation but left the ambivalence for Abel Dottin, absentee owner of the estate, to reconcile.

An outstanding feature of the battle at Lowthers was the great courage and loyalty displayed by the free coloured men of the Christ Church militia under Colonel Best's command. When news of the rebellion spread throughout southern Barbados, the free coloured men, with little or no hesitation came to the assistance of the white community. It is not known what percentage of the some 3,007 free coloured population had enrolled for militia service but Colonel Best had many within his detachment. Throughout the years of the war with the French, the propertied and 'respectable' members of this community had adopted a posture supportive of the planter elite in order to gain political support for their objectives. They did not aggressively confront the white community but were generally moderate and humble in their political demands. Unlike the free coloureds in other islands whose ideological expressions in relation to slaves and whites show much ambivalence, in Barbados their leadership was firmly pro-planter. Colonel Best believed that his free coloured men were instrumental in the defeat of the blacks at Lowthers and during the subsequent mopping up operation. He wrote:

> The free colour'd people behaved admirably. They, as well as the white soldiers that I commanded were devoted to me... They would dash singly into a house full of rebels without looking behind for support and dig out the fellows. It was this intrepid courage that appalled the blacks.[74]

The Christ Church militia, having killed 30 rebels at Lowthers on Monday afternoon, continued to track down scattered groups throughout the night and the following Tuesday morning. By Tuesday midday, Colonel Best reported that another 10 were killed in combat. He was, however, alarmed by the shift in the rebels' strategy. Unable to make any headway against the militia forces, the rebels, according to Best, resorted to a more extensive system of arson in order to inflict maximum damage upon the planters. Best wrote:

> Large quantities of canes were burnt and I think more on the second night than the first, which proved that although the rebels were subdued by the armies, they were nevertheless determined to do all possible mischief. Houses were gutted and the very floors taken up. The destruction is dreadful, the plundering beyond anything you can conceive could be effected in so short a time.[75]

Nonetheless, Colonel Best continued,

> Our success at Lowthers and our subsequent rapid movements on that day stopped the progress of the rebellion in Christ Church. The news of our success passed quickly to the rebels in the upper part of St Philip and struck dismay.[76]

In comparison, however, the progress of the imperial troops was rather less than exemplary. Colonel Codd, commandant at the Garrison, stated that he had received information concerning the rebellion about 2.00 a.m. Monday and about "10.00 a.m., having waited in vain for authentic information of the strength and position of the insurgents... deemed it necessary to march off to the quarter of the country where the alarm had first spread".[77] This suggests either a breakdown in military intelligence or a lack of keenness to be involved in the affair. He moved with a force consisting of three field pieces under the command of Major Brough and in order not to expose his men to what appears to be fanatical slaves, he called out 150 [black] men of the first West India Regiment under Major Cassidy's command to support the 200 men of the 15th regiment under the command of Lt Colonel Davidson. Also accompanying this force were the 250 men of the Royal Regiment of the St Michael militia under the command of Colonel Mayers. Left behind was "a force fully adequate to the protection of the Garrison and town under the command of Lt Colonel Edwards of the Bourbon Regiment".[78]

On his way to the thicket, Colonel Mayers received intelligence that a body of rebels had made a stand there.[79] But before reaching the area his detachment met up with men from the St Philip militia, who were being attacked by a rebel group from Sandford plantation. Both militia groups withdrew and rested the night. At daybreak they

3 The struggle for freedom in Barbados, 1800-1833

jointly attacked the rebels in Sandford plantation yard and the rebels were dispersed – some were killed and prisoners were also taken. These Sandford slaves, unlike those at Lowthers, did not form lines of attack but tried to ambush the militiamen in the plantation yard.[80] Some of these rebels were armed with muskets. Charles, their chief driver, and also leader of the plantation, was on horseback giving orders and waving his muskets.[81] It was during this battle that Brewster, the militiaman, was killed.[82]

The West Indian Regiment arrived outside of Bayleys plantation Monday evening before sunset. Major Cassidy sent a message to Colonel Codd, who was only seven miles away, informing him that he had identified a large party of insurgents but as he could not ascertain their numbers, he desired whether he should await his coming or attack them immediately. Colonel Codd, not surprisingly, informed Major Cassidy that he must act to the best of his judgement but that he would not bring his troops until daybreak.[83] At dawn the battle at Bayleys, between an estimated 400 rebels and 150 men of the 1st West India regiment, commenced.[84] It was during this battle that Bussa was probably killed. One white soldier stated that the rebels, on seeing the black regiment approaching, were temporarily confused.[85] There had been many rumours in the slave ranks that a Haitian revolutionary army would be landing at Barbados to assist with their struggle for freedom.

The experiences of Loveless Overton illustrate the impact which the Haitian revolution had on the Barbadian slaves, some of whom believed that King Christophe would have sent troops to assist them in their struggle. Overton, a free coloured man, trumpeter in the King's Dragoon Guards, landed at Bridgetown on February 20th, 1817. The following day, while walking through the town wearing his uniform, he saw a white man beating his slave. He ventured to assist the slave. The following day he was arrested for being "an emissary from St Domingo". Overton noted that his arrest "caused a great sensation among the slaves who now seemed to believe that [he] was an emissary". Many slaves, he noted, believed that "my arrival was in some measure connected to them". While in gaol many slaves approached his cell desiring to know what his instructions were. He also noted that the free coloureds who had been anti-rebellion informed him that his life was in danger, given the slaves' anxiety over his presence and the fears of the whites. He was eventually released by an officer of his regiment but was re-arrested two weeks later as rumours circulated in Bridgetown that the country Negroes who saw him were of the opinion that his intentions were to revive rebellious sentiments.

The next day he was shipped out to England.[86]

Some rebels at Bayleys on seeing the black soldiers in red uniforms were probably under the impression that these men were their Haitian reinforcements. It is also plausible that some of the rebels knew exactly who these soldiers were but probably thought that racial solidarity might have prevailed instead. In any event, there was some initial confusion in the ranks. The soldier wrote:

> The insurgents did not think our men would fight against black men, but thank God they were deceived... The conduct of our Bourbon Blacks, particularly the light company under Captain Smith (an old twelfth hand) has been the admiration of everybody and deservedly.[87]

When the rebels realised that the 'Bourbon Blacks' were there to defeat, rather than assist them, they fired and immediately killed two of them, badly wounding another. The fire was returned and after much exchange, 40 rebels were killed and 70 taken prisoner. Most were dispersed, once again, as a result of superior firepower. A large group fled north and reassembled at Golden Grove plantation, some three-quarter mile away. They took cover at the plantation's 'great house', owned by assemblyman, Mr. Grasset. The 'Bourbon Blacks' pursued them and surrounded the house, from which the rebels fired upon them. According to the soldier's narrative, the rebels "were soon dislodged, many of them killed and wounded leaping from the windows and rushing through the doors".[88]

About 8.30 a.m., after the rebels were defeated, Colonel Codd arrived at Bayleys with his white soldiers. He was quick, however, to order his men to take over the mopping up operations in the area. He informed the Governor:

> The only plan I could then adopt was to destroy their [slaves] houses in order to deprive them of some of their hiding places and resources, and to recover their plunder. After diligently scanting them, I set fire to and consumed several on those plantations where little else remained.[89]

During the operation, Colonel Codd noted that some of the militiamen of the parishes in insurrection, "under the irritation of the moment and exasperated at the atrocity of the insurgents... were inclined to use their arms rather too indiscriminately in pursuit of the fugitives".[90] Slaves not in rebellion were killed in this rampage; many of them had return to their estates having been out in hiding from the rebel forces.

During the morning, while these purges were taking place,

3 The struggle for freedom in Barbados, 1800-1833

Colonel Codd received "the most alarming account" from Lt General Hayes of the militia that the rebels were consolidating their forces in St John where great damage was being done to the estates and that a "body of insurgents had threatened the town and thrown it into the greatest confusion".[91] The slaves were now taking the core of the rebellion into the outer regions of St John, St George and St Thomas. Some rebels who had escaped the Christ Church militia at Lowthers were preparing to make an onslaught on Bridgetown. Colonel Codd immediately called up Colonel Mayers of the St Michael militia to fall back on Bridgetown with a party of the 15th regiment, taking all prisoners who were captured at Bayleys, Thickets and Golden Grove.[92]

Colonel Codd documented his movements for Tuesday afternoon as follows: "Having secured my position at Bayleys, the rendezvous of the insurgents, I marched off in the direction of St John to offer protection in that quarter."[93] He arrived there about 4.00 p.m. that afternoon (Tuesday) and was soon "perfectly satisfied" that "the insurgents were not in a position strong enough for attack or defence".[94] Still worried that rebel slaves out in the field would double back on Bayleys, as they had done during the Lowthers battle, Colonel Codd returned there with a party of 70 men and a field piece. By Tuesday night, according to Colonel Codd, conflagrations had ceased "and the dismay and alarm which had seized the colonists in a great degree subsided".[95] He returned to headquarters on Wednesday. By this time at least 150 blacks were killed, four free coloureds and over 400 blacks arrested and pending trial.[96] The Bridgetown scare was short-lived and mopping up operations continued swiftly in the central parishes.

By Wednesday morning the St Lucy rebels were also quelled. They had entered the rebellion, not on the Sunday night, but during the following Monday. The limited information relating to the rebellion in this parish suggests that a small group of slaves had set about burning selected estates. Three estates in all were extensively damaged. Bourbon plantation was the most damaged. No fighting between rebels and militia was reported. It seems that these slaves withdrew as a detachment of the St Lucy, St Andrew, St Thomas and St Peter militias arrived in the area. By midday Wednesday the rebellion was perceived by Colonel Codd to be squashed as group resistance and arson had ceased. For their loyalty to the whites, the free coloured people were given legal right to give testimony in courts in all occasions – an objective they had pursued with great vigour since 1801.

The rebellion was not sudden and without prior evidence of its making. Since the turn of the century, the slaves had been becoming increasingly anxious and restless as they perceived the possibility of obtaining legislated freedom to be unlike all previous times, fairly good. Parliamentary discussions in England were serious and fruitful as seen in the 1807 Abolition Act and subsequent amelioration measures. Then there was also the example set by the Haitians, which, according to Watson, though it is difficult to measure, must not be undervalued in terms of its psychological impact upon the slaves in the region. Mrs Fenwick stated that in the years prior to the rebellion, the slaves did not only seem restless but many were visibly refusing to be co-operative. This was especially so among the artisans and the domestics, the elite slaves who were closer to both full freedom and political information. These were the ones who seemed to have had much political and social influence over their communities.[97]

Some planters were aware of the growing agitation and increasing social tension. During the House of Assembly debate of December 10th, 1810 it was noted that "the increase of arrogance and vice among the slaves" particularly those in Bridgetown who were more aware of the activities of Mr Wilberforce "has occasioned, nay demanded punishment".[98] For the first time since the early eighteenth century, serious discussions were taking place in the Assembly concerning the "relaxed state of the police and the effects which it produces amongst the slaves".[99] From 1804, when the Haitian revolutionaries declared their independence from France, House Assembly debates became increasingly focused upon the apparent increase of insolence among the slaves. Robert Haynes, planter-assemblyman, stated that he knew there was something "brewing up in their minds" but never suspected it to be of rebellious proportions.[100] It was generally thought that a tightening of police systems was all that was necessary to restore the traditional order.

The extensive growth of general slave aggression to planter authority during this period is now well established in literature. In Barbados, this was reflected in an increased level of anti-planter activity such as an expansion in the numbers of runaway slaves. It could be suggested that the incidents of the *marronage* cannot be considered a good indicator of the slaves' specific rejection of the planter-authority but represents more of an increased desire for leisure and social activity. However, when it is realised that many of these slaves in this period who attempted *marronage* were executed, unlike the eighteenth century when punishments for *petit marronage* (temporary absence from the estate) were generally corporal in nature, the obvious seriousness of this political development can be appreciated.

3 The struggle for freedom in Barbados, 1800-1833

For example, on January 14th, 1831, William Adamson was paid £25 by the island's treasurer for his slave, Abel, who was executed at Law for running away.[101] In August of the same year, Cuffy, a slave belonging to Thomas Grassett, owner of Golden Grove plantation in St Philip, was executed at Law for running away. Grassett was paid £25 and the constable, Jacob Norm, received £2.10 for his capture.[102]

Between 1808 and 1815, the system of slave control came under increased pressure and this resulted in the development of new forms of social control. Slave unrest reached a stage whereby plantation managers were unable to impose discipline in an effective manner without resort to public facilities such as prisons and the Bridgetown Cage; the latter was an institution, which was used from the seventeenth century to confine runaway slaves while the process of law was being implemented.[103] In April 1811, the Speaker of the House of Assembly, John Beckles, while accepting the need to improve the efficiency of slave control, the result of increased slave resistance, informed the House that the practise of owners sending their slaves to the Cage as a general punishment was illegal.[104] Beckles insisted that only captured runaway slaves and not general insubordinate slaves should be confined to the Cage.[105] The Bridgetown Cage was soon reported to be filled with captured runaways and other rebellious slaves. This was a new development. One constable informed the House that for the following month of May 1811, 28 slaves were imprisoned in the Cage for running away, 24 lodged there by their owners for general insubordination and nine legally committed for committing serious public offences.[106] Between 1811 and 1816, the names of over 200 slaves were listed in the *Barbados Mercury* and *Bridgetown Gazette* as captured runaways, some of whom were executed for rebellion. Many owners refused to repossess their captured slaves and some insisted that the full force of the law be applied, that is, capital punishment especially for those who committed public crimes while absent.

An analysis of the above-mentioned lists illustrates that a substantial portion of runaways were elite slaves, particularly, artisans and also that many were mulattos. These were the elite slaves upon whom the plantations depended for smooth operation and social stability. Their increasing restlessness and hostility to planter authority was illustrated by the full range of actions from negative work attitudes to open rebellion. Many advertisements for elite slave runaways, appeared in newspapers in 1815-1816. For example, notices appeared for Ben Stuart, "a runaway mulatto carpenter, who looks very much like a white man with light straight hair and grey eyes";[107] for Joe, a fisherman, popularly known in Bridgetown, St Thomas and Christ Church;[108] for April who "has a very English tongue".[109] Also listed in the minutes of Council were those runaways executed at Law. For example, in 1811, Issac Parfitt and James Moore petitioned the Council for £25 each for the value of their rebellious slaves executed at Law.[110] The increased number of executions suggests that this upsurge of maroon activity was not simply the result of slaves' desire for a few hours or days respite from the plantations. These were the elite slaves who led the rebellion.

Under martial law during June and early July, slaves continued to be arrested and tried. In September, some were arrested for trying to organise a second insurrection. Colonel Best, who sat on the court martial which tried slaves arrested for planning this aborted September rebellion, informed Abel Dottin:

> The Negroes have hatched up another conspiracy... Murder was to have been the order of the day. As a former occasion, the drivers, rangers, carpenters, and watchmen were chiefly concerned and free field labourers... I am under no apprehension as to the consequences ... It is no longer delusion amongst the slaves... I once thought before, I am now convinced that they are not entirely, if at all, led away in the last business by delusion. They conceived themselves to be sufficiently numerous to become the masters... of the island.[111]

The captives, according to Best, confessed that on the last occasion their tactics were wrong. Instead of engaging the entire militia in open combat, they should have aimed at and killed only the mounted officers and by this means the rank and file would flee.[112] This was the plan for the September affair but it was betrayed by a slave who informed the militia that he was offered any position in the rebel organisation which he desired.

Thomas Moody stated that this September affair, which originated in the parish of Christ Church, "excited much alarm and uneasiness in the minds of the inhabitants".[113] When the Secretary of State for the Colonies, however, requested Governor Leith to send all information relating to the insurrectionary attempt, it seems to have caused him much difficulty. He replied: "It does not... appear that the affair in question is of any extent to cause alarm, and may more properly by regarded as the result of one or two turbulent men, disappointed in their failure, endeavouring ineffectually to reproduce unsubordination."[114]

The aborted September affair suggests, however, that slaves persisted with attempts to overthrow the planters' regime and by that means gain their freedom. It became clear to the planters that

3 The struggle for freedom in Barbados, 1800-1833

much greater repression was necessary to keep the slave in subjection. John Beckles summed up the debate in the House concerning the crisis in slave control by stating that the rebellious "spirit" of the slave was

> not subdued, nor will it ever be subdued whilst the dangerous doctrines [of the abolitionist lobby] which have been spread abroad continue to be propagated among them. It behoves us to be upon guard, to keep a watch that we may not again be caught so shamefully unprepared. The comfort and happiness of our families require it – the safety and tranquillity of the island call for it. It is a duty which we owe our country.[115]

The last remaining captives were not dealt with until January 1817. About 1 o'clock Saturday afternoon, January 25th, 123 rebels were removed from gaols, escorted by the flank companies of the Royal Regiment to the Bridgetown wharf where they were conveyed on board the ship *Francis and Mary* in which they were to be transported to Honduras, presumably to be employed in cutting down the valuable mahogany forests in that colony. The Lt Governor of the colony refused to accept them on the grounds that his police system was inadequate. They were eventually shipped out to Sierra Leone in West Africa – the ironic punishment of attempting to gain their freedom.[116]

Following the death of Governor James Leith, Lord Chambers Combermere was appointed Governor. He arrived at Barbados on June 3rd, 1817 and assumed the government the following day. The bill, which had become law on February 5th, in spite of "some angry debates" in the House, "allowing the testimony of free Negroes and free people of colour to be taken in all cases", had exacerbated the anxiety of black slaves over their own amelioration and freedom.[117] As a result, Lord Combermere's reign (1817-1820) was characterised by his effort to respond to both the demands of the increasingly restless slaves and the need to strengthen the system of slave control on the island. In his address to the Legislature on June 17th, 1817 he congratulated the House for the February 5th decision and then informed the members of the two policies which he intended to pursue as governor.

First, he noted, the island needed the establishment of a well constituted police system to ensure security and order; secondly, the "political happiness of the island" rested upon the extensive diffusion of religious instructions to slaves and free blacks. On September 9th that year, shortly after the elections, Combermere reiterated his policies to a full but seemingly disinterested House. When the new

Assembly convened on November 3rd, once again the Governor's speech carried the same message. On this occasion, however, the Assembly saw it fit to respond and the Speaker of the House made the following remark:

> We shall not fail to notice your Excellency's remarks on the propriety of revising, correcting and consolidating such of our laws as relate to the treatment and government of slaves – the first step to which, it will be in the recollection of your Excellency, was taken by the House of Representatives at their last sitting, by the repel and expulsion from our statue-book of some of the most disgraceful and obnoxious clauses.[118]

Schomburgk noted that this was the last friendly address which the Governor was to receive from the House. Some members suggested that his policies were merely stirring up the old troubles of 1816 and tending towards the renewal of political instability. The House did not believe that any further ameliorations were possible and thought that it had bent to the request of the imperial government, the slaves and free coloureds, to its maximum. The policy was now clear: any insurrection of slaves or free coloureds would be met with the full military power available. Furthermore, that the threat of insurrection was not an acceptable reason for any further amendments. The Governor, defeated in his endeavours, withdrew and departed from the island with his family on June 12th, 1820. Before his departure, however, he made an address to the House, which was concluded as follows:

> Mr. President and Gentlemen of the Legislative Council, Mr. Speaker and Gentlemen of the House of Assembly.
> A spirit of insubordination has been planted, the fruit of which may one day be gathered with sorrow and repentance, unless the returning good sense of the people provide timely remedy.[119]

On June 10th, 1823, Governor Sir Henry Wade published a proclamation in which he tried to discredit the view made popular among slave communities by an unidentified small group of "disloyal slaves" that freedom was shortly to be issued by the imperial government. The Governor warned the slaves that they must not become victims, as they had done in April 1816, of such propaganda and that all such publicity should be viewed as their enemies.[120] On this occasion, no attempted insurrection was reported and much caution seemed to have prevailed in the slave communities in relation to the information. On August 30th, the news of the slave insurrection in Demerara reached Barbados. The Governor, General Murray, seemed to have

3 The struggle for freedom in Barbados, 1800-1833

been expecting the insurrection as martial law had been proclaimed since August 18th. Information publicised in Barbados stressed the easy suppression of the rebellious attempt rather than the details of its organisation, motives and leadership. This was designed to impress upon the Barbadian slaves the folly of such actions and to remind them that only by a peaceful performance of their duty could they, in the words of the late Governor Leith in 1816, hope for any further "amelioration to their condition."

Meanwhile, white society lived in anticipation of a slave revolt and the memories of April 1816 were still fresh. The free coloureds used this opportunity, as they had done in 1816, to press the Legislative Council for an extension of their civil rights. In December 1823, a petition signed by 372 of them addressed to the Governor, stated that as British subjects, there were still parts of the colonial code, which deprived them of participating with their "white brethren" in certain privileges and that because of the present unstable political condition of the colony they were prepared to make only moderate claims. The Legislative Council, angered by what it considered to be the audacity of the free coloureds, issued a resolution, which stated:

> This House in the most positive and unequivocal manner denies that the free coloured inhabitants of this island are entitled to any rights and privileges except those granted to them by the Council Legislature, the continuance of which depends entirely on their good conduct.[121]

The refusal of the West Indian legislatures to ameliorate slave conditions by legal reform was identified as responsible, not only for the 1816 rebellion, but also the 1823 Demerara insurrection. Thomas Fowell Buxton, the principal spokesman for the parliamentary humanitarian lobby, charged in 1823 that the present brutal and illiberal conditions under which the West Indian slaves exist, were not only an affront to the spirit of the Christian religion but the natural bedrock for insurrectionist attitudes. He then called for the prompt abolition of slavery in all its variations in the British Caribbean. In this year, fears of insurrection continued to sweep through the Caribbean. In Trinidad, St Lucia and Dominica, reports of such fears were made to the Colonial Office and in Jamaica, 11 slaves were executed for plotting to destroy the white inhabitants.[122]

The House of Commons debate on May 15th, 1823 on a motion for the mitigation and gradual abolition of slavery throughout the British Empire had placed much emphasis upon the growing agitation of slaves and the inevitability of insurrection. Buxton tried to impress upon the House the full significance of the Haitian revolution upon the British slaves. This was not new to the Barbadians, who in 1816 had suspected some degree of Haitian participation in the insurrection. He told the House that it should not be difficult to imagine the political attitudes of slaves in the British islands, knowing that on a nearby island some 800,000 blacks (men, women and children) exercise all their rights and enjoy the innumerable and incalculable blessings which freedom gives.[123]

Parliamentarians were not convinced by Buxton and his colleagues that immediate emancipation was in the interest of the slaves and their masters but Colonial Secretary Bathurst was given leave to urge the legislatures of the various colonies to adopt measures to significantly ameliorate the conditions of the slaves. Bathurst recommended that each colony should appoint a protector to safeguard the slaves from extreme maltreatment and slaves should have the right, now enjoyed by the free blacks and free coloureds, to testify against whites. Overseers and drivers should not be allowed to inflict corporal punishments and a record should be kept of all such punishment administered on the estates. The breaking up of slave families should be prohibited and slaves should be encouraged to attend church on Sundays.[124]

The Barbadian planters rejected these proposals. They argued that these were concessions to the slave which would tend towards the creation of a widespread insurrectionist attitude that did not already exist. If the slaves were given these rights, they would openly confront their masters and dare them to retaliate; it would be giving legislative support to the fomenting insubordinate ideas of the minority of rebels in the slave communities. The Governor, Henry Wade, supported the planters' rejection of Bathurst's plans. The Legislative Council implied that Bathurst had become an agent of the Wilberforce movement, which was committed to their destruction. In a letter to the Colonial Office, the Council stated quiet firmly that the island would not allow "fanaticism, prejudice and injustice" of the humanitarian movement to sign their death warrant and that "neither threats nor persuasion will ever induce them to put the finishing hand to their political, perhaps natural existence".[125]

In 1824, however, the Speaker of the Assembly introduced a bill to consolidate and improve the slave laws of Barbados with an attempt to secure the more effective management of the slave population. The bill was debated by the House for about ten months. Its provisions were moderate in nature and fell short of those demanded by Bathurst. The bill made the following concessions to the slaves: they

3 The struggle for freedom in Barbados, 1800-1833

could give testament in courts against whites, thus putting them on equal status with free coloureds and free blacks; they could now legally own property in courts, even though they themselves were, by law, real estate; in addition, the fees for manumission were greatly diminished. In the event of slaves using such rights to increase their insubordination or to become insurrectionist, the bill also provided that any slave who threatened to strike their white master would be guilty of a capital crime; in addition, any white who killed a slave who was in the act of insurrection would be immune from persecution.[126] After the Act was rejected by the Colonial Office, it was amended by the Council. The immunity clause, which protected whites, was removed and the Act was accepted.

Meanwhile, according to Schomburgk, "The agitation amongst the labouring class continued."[127] In 1824, a slave by the name of Joseph Griffith was charged with inciting other slaves on the island into acts of rebellion. A court martial, however, was not assembled, as the members of the House considered the incident to be of minor significance. Nonetheless, the want of a police presence for preserving order in Bridgetown became daily more apparent: attacks on the property of white inhabitants were almost nightly committed; windows were broken, "without the offenders being brought to justice".[128] Most of these offences against property were blamed on the large number of urban blacks, both slave and free, who from the early nineteenth century, were identified as a criminal element. The growing aggression of the blacks was not confined to those in Bridgetown. Cases of plantation larceny were cited to be on the increase and the slaves' growing disregard for the traditional authority of overseers and mangers was generally recognised.

During the December Grand Session of 1826, John G. Archer was indicted for the murder of a slave. This case occupied the attention of the black and white population throughout its duration as it was of critical significance to the future of the legal aspects of race relations in the colony. According to a law of 1805, the wilful murder of a slave was a capital felony but to procure evidence to gain a conviction was almost impossible. Archer was a man of substantial property and the court was faced with the difficulty of finding a jury that would be impartial to the case. The Governor appointed the Honourable Renn Hamden to preside over the case as he was noted to possess an "independent and manly character."[129] Archer was found guilty of manslaughter and sentenced to one year imprisonment. Subsequent to this judgement, a few whites were convicted upon the evidence of slaves and sentenced to imprisonment. The slaves had entered the system, a significant achievement, and this traditional cornerstone of white supremacy in Barbados was undermined.

As the legal rights of slaves increased, the free coloureds and free blacks became increasingly militant about the extension of their own civil rights. Their objective was to maintain that distance of privilege, which they enjoyed over the slaves. On February 22nd, 1831, Mr. Robert Haynes, member of the House for St John, introduced a bill into the Assembly, the objective of which was to give full civil rights to the free coloured peoples. The bill was passed by the House on June 7th, only four members voting against it. The Act conferred upon the free coloured people equal legal rights with the whites such as, to elect members to the House of Assembly and Vestries and to serve on juries, providing they met the property requirement and were Christians.[130]

These legislative events, Schomburgk noted, took place against the background of a "constant dread of insurrection" in the island.[131] On August 1st, 1833, the imperial government passed an Act abolishing slavery in the British Empire. The Act provided that from August 1st, 1834, all persons registered as slaves, of the age of six and above, shall become apprentice labourers in the employ of the persons previously entitled to their labour. Those under six were immediately fully freed. The apprenticeship of domestics, artisans, and other non-praedial labourers was to cease on August 1st, 1838 and those praedial labourers attached to sugar cultivation, on August 15th, 1840. In 1838, however, after much criticism of the apprenticeship system, all labourers were fully emancipated in the British West Indies.

It would not be an exaggeration to state that the reform of legal relations in Barbados after 1816, particularly the 1817 concessions to free coloureds and free blacks, and the 1826 Consolidation Laws were related to the rebellion. In the case of the former reform it was total but only partly so in the case of the latter. The rebellion did destroy the social and political complacency of the white ruling class in Barbados, in spite of their politically motivated statements to the contrary. Social tension did increase in the years after the rebellion and occasional incidents intensified that tension. Though the whites remained confident that they could defeat the slaves in combat, they were, nonetheless, unprepared to suffer the human and material cost that would result from such a confrontation. The Consolidation Act of 1826 was part of the Assembly's response to the demands of the slaves, which though not articulated by them, were clear to the ruling class.

Under pressure from below in the case of slaves, and above, in

3 The struggle for freedom in Barbados, 1800-1833

the case of the imperial parliament, the planters had no choice but to make these fundamental concessions. The free coloureds, by giving their military and verbal loyalty to the whites, won their rights on the back of the blacks but the slave continued to ride close behind them in the pursuit of their full human rights. The Emancipation Bill of 1833 was fought for by the slaves in Barbados, Demerara and Jamaica in 1816, 1823 and 1831, respectively. In addition, the rebel slaves provided the abolitionist movement with information and a socio-political climate in the colony, which they could manipulate positively in the House of Commons. Parliament was convinced in 1832 that the colonies were now irretrievably destabilised.

Barbados, generally referred to as the most ancient and loyal colony by the Colonial Secretaries, the showpiece of their New World empire, had become socio-politically unstable as a result of insurrectionist attitudes among slaves. It seemed that the last outpost of efficient and commended slave control had finally joined the ranks of the other problematic colonies such as Jamaica. Reform and eventual emancipation were linked to this development. The slaves might not have won emancipation directly but they made its occurrence far earlier than it would otherwise have been. They allowed the imperial government to enact general emancipation in a state of humanitarian glory rather than in a state of shameful and extensive bloodletting.

Notes

1. The term 'free coloured' is used here to refer to any free person of mixed racial ancestry; it does not, therefore, include free blacks, that is, persons of solely Negroid ancestry. The term, therefore, suggests not only legal status but also specific phenotypic or racial characteristics. Handler used the term freedman collectively to include both free coloureds and free blacks. In the Spanish Caribbean and the English islands once under Spanish rule, such as Jamaica, the free coloureds were phenotypically graded between white and black and terms such as mulatto, sambo, octoroon, quadroon and mustee were used. In Barbados, these terms were not used for reasons of social classifications though sometimes mulattos were specifically identified. No matter what the level of grade between black and white, the term coloured was generally used. See J. Handler, *The Unappropriated People: Freedmen in the Slave Society of Barbados* (Baltimore, 1974), pp.1-6.
2. See G. Heuman, "White over Brown over Black: The Free Coloureds in Jamaican Society during Slavery and after Emancipation," *Journal of Caribbean History*, vol. 14, 1981, pp.46-69.
   Also, A. Sio, "Race, Colour, and Miscegenation: The Free Coloured of Jamaica and Barbados," *Caribbean Studies*, vol. 16, April 1976, pp.5-21.
3. J. Handler, op. cit., p.73.
4. Petitions were made by the free coloureds to give testament in Courts in 1801 and 1811. On both occasions the Assembly refused outright. See Minutes of the Assembly, Oct. 13th, 1801, and Feb. 19th, 1811, Barbados Archives. Also, Address of free coloureds to John Beckles, Speaker of the House, March 5th, 1811, CO 31/45.
5. Governor Seaforth fought a tough battle with the Assembly between 1801 over the issue of making the murder of a slave a capital felony. He succeeded in 1805 but only after the Secretary of State for the Colonies threatened to take measures against those assemblymen who opposed the Governor's bill. See Lord Seaforth to Secretary of State, Nov. 13th, 1804 CO 29/29, ff.44-47. Secretary of State to Lord Seaforth, Jan. 21st, 1805, CO 29/29, ff. 49-49.
6. Governor Seaforth to Secretary Camden, May 4th, 1805, CO 28/72, ff.121-122.
7. See J. Handler, op. cit., pp.41-42.
8. [John Poyer] A letter addressed to ... Lord Seaforth by a Barbadian [Bridgetown, 1801].
   See also his book, *History of Barbados from 1801 to 1803, Inclusive* (Bridgetown, 1808), pp. 9-15.
9. See K. Watson, *The Civilised Island, Barbados: A Social History 1750-1816* (Bridgetown, 1979), p.104.
10. The bill prevented both free coloureds and free blacks from owning more than 5 slaves or owning more than 10 acres of land. They would not be allowed to bequeath any property to their progeny or other freed persons. See Minutes of the Barbados Assembly, Nov. 9th, 1802, Barbados Archives. See also, J. Handler, op. cit., p.78.
11. The petition of the Free Coloureds, Minutes of Council, Nov. 1st, 1803. Lucas MSS.
12. Minutes of Council, Nov. 1st, 1803, Barbados Archives.
13. *Barbados Mercury and Bridgetown Gazette* (*BMBG*), Tuesday, September 10th, 1816.
14. *Remarks on the Insurrection in Barbados and the Bill for the*

3 The struggle for freedom in Barbados, 1800-1833

Registration of Slaves (London, 1816), f.7.
15. Ibid.
16. Ibid., f.4.
17. Ibid., f.1.
18. See *The Report from a Select Committee of the House of Assembly Appointed to inquire into the Origins, Cause, and Progress of the Late Insurrection – April 1816* (Barbados, 1818). (Hereinafter referred to as *The Report*).
19. Ibid.; see also *An Account of the Late Negro Insurrection which took place in the Island of Barbados on Easter Sunday, April 14th, 1816.* New York Public Library, MSS. Division. (NYPL).
20. Governor Leith to Bathurst, April 30th, 1816, CO 28/85, f.8.
21. Governor Leith to Bathurst, September 21st, 1816, CO 28/85, f.36.
22. *An Account of the Late Negro Insurrection…*
23. Colonel John Rycroff Best to Abel Dottin, Barbados, April 27th, 1816 (NYPL) The letters by Best are found, bound to the back of John Poyer's *History of Barbados* (1808), in the MSS. Division of the NYPL. See J. Handler. *A Guide to Source Material for the Study of Barbados History 1627-1834* (Carbondale, 1971), p.179.
24. Ibid.
25. *The Report*, Evidence of Major Oxley, p.32.
26. Mrs. Fenwick to Mary Hays, September 26th, Barbados, 1816, in A.F. Wedd (ed.), *The Fate of the Fenwicks; Letters to Mary Hays 1978-1828* (London, Methuen, 1927), p.179.
27. Colonel Codd to Governor Leith, April 25th, op. cit. See also for a detailed account of the battle at Bayleys Plantation: Extracts from a Private Letter dated April 27th, 1816, St Anns Garrison, Barbados, CO. 28/85, ff.22-23.
28. *The Report*, pp.4-5.
29. Governor Leith to Lord Bathurst, April 30th, 1816, CO. 28/25, f.9.
30. Ibid.
31. Colonel Best to Abel Dottin, April 27th, op. cit.
32. Ibid.
33. See W. Dickson, *Mitigation of Slavery* (London, 1814), p.439.
34. See M. Craton, *Testing the Chains: Resistance to Slavery in the British West Indies* (Ithaca, 1982), pp.254-55. Also, K. Watson and H. Beckles, "Concessionary Politics: Slave Resistance in Eighteenth Century Barbados," unpublished manuscript.
35. Minutes of the House of Assembly, January 7th, 1817; see also, *Barbados Mercury and Bridgetown Gazette (BMBG)*, March 30th, 1816.
36. Robert Hayes to Thomas Lane, September 23rd, 1816, Barbados, Newton Estate Papers, 523/781, Senate House Library, London.
37. Governor Leith to Lord Bathurst, CO 28/85, f.8.
38. See K, Watson, op. cit., p.129. The Select Committee stated in *The Report* that the slaves were engaged in the planning since December.
39. *The Report*, f.9.
40. The 1819 census of the island recorded that only 7% of the Black population was African born. Barbados Archives.
41. These data are taken from the evidence of slaves who confessed to the Select Committee investigating the Rebellion. See the evidence of Daniel, Cuffee Ned, Robert, and James Bowland, in *The Report*.
42. *The Report*, f.34.
43. Ibid.
44. Ibid., f.27.
45. Ibid., ff.36-37
46. Ibid., f.57.
47. Ibid., f.29.
48. Ibid., f.26.
49. Ibid.
50. Ibid., f.9.
51. These biographical data are from H.A. Vaughan, "Joseph Pitt Washington Franklyn, 1782-1816," Part 2, *The Democrat*, Wednesday,

99

December 23rd, 1970.
52 Petition of Free Coloured People, March 4th, 1817, CO. 28/86 ff.6-7.
53 Vaughan, op. cit.
54 This is one of the important comparative points made by Craton. See his "Slave Culture, Resistance, and the Achievement of Emancipation in the British West Indies, 1783-1838" in J. Walvin (ed.), *Slavery and British Society 1776-1846* (London, 1982).
55 These data are also taken from the evidence supplied in *The Report*.
56 CO 28/85, ff.11-14, Colonel Codd to Governor Leith, April 25th, 1816; see also, *BMBG*, April 30th, 1816.
57 Ibid., Extracts from a private letter, dated April 27th, St Anns Garrison, Barbados, CO 28/85, ff.22-23. Also, Evidence of Colonel Eversley, *The Report*, pp. 28-29.
58 Ibid.
59 Ibid.
60 Ibid., Colonel Codd to Governor Leith, April 25th, 1816.
61 CO 28/86, Census of Barbados, 1817 (October 31st).
62 See Minutes of Council, January 13th, 1812, CO 31/45. Also, CO 28/86, f.76, An account of the islands population.
63 The decennial age and sex composition of the slave population is given in the 1817 census. I have estimated that at least 30% of all slave males were under 16 and over 60 years of age. See also J. Handler and F. Lange, *Plantation Slavery in Barbados: An Archaeological and Historical Investigation* (Cambridge, 1978), pp.67-72.
64 Watson, op. cit., p.132, suggested without providing any form of calculation, that the number of rebels did not exceed 5,000.
65 CO 28/86, Census of Barbados, 1817.
66 See *The Report*, evidence of Colonel Eversley, pp.28-29. Also, Colonel Best to Abel Dottin; two letters dated April 27th and September

28th, 1816, Barbados. New York Public Library (NYPL), op. cit.
67 *BMBG*, April 30th, 1816, Report on the progress of the rebellion.
68 Ibid., Colonel Best to Abel Dottin, April 27th.
69 Ibid.
70 Ibid.
71 Ibid.
72 Ibid.
73 Ibid.
74 Ibid.
75 Ibid.
76 Ibid.
77 *BMBG*, Colonel Best to Governor Leith, April 25th, 1816.
78 Ibid.
79 *BMBG*, Colonel Best to Governor Leith, April 25th, 1816.
80 Evidence of Major Oxley, *The Report*, p.32.
81 Ibid.
82 Confession of Robert, a slave, *The Report*, p.30.
83 Evidence of Major Oxley, *The Report...*
84 Colonel Best to Governor Leith, April 25th, 1816, op. cit.
85 "Extract from a private letter," op. cit.
86 Loveless Overton to Lt Colonel Teedale, June 30th, 1817, CO 28/26, f.153.
87 "Extract from a private letter," op. cit.
88 Ibid.
89 Colonel Codd to Governor Leith, April 25th, 1816, op. cit.
90 Ibid.
91 Ibid.
92 Ibid.
93 Ibid.
94 Ibid.
95 Ibid.
96 Ibid.
97 Eliza Fenwick to Mrs. Fenwick, January 10th, 1812. Also, December 11th, 1814 to Mary Hays, in A.F. Webbs (ed.), *The Fate of the Fenwicks*, op. cit., pp.75-76, 163-64.
98 Minutes of Assembly, December 10th, 1810, CO 31/45.
99 See Lord Camden to Governor

3 The struggle for freedom in Barbados, 1800-1833

Seaforth, November 24th, 1804, CO. 29/29, f.43.
100 Robert Haynes to Thomas Lane, September 23rd, 1816.
101 Minutes of the Assembly, November 20th, 1813 CO.
102 Minutes of the Assembly, September 28th, 1813 CO.
103 Minutes of the Assembly, April 13th, 1811, CO 31/45.
104 Ibid.
105 Ibid.
106 Ibid.
107 *BMBG*, January 13th, 1816.
108 Ibid., May 6th, 1815.
109 Ibid., May 20th, 1815.
110 Minutes of Council, April 8th, CO 31/45.
111 Colonel Best to Abel Dottin, September 28th, 1816, op. cit.
112 Ibid.
113 Thomas Moody to H. Goulburn, October 14th, 1816, op. cit.
114 Governor Leith to Bathurst, September 21st, 1816, CO 28/85, f.36.
115 *BMBG*, January 25th, 1817. See also, E. Stoute, "Glimpses of old Barbados," *Advocate News* (October 18th, 1970).
116 See M. Schuler, *Alas, Alas, Kongo: A Social History of Indentured African Immigrants into Jamaica, 1841-1865* (Baltimore, 1980), pp.5-6.
117 R. Schomburgk, *The History of Barbados* (London, 1848), p.401.
118 Ibid., p.403.
119 Ibid., p.409.
120 Ibid., p.416.
121 Ibid., p.417.
122 C. Levy, *Emancipation, Sugar and Federalism in Barbados and the West Indies*, (Gainsville, 1980), p.21.
123 *Substance of the Debate in the House of Commons on the 15th May, 1823, on a motion for the mitigation and gradual abolition of slavery throughout the British dominions* (Dawson of Pall Mall, London, 1968 edition.), p.9.
124 C. Levy, op. cit., p.21.
125 Ibid., p.22.
126 Ibid., p.23.
127 R. Schomburgk, op. cit., p.417.
128 Ibid., p.418.
129 Ibid., p.422.
130 Ibid., p.452.
131 Ibid., p.458.

CHAPTER FOUR

Free Workers and Sugar Estates in Trinidad, 1838-1845

Kusha Haraksingh

The relationships between the constituent groups of the sugar plantations of the Caribbean have become a dominant theme of West Indian history. There is no great mystery in this, for the real character of those two overwhelming systems – slavery and indentureship – which have so powerfully moulded the life of the region was decided by the day-to-day interaction in the barrack lines, the cane pieces and the boiling houses of the sugar estates. Thus, even those who have attempted to arrive at the real nature of slavery or indentureship through the respective laws and ordinances imposed by the authorities have had nevertheless to come to terms, albeit in varying measures, with the play of forces on the ground. In the period following emancipation and before indentureship was firmly established, a new dimension was added to the existing lines of interaction; this involved the struggle between the freedmen on the one hand, and the plantations on the other. A horizontal plane was welded on to the already vertical axis of stress. The relationships which emerged have been described first in terms of drift and withdrawal and, secondly, in terms of unequal competition between an emergent, progressive but disadvantaged peasantry and an unyielding, reactionary and grasping plantocracy. This paper considers the first part of this theme in relation to Trinidad.

The story as we have it so far is that "the majority of ex-slaves wished to remove themselves from the estates on which they had suffered so much in the days of bondage".[1] The degree to which they were able to translate this desire into reality depended largely on the available alternatives to estate labour, and in this connection a convenient line of division based on the ratio of man to land has evolved. Thus, W.A. Green applies the designation "high density colonies" to those like Barbados and Antigua where the planters controlled virtually all arable land and where the freedmen therefore

4 Free workers and sugar estates in Trinidad, 1838-1845

remained circumscribed to the estates. At the other end of the scale, he uses the description "low density colonies" to refer to places like Trinidad and British Guiana where huge tracts of land were available for squatting and for subsistence agriculture.[2] According to Green, "differences in population density coincided with distinctions which arose in the supply and quality of estate labour". In the low density colonies, the various ways in which the freedmen responded to new opportunities resulted in a depletion of the pool of labour available to the plantations. In those areas loss of labour was greatest, and in Trinidad in particular there were acute labour shortages.[3] Thus the flight of labour from the plantations seems to have been established.

Several components have gone into the making of this picture. For some, it was but natural and expected that the freedmen would desert the plantations wherever that was possible. In the words of Hugh Tinker: "Where there was any alternative, the newly-freed Blacks departed... Wherever possible, the Creole Black, whether in the Caribbean or in the Mascarenes, took himself away from the Plantation forever."[4]

The rationale for this movement of withdrawal has been discovered more in the realm of psychology than in the sphere of economic reward. As Riviere claims: "Psychological forces determined labour mobility to a large extent and this was reflected in the preference of large numbers of ex-slaves for subsistence farming to estate labour which promised greater financial rewards."[5]

Apparently, the implications of the seamless cloth of which the history of sugar, slavery and the plantations was woven were not lost on the freedmen.[6] They had lived through that connection, and "knew instinctively that slavery was the plantation and the plantation was slavery; if they wished release from the one they must manage to quit the other".[7] Or, as Riviere puts it, to the ex-slaves "real freedom meant disassociation at any cost from the symbol of enslavement, the plantation".[8] In this vein, the process of withdrawal has sometimes achieved the status of a logical imperative, and the claim has been advanced that so overwhelming was the aversion of the freedmen to the estates that they wished to have no part of it at any price whatsoever. Not only that, but no occupational pursuit which smacked of slavery would be countenanced.

Freedmen behaviour in the aftermath of emancipation has sometimes been imbued with a quality of romance which also tends to reinforce the impression of desertion. The ex-slaves are depicted as moving into new and untamed territory, there heroically to combat not only the forces of raw nature but also the scheming of the planter-prompted officialdom. In this frontier-like saga, the freedmen are engaged in a contest to establish and sustain an existence in plots and villages outside the orbit of the plantations. It is a struggle in which initiative and dynamism are restored to a population which heretofore had existed in circumstances where neither was encouraged; as a matter of fact, the circumstances were such that if either was displayed it tended to attract punishment rather than reward. The freedmen moved not only outward in space but also inward to resurrect deep-seated cultural traditions, and thus, to reconnect with an ancestral heritage. Both movements necessarily are synchronised; the one cannot proceed without the other, and both are employed in setting the perimeters of the emergent peasantry.

Planter activity after 1838 leads one to the same conclusion regarding the withdrawal of labour from the estates. In anticipating emancipation, the planters had sketched troubling pictures of impending disaster. Thereafter, they began persistently to complain about "the great ruin of freedom". To hear them speak, life had become impossible and the obvious and only remedy was to replenish the labour supply through immigration. Consequently, studies of immigration which take planter claims as their point of departure reinforce the general impression of drift. For the logic of the following progression – importation of labour for the estates, which is necessitated by the shortage of the domestic supply, which in turn arises from a withdrawal of the freedmen from the plantations – assumed irresistible proportions. As Laurence puts it: "... with the coming of full emancipation in 1838 the long anticipated flight of the Negroes from the estates immediately created an acute shortage of labour. The obvious remedy was immigration..."[9]

Perhaps unwittingly, studies which are concerned with establishing the harshness of slavery tend to support planter claims regarding a serious deficiency in the labour supply following emancipation. For to have said that the Blacks would have done anything but remove themselves from the estates, where that could be accomplished, would have been in a sense to raise vexing queries about conditions during the slave period. These questions have in fact been raised in studies of the American South and the controversy which they have aroused is still to be abated.

Several other questions arise in respect of the foregoing picture. Most immediately, it is the nature of the evidence which invites closer scrutiny. For the most part what happened to labour is reconstructed from the statements of planters, as yet the only vocal group in the drama. Thus, when Blouet remarks that "the documents contain

4 Free workers and sugar estates in Trinidad, 1838-1845

persistent references to the diminution of the labour force"[10] this is simply another way of saying that the planters consistently claim that labour is insufficient. Interestingly enough, the planters would make the same claim before the Sanderson Committee of 1910, when the attack on indentureship had begun to gather momentum and when, by other accounts, there was a substantial surfeit of plantation labour.[11] What may be seen as the voracious appetite of the plantocracy for more labour just before the close of indentureship when there was serious underemployment on the estates, raises the possibility as to whether, in the earlier periods following emancipation, their statements ought not to be regarded more in the nature of propaganda for a cause than as a description of actual conditions. The cause would evidently be based on their total irreconcilability to the loss of servile labour, and hence, their determination to secure a system of labour procurement and management which would resemble that to which they had been so long accustomed.

The physical environment as depicted in the arguments and statements of the planters seemed on the surface to add weight to their claims, especially when combined with contemporary theories about settlement and the preferred lifestyle of the Blacks. Great play was made of the size of Trinidad and of the potential for expanded sugar cultivation if only the required labour was forthcoming. As Robert Bushe, who owned estates in Trinidad and who acted as an attorney for several other proprietors, said in 1842: "The colony of Trinidad is very large; they say there are a million acres that are fit for sugar cultivation, but there are not 20,000 acres of sugar cane at this moment in the whole island."[12]

A million acres was a gross exaggeration. It took no account of the true potential of the land or of the existing technology in relation to either transportation or processing, but it added weight to the planters' contention. The fertility of the soil and its bountiful nature were also emphasised (indeed, a visitor in the 1860s would speak of several people obtaining a living by selling "the spontaneous growth of the fruit trees").[13] Put anybody in this situation, especially a people naturally given to shiftlessness, the planters argued, and the result must be a persuasive disinclination to work.

But though the planters viewed the freedmen as heirs to a particular cultural baggage, they too operated within certain well defined terms of reference. For them, labour was not an abstract phenomenon to be spoken about in indefinite terms but an entity which was to be understood only in relation to certain established qualities. The preferred position was a situation in which labour was both submissive and disciplined; at the least, however, labour had to be manoeuvrable or it was not labour at all. Thus, the planters were not really saying that there was a problem of manpower but that labour, as they construed it, was not adequate. This explains their preoccupation with contract labour which schemes of immigration would provide. In the meantime, they could begin to rationalise their operations. Emancipation had relieved them of certain obligations, and now, perhaps unwittingly had given them some room to manoeuvre. Since productivity was a function of many variables, the planters could use this new flexibility to try to weed out those factors which hindered efficiency. Perhaps they would begin by pushing out at their own pace freedmen who did not conform to their idea of labourers. Associated with this strategy might be several other measures which, when taken together, would raise the possibility that rationalisation, not flight, might more adequately explain labour conditions in the immediate post-emancipation years.

In any reconstruction of the period following emancipation the fate of labour cannot be understood apart from the annual rhythm of sugar cultivation and the activities which are involved. This is especially the case with Trinidad where conditions differed from those encountered in the neighbouring territories. The relative newness of sugar cultivation in the island was one factor making for differences; the weather pattern, another. So, too, was the quality of the soil. As David Lockhart, the experienced and widely-travelled head of the island's botanical garden said:

> The only place which can bear any comparison is Cuba; but altogether I have seen nothing equal to Trinidad in the great variety and excellence of the soils; and particularly in its seasons; which, from its situation, exempts it from the droughts to which all the other islands, from Barbados to Cuba, must be occasionally subject.[14]

Soil conditions especially were so favourable that a certain level of inefficiency in field operations could be tolerated and indeed visitors from the smaller islands were often amazed at what they considered the wasteful agriculture practices of the Trinidad planters.

In 1838, in Trinidad there were 206 sugar estates of varying sizes, some more favourably located than others with respect particularly to cartage and to room for expansion. In that year the colony exported 20,721 hogsheads of sugar[15] which, given an average output of 1.5 to 2.0 hogsheads per acre[16] and assuming that there was no left over sugar from the previous year, would put the harvested area at between 10,000 and 14,000 acres. For some years prior to emanci-

4 Free workers and sugar estates in Trinidad, 1838-1845

pation the Trinidad planters had adopted the double crop system whereby only half of the canes were harvested in any one year, and the remaining half allowed to 'stand over' for the subsequent year's crop.[17] Thus, the total area devoted to cane in 1838 could be estimated at around 24,000 acres. In addition, the estates had lands attached for the works, buildings and for keeping stock as well as provision grounds and woodlands.

By the mid-1830s cane planting had ceased to be a widespread activity in Trinidad. Most of the estates would put in a few acres of new canes every year, but otherwise they relied heavily on their ratoons. The immense fertility of the soil permitted productive ratooning for up to thirty years on average, and in the South Naparima district, forty years was not unknown. In that area, the majority of the estates were not more than twenty years old, so that, except in terms of an extension of cultivation or where the ratoons might have been damaged from one cause or another (usually by stray animals), the estates did no replanting. It is true that the planters thus relinquished the higher yields obtainable from plant canes, but what they so lost on the swings they gained on the roundabouts in terms of having saved the expense of planting and of looking after new canes.

Where planting did take place the first task was usually clearing the land, for new canes were normally set in virgin soil. Ratoons which had ceased to be productive were simply abandoned and the land which had been so occupied was left idle for about six years. The method of planting in Trinidad was unique; as described by a planter, "You merely make a small hole with a hoe... you then put in the plants in new land." It was, nevertheless, a labour intensive activity and if carried out on any great scale could "consume a greater part of the labour upon the estate". Planters estimated that about 2,700 cane-holes per acre was the norm. The new canes were weeded about three or four times before harvest and the cuttings not more than twice. Most of this would be done in the first year of growth. Trenching, or digging of drains, was indispensable in the new cane lands, but in the ratoon areas the drains merely had to be maintained. Stand-over canes, that is, ratoons in the second year of growth, could in fact endure some amount of surface moisture without any significant lessening of sugar yield. Manure was hardly applied either to new or old canes, and in any case never in the second year of growth. Indeed, stand-over canes required almost no attention though it was reckoned that they benefitted from stripping of the dried leaves. Thus, a resident on a typical Trinidad estate during 1838 would have been able to describe the following cultivation profile:

	(1)	(2)	(3)	(4)	(5)
1840	H	H	-	R	H
1839	R	R	H	H	-
1838	H	H	R	-	P
1837	R	-	H	P	-
1836	H	P	R	-	-

(1) ratoon canes in the second year of growth (stand-over canes last harvested in 1836 and awaiting harvest in the current year);

(2) canes planted in 1836 (awaiting first harvest in the current year);

(3) ratoon canes in the first year of growth (last harvested in 1837 and to be harvested again in 1839);

(4) canes planted in 1837 (to be harvested in 1839 for the first time);

(5) new canes planted during the current year (to be harvested in 1840 for the first time).

The acreage under items (2), (4) and (5) would be small compared to items (1) and (3). Item (5) would require special attention, items (2), (3) and (4) some attention, and item (1) little or no attention.

At harvest time there was a frenzy of activity on the estates. The canes to be reaped were cut by task and transported to the mills either by cart-loads or by crooking, that is, on the backs of mules. The planter normally aimed at employing his mill to the fullest, whether it was powered by water, or by draught animals, or by steam. The first was rare in Trinidad, the second accounted for the greater number of mills, and the third would increase in prominence following emancipation. By 1838 a well-established routine marked the manufacturing process, with the final stage being the filling of the hogsheads for transport to the shipping places.

The feverish activity was dictated by the expected arrival of the rainy season around the middle of the year. The rains themselves posed no threat but it was the effect which they had on cartage which was the planter's nightmare. One planter, who was also a road commissioner, graphically presented the problem by describing the road surface in South Naparima following the rains as "deep and stiff and so tenacious that it will occasionally pull off a horse's shoe when at all loose in passing through it."[18] The situation was not quite so bad in the northern areas, but even there an untimely onset of the rains would curtail the harvest and result in ripened canes having to be stood-over for the following year. The extended period of growth occasioned a reduction in the sucrose content. Frequently, too, early rains would jeopardise the transportation of already filled hogsheads

4 Free workers and sugar estates in Trinidad, 1838-1845

to the shipping places. To avoid this, the majority of planters resorted to carting off the greater part of their crop to the embarkation points before it was "sufficiently drained... by which a considerable loss of molasses" was sustained. For the planter caught by the rains, two options were open. He could decide to persevere, in which case, he had to empty the contents of the hogsheads and fill them into bags which could then be carried on mule-back. The empty hogsheads were then refilled at the shipping point. The whole process was "expensive and troublesome" and the planter often adopted the second alternative which was simply to store the hogsheads on his estate until the subsequent shipping season. In that case, though, the sugar deteriorated "much in quality and quantity". One planter who was so trapped by the rains reported that fourteen hogsheads which had remained on one of his estates had been reduced to ten when finally shipped.[19]

A number of features which emerge from the operations as described have to be borne in mind when we try to reconstruct the actions of both planters and freedmen in the immediate post-emancipation years. The most obvious is the diffused labour requirements on the estate, characterised by variations in terms of space, time and type of activity. Requirements were demanding in the manufacturing process but relatively relaxed in the cultivation; high in the first half of the year but low in the second, somewhat special in relation to plant canes but relatively routine otherwise.

Thus, the initial reaction of the Blacks to the emancipation proclamation was in itself no cause for alarm. The time was August when much of the work was already done, and if the freedmen left the estates to rejoice for a while that did not unduly disturb plantation operations. Of course, some of the planters were anxious over what they regarded as the existing potential for social upheaval, but that was a different matter. Provided that a sufficient number of freedmen returned in time for the start of the crop in January 1839, the manufacturing process would not be impaired. In the event, production figures seem to indicate that the planters indeed managed to secure all the hands that they required, for sugar exports in 1839 were only 6 per cent down from the previous year, an insignificant variation considering the number of random factors which impinge on sugar output. The statements of the planters, however, contain no qualification which could amend the impression which they sought to convey of a spontaneous exodus of Blacks during August leading to a confirmed loss of labour; they seldom refer to the return of the labourers. But the movement of the population in August 1838 did not represent a picture of final withdrawal, which some of the planters would have us believe. Instead, it merely marked the start of an emerging pattern of seasonal drift and return into which many of the freedmen would eventually settle. Indeed, this is the pattern which would come to characterise the continuing relationship between freed Blacks and the sugar estates.

There were good reasons why the planters themselves should encourage seasonal migration. During the period of slavery they had operated on the highest common denominator with regard to manpower requirements In other words, their labour force had been based on calculations relevant to the high crop-time demand, and they were therefore overstaffed during the growing season. Freedom provided the opportunity for real flexibility in tailoring the number of workers to quantity of work. In this connection, the established regimen of task work was useful. But the crucial enabling move would be the untangling of the tie between residence and employment.

Task work, or at least its underlying principle, was more widespread on the estates than has been generally supposed. During slavery, a task was considered a day's work; in freedom it came to be applied normally only to field operations. Even in the field, though, special arrangements were sometimes made for particular activities and designated as job work. In the manufacturing process, day work, of 9 hours duration, became the pattern. But the job was really a large scale version of the task and in the mills, despite the 9-hour gauge, workers were expected to achieve a certain measure of productivity. As one planter explained: "On a cattle-mill estate, we expect them to grind 2,400 gallons; on a steam-engine estate, we expect them to grind 4,000 gallons liquor."[20] So quantity was the key, though quality was not overlooked. As W.H. Burnley, a member of the Legislative Council and himself a leading member of the plantocracy, explained: "The planter need not pay for the work until it is well done and could call upon the labourer to repair it."[21] Thus, the time spent was one element in job computation but the crucial thing was that the unit of work had to be satisfactorily completed.

For the planters and their attempt to streamline operations, the elasticity of the task system was its cherished characteristic. In the nature of things there could be no standard task, for conditions were not uniform, either from field to field or from day to day. It is not a matter for surprise, therefore, that Lionel Lee, part owner of Orange Grove Estate, was able to increase the size of the weeding task on his estate from 3,000 square feet in 1840 to 5,000 square feet in 1841. (Both attracted the same rate of fifty cents). His explanation was "the

4 Free workers and sugar estates in Trinidad, 1838-1845

fineness of the season, and the grass and weeds being not so heavy".[22] Lee and other planters made full use of the freedmen's preference for task-work. This has been explained by the view that in working according to the task, the labourer enjoyed the advantage of knowing how much he had to do and could get home presumably to look after his own affairs. But perhaps a more convincing explanation lay in the opportunity to bargain which was inherent in settling the dimension of a task. There is little evidence for believing, though, that the freedmen fared well in those negotiations.

There was some common ground between planters and freedmen, too, in divorcing the location of residence from that of employment. A number of ex-slaves, while willing to continue plantation work, preferred to live off the estates. In the case of others, from whom the planters had earlier obtained more useful services or whose productivity did not measure up to planter expectations, there was perhaps less mutual agreement. Thus, old men or the weak and infirm, or the recalcitrant or frequently absent labourer were shunted off the estates. The process of ejectment began with a week's notice; if there was no compliance, the stipendiary magistrate was applied to and he ejected them by sending over the constabulary.[23] The planters had to be careful, though, not to go too far with ejectment; they never lost sight of the need to retain a core of labourers on the estate. To this end, they were able to exercise some selectivity and also to channel selected workers into 'specialist' activities. The grant of rent-free accommodation as well as certain other allowances has to be seen in this context. It is not, then, that "conciliation provoked an exodus of plantation labour in Trinidad",[24] but that those who found themselves outside the pale, as it were, also found themselves outside the estate.

The foregoing analysis has attempted to establish the possibility that planter rationalism might have been the dominant force influencing freedmen behaviour in the post-emancipation period. If this was really so, that is, if push factors emanating from planter activity were more powerful than other considerations, then two things would follow. First, sugar production would at least remain constant for it would have been foolhardy for the planters to push so far or so fast that the output suffered. They could hardly be expected to cut off their noses to repair their faces; instead, they would have regulated their activities so that the level of output did not fall. Secondly, evidence of freedmen attachment to the estate would be present; this is inherently more difficult to measure but not impossible to establish.

The planters attempted to use the data on sugar exports to prove that a decline in output had occurred. In their calculations, as presented by W.H. Burnley on behalf of the Agricultural and Immigration Society, the years 1831-1833, 1835-1837 and 1839-1841 were selected as representative of slavery, apprenticeship and freedom, respectively. On the basis of simple averages the argument was postulated that exports had fallen from 18,923 tons in the first period to 14,828 tons in the third period – that is, a decline of 22 per cent.[25] One could accept export figures as a surrogate for information about production; in fact, one has no choice in this matter. And of course, the mathematics of the planter's computation cannot be faulted. But the process is inferentially misleading. It did not adequately reflect the complexity of operations on the estate. For one thing, output for 1831, for example, would have been affected directly by events since 1829. For another, the host of random factors which influence final production and thus export figures – such as the timeliness of the rainy season, the intensity of sunshine during the harvest, the outbreak of cane fires, the occurrence of breakdowns in the mills, and so on – cannot be handled by crude averages. In order to weed out chance factors, the calculation of first differences and moving averages is necessary.

The list of first differences, as presented in Table 1, reveals year-to-year fluctuations in sugar production of varying measure, spread throughout the period 1830-1845 in a haphazard manner. There is no discernible pattern except that the production curve seems to be on a downswing between 1836 and 1840 but on an upswing from 1840 to 1843. Perhaps a longer time series might have revealed the presence of cyclical movements, but there is nothing here to establish decline in freedom as opposed to slavery.

4 Free workers and sugar estates in Trinidad, 1838-1845

Table 1
Sugar Production 1830–1845

Year	Sugar Production (tons)	First Difference (tons)
1830	10244	–
1831	16358	+ 6114
1832	15613	– 745
1833	14315	– 1298
1834	16980	+ 2665
1835	14469	– 2511
1836	15607	+ 1138
1837	14768	– 839
1838	14312	– 456
1839	13433	– 879
1840	12289	– 544
1841	14080	+ 1191
1842	14300	+ 220
1843	16168	+ 1868
1844	13729	– 2439
1845	18207	+ 4478

Source: N. Deerr, *History of Sugar*, Vol. 2, pp.201-202

Table 2
Sugar Production 1830–1845: Five-Year Moving Average

Year	Five-Year Moving Average (tons)
1828	–
1829	–
1830	13908.2
1831	14114.2
1832	14702.0
1833	15547.0
1834	15396.8
1835	15227.8
1836	15227.2
1837	14517.8
1838	14081.8
1839	13776.4
1840	13682.8
1841	14054.0
1842	14113.2
1843	15296.8
1844	16013.6
1845	17088.8

Source: N. Deerr, *History of Sugar*, Vol. 2, pp.201-202

More interesting still are moving average figures, as shown in Table 2. A five-year span was selected as an appropriate time frame, having regard to the continuum of operations on the estates. In the immediate pre-apprenticeship period 1829-1833, average annual production reached the level of 14,114 tons; in the immediate post-emancipation period 1839-1843, it was 14,054 tons, a difference of 0.4%. One normally expects a close relationship between output and expected returns. However, when export figures are related to the selling price of muscovado sugar on the London market in the equation:

$$y = a + bx$$

(where y represents quinquennial moving averages for exports, 1830-1845, and x represents quinquennial moving averages for prices, 1830-1845) the regression coefficient is only .003. Variations in selling price do not at all help to explain variations in output. This could only be understood in relation to the massive rigidity which characterises commitment to sugar production. Once the original investment has been made in terms of stock, works, and the canes on the ground, the planter soldiers on, taking the good with the bad and forever hoping for better prices. The end result is consistency in production figures, as revealed by Table 2.

The ability of the planters to maintain an even keel demonstrates that labour was not the intractable problem which they made it out to be. Other evidence exists in addition, which not only invites a reappraisal of the impression of decisive Black withdrawal but also tends to establish freedmen attachment to the estates. The material concerns mainly the preferred settlement areas of the Blacks, whether as squatters or as landholders, and the outbreak of strikes and other industrial disputes on the estates. There is some information, too, about productivity and wage rates, but it is not free from serious deficiencies which make year-to-year comparisons exceedingly difficult and is therefore better left alone.

Although a number of freedmen withdrew from the estates in terms of residence, some continued to live and work there, attracted by planter inducements. Thus, Robert Church of Paradise estate revealed in May 1842 that "nearly all" his resident labourers had been slaves.[26] Evidently, he had succeeded in retaining his slaves for plantation work. Where resident labourers are concerned, the attachment to the plantation is of course not in doubt. But even where there was a residential drift, the overwhelming preference of the freedmen was to settle close to the estates. When Burnley was asked in 1842

4 Free workers and sugar estates in Trinidad, 1838-1845

whether, in view of the large proportion of uncultivated and waste land in Trinidad, the freedmen were "in the habit of withdrawing to any distance from the civilised and cultivated parts and squatting in the wilder parts of the country" he responded, "not in the slightest degree".[27] His remarks were echoed by William Knox, a barrister and sometime plantation manager.[28] Geographical proximity could be interpreted simply as a mark of attachment to familiar surroundings but more importantly it facilitated working on the estates. Several planters attested to this; Lewis Pantin, proprietor of Bonne Aventure Estate, for example, disclosed that squatters in the neighbourhood were the source of much of his manpower.[29] Obviously, the decision to live near the estates was also a decision to work on them.

The freedmen who had managed to secure the wherewithal to buy land also demonstrated, through the location of their purchases, their attachment to the estates. It is true that the planters, who are reported in 1842 as "selling land to the labourers every day", are the ones who dictated which parcels of land were put on the market and it is also true that they chose to sell lands in the vicinity of their estates. But the fact is that buyers could be found, and that the planters sold mainly as a means of retaining labour. As Burnley explained, when planters sell plots of land to freedmen, they do so with "the ulterior view of gaining an advantage over the proprietors by congregating a larger number of labourers upon their own estate".[30] Apparently, the strategy proved successful, for according to the evidence of stipendiary magistrate Joseph Guiseppi, the planters in 1841 had twice as many freedmen working and living off the estates as they had resident labourers.[31]

It is often argued that the planters had not utilised the apprenticeship period in making preparations for freedmen. Instead of laying the groundwork for new labour relations, the "term of apprenticeship had been wasted... by the planters, in exacting the utmost amount of work from the prospective free labourer".[32] In view of the historical legacy, as well as unfamiliarity on all sides with free labour arrangements, it is not surprising that industrial disputes were commonplace in the early years of freedom. Magistrate Guiseppi disclosed that he had received several complaints from labourers against their employers. And several planters spoke of frequent work stoppages and of the labourers downing their tools for 'triffling' reasons. Richard Darling, attorney for Retrench Estate, recounted how a gang of his workers who had been usually employed in weeding initially refused to do the work of cutting the canes and finally agreed to do so only on the condition that they were "allowed to cut what piece they pleased".³³ The cry was often heard that the workers were not performing up to their limit, that they came out to work late, and that productivity (however measured) left much to be desired. Evidently, the freedmen were taking steps to improve their working conditions. In modern terms this could be regarded as "industrial action" and like residence, it is a powerful indicator of attachment to the estates. For had the freedmen been alienated, they would not have bothered to argue or strike when confronted with unsatisfactory conditions; instead, they would have "voted with their feet" and abandoned estate work.

The roving bands of freedmen which are supposed to have arisen in the wake of emancipation have to be considered in the above light. The number of these 'migrant' workers has never been clear but their motivation seems straightforward enough. Frederic Maxwell, himself an ex-slave and in the 1840s manager of an estate, believed "they do not like their work to be closely looked after, and so remove to another estate, where they think they will be allowed to do it more quickly and superficially".³⁴

The implication, here, though Maxwell does not pinpoint it, is that the migrant workers too were involved in the search for improved conditions of service – improved, that is, in the sense of a higher ratio of reward to effort. This search occurred within the sugar industry. When they moved, it was from estate to estate.

This reappraisal of freedmen behaviour has to contend with several impressions associated with the period which have usually been taken for granted. The first concerns the story of land for foodstuffs, the second the tale of urban expansion, and the third the woe of abandoned estates. These also are building blocks of which the general edifice of freedmen desertion is constructed.

The availability of land for growing food has been held out as a force which either attracted the freedmen out of the plantations or created competing demands upon their labour. Yet the contemporary evidence is full of references to falling food production. Burnley, collating the evidence of several planters in 1842, insisted that "the freedmen do not cultivate to any extent, for provisions are now scarcer in the colony than they ever were before". Martin Sorsano, from his vantage point as surveyor-general, was impressed with the low level of land and effort devoted to food. And harbourmaster Richard Stewart was able to provide impressive quantitative evidence to establish a heavy increased importation of food since 1838. He revealed also that both Port of Spain and San Fernando depended largely on imports from Venezuela where previously they

4 Free workers and sugar estates in Trinidad, 1838-1845

had been domestically supplied, and that in fact ex-slaves who had once kept the towns in stock were in the 1840s among the buyers.[35] With respect to competing demands, some writers have argued that the busiest time on the food grounds coincided with the busiest time on the plantations.[36] Whether that was true or not, for all kinds of food crops, is questionable. Yet it is remarkable how persons employed nowadays in the sugar industry manage without great stress also to work provision grounds and, not infrequently, even private cane fields.

Urban expansion has often been seen as a corollary of estate withdrawal. The qualitative evidence for this is extremely suspect, for it is well known that officials and the elite residents of the towns had a way of seeing more Blacks than there actually were. The quantitative evidence for Port of Spain, based on Cabildo records, reveals that the population expanded by 28 per cent between 1838 and 1842. The number of people involved was 3,304 but the records do not disclose how many of these were Trinidadian ex-slaves. However, one study[37] has concluded that "a major component" of this growth was White, comprising British administrators and merchants, other European landowners and Venezuelan emigres. Of that percentage which was Black, a large proportion were migrants from other West Indian islands who had made the trek via the rural plantations which they had quickly abandoned. From the heavy imbalance of males to females, as revealed by the 1842 census of the town (734 males per 1,000 females), it seems that a large number of the Trinidadian ex-slaves who came to town were women. And from the age structure of the population, which shows a high proportion of children under ten, it appears that the mothers were accompanied by their offspring. When the appropriate discounting is done, then, it seems that in the town's growth, able-bodied male Trinidadian ex-slaves were few in number. These were of course precisely the element that the planter engaged in a process of rationalisation would try to have around him, and these are the people whose responses are crucial in establishing any scenario of drift and withdrawal.

In their anxiety to demonstrate how scarce labour was, some planters referred to the abandonment of estates for want of labour. Omitting the fact that some measure of abandonment could be deliberate, either in terms of unproductive ratoons or of consolidation, the evidence shows that the planters under close questioning often backtracked on the general impression which they wished to create. For example, Robert Bushe, when asked if he knew of any estates that had been abandoned, replied that he himself had abandoned two.

He later admitted that he had really sold one to another estate. He also conceded that where estates had been abandoned, the labourers had generally gone to other estates and that their work had become more concentrated and productive.[38] More revealing is the transcript of Burnley's evidence before the Parliamentary Committee of 1842. Part runs as follows:

Q: Have any estates been abandoned?
A: I think some one or two estates may have been abandoned.
Q: Can you state positively whether they have or have not?
A: I can state positively that I know of one that has been abandoned.

Burnley was speaking as Chairman of the Agricultural and Immigration Society. He, if anyone, would know about the extent of abandoned estates. But he could only point to one, and furthermore would later admit that there were special circumstances involved: the proprietor of the abandoned estate owned three others, and had ceased to cultivate that one because "it was less profitable".[39]

The planters not only insisted that labour shortages had led to a fall in production but also that expansion had been hampered. There is no doubt that a larger labour force was necessary if the sugar industry was to expand, but it was not fair to use labour as the whipping-boy. The crucial bottlenecks preventing expansion lay elsewhere, in mill capacity and in the problem of cartage. The former was being slowly upgraded in the post-emancipation period but not to the extent which Lodbell in his study of investment in the British West Indian sugar industry has claimed.[40] When Burnley was asked whether "any material change had occurred in the making of sugar or in the cultivation of sugar estates" his response was: "I may say safely, decidedly none."[41] Trinidad planters were clearly unwilling to invest in new machinery without the safeguard of a tractable labour force. As for the problem of transportation, even if more labourers were forthcoming it would have curtailed expansion even in the fertile Naparimas. That bottleneck would not be widened and the constraints eased until schemes of railway construction were implemented.

In Trinidad, emancipation was the signal for the start of a process or rationalisation by the owners and managers of sugar plantations. This involved initially the tailoring of the labour force to the fluctuating seasonal demands of estate labour. The process was selective; some freedmen were induced to remain on the estates, and among these some were channelled into 'specialist' occupations, thereby, creating a body of key workers especially for the requirements of crop-time. Others were removed from the estates; some removed themselves but enough of this group stayed in the vicinity of the plantations to provide a pool of labour which helped to maintain the level of production. Abandoning the estate in terms of residence was not the same as withdrawing from the estate in terms of labour. The Blacks, too, were using the new opportunities of freedom to decide where they would live and where they would work. But it would appear that the pace of rationalisation was dictated by the planters for, despite the attendant uncertainties traditional to sugar cultivation, they did manage to handle the situation so that output did not suffer.

While rationalisation was in train, however, the planters kept insisting that labour was inadequate and not continuous. The first complaint laid the groundwork for the essence of their plans, which was the replacement of free labour by labour not so free. The second claim, based on the planters' formula that the more the freedmen earned the less they worked, prepared the way for keeping wage levels low. Both goals were to be fully achieved under the scheme of Indian indentureship which began in 1845.

Notes

An earlier version of this paper was presented to the 11th Annual Conference of the Association of Caribbean Historians in 1979.

In the following references *PP 1842* refers to the report of the *Select Committee of the House of Commons on the West Indian Colonies, 1842*.

Burnley (ed.) refers to W.H. Burnley (ed). *Observations on the Present Condition of the Island of Trinidad* (London, 1849).

[1] For a fuller review of the literature see D. Hall, "The Flight from the Estates Reconsidered: the British West Indies 1838-42," *The Journal of Caribbean History*, Vols. 10 & 11 (1978). See also G.L. Beckford, *Persistent Poverty: Underdevelopment in Plantation Economies of the Third World* (London, 1972), pp.88-97.

[2] W.A. Green, *British Slave Emancipation* (Oxford, 1976), p.193.

[3] W. Emanuel Riviere, "Labour Shortage in the British West Indies After Emancipation," *JCH*, Vol. 4 (May 1972), p.5.

[4] H. Tinker, *A New System of Slavery* (Oxford, 1974), p.18.

[5] Riviere, "Labour Shortage", op. cit., p.4.

[6] The imagery is from M. Craton et al., *Slavery, Abolition and Emancipation* (London, 1976), p.ix.

[7] Tinker, *New System of Slavery*, p.2.

[8] Riviere, op. cit., p.4.

[9] K.O. Laurence, "Immigration in Trinidad and British Guiana 1834-1871," PhD Dissertation,

Cambridge University (1958), p.iii.
[10] B.W. Blouer, "Land Policies in Trinidad 1838-50," *JCH*, Vol. 9 (1976), p.46.
[11] See the evidence before the Sanderson Committee of 1910; and also K. Haraksingh, "Estates, Labour and Population in Trinidad 1870-1900," paper presented to the 10th Annual Conference of Caribbean Historians, St Thomas (1978).
[12] *PP 1842*, p.285.
[13] E.B. Underhill, *The West Indies: their Social and Religious Condition* (London, 1862), p.36.
[14] Burnley (ed.), p.104.
[15] D. Hart, *Trinidad and the Other West Indian Islands* (Port of Spain, 1866), p.149.
[16] *PP 1842*, pp.108-109.
[17] *PP 1842*, p.95. This description of sugar cultivation is based largely on the evidence of Robert Church before the committee.
[18] Burnley (ed.), p.103.
[19] Ibid.
[20] *PP 1842*, p.276.
[21] Burnley (ed.), p.116.
[22] D. Wood, *Trinidad in Transition* (Oxford, 1968), p.52.
[23] *PP 1842*, p.93.
[24] Riviere, "Labour Shortage", op. cit., p.9.
[25] *PP 1842*, p.55.
[26] *PP 1842*, p.100.
[27] *PP 1842*, pp.69-70.
[28] Burnley (ed.), p.110.
[29] Burnley (ed.), pp.99-100.
[30] *PP 1842*, p.105.
[31] Burnley (ed.), p.82.
[32] Underhill, *The West Indies*, op. cit., pp.66-67.
[33] Burnley (ed.), p.64.
[34] Burnley (ed.), p.53.
[35] Burnley (ed.), pp.108, 122-23.
[36] Green, *British Slave Emancipation*, op. cit., p.194.
[37] S.S. Goodenough, "Race, Status and Residence in Port of Spain, Trinidad: a Study of Social and Residential Differentiation and Change," PhD Thesis, University of Liverpool (1976).
[38] *PP 1842*, pp.276-77, 281.
[39] *PP 1842*, p.82.
[40] R.A. Lobdell, "Patterns of Investment and Sources of Credit in the British West Indian Sugar Industry 1838-97," *JCH*, Vol. 4 (May 1972), p.34. He cites the evidence of Robert Bushe before the 1842 Committee to substantiate the following statement: "... cultivation machinery is said to have become widespread in Trinidad by the mid-1840s..." This is a misreading of Bushe's evidence.
[41] *PP 1842*, p.75.

CHAPTER FIVE

Freedom without Emancipation: the Rise of Large Maroon Communities in Suriname

H.A.M. Essed

Throughout the period of slavery in Suriname, from about 1650 to 1863, there was resistance to this inhumane economic system. Indians, slaves and Maroons rebelled in their own way against slavery and never accommodated to it. As early as 1686, Governor van Sommelsdijck was forced to conclude peace treaties with the Caribs, Warous and Arowaks "who greatly disturbed the colony..." Under this peace treaty they "were declared free men who could never, but for crimes, be reduced to slavery".[1] In 1760, Governor Litchtenbergh wrote about the slaves to the States of Zeeland: "...those people, who are a large number of sly fellows can hardly be controlled by the few whites that live here as yet".[2] In 1765, Governor Nepveu wrote about "... the numerous runaway slaves and rebellions... and... the mood that has prevailed among the people in the last few years..."[3] In 1862, one year before slavery was abolished, slave rebellions broke out on the plantations Berg en Dal[4] and Rac à Rac.[5] It was the Maroons, however, who through their regular warfare became the most formidable enemy of the colonial slave drivers and brought the colony to the brink of ruin.

In their attempts to subdue the Maroons the colonial rulers raised a large, well-organised colonial army. By 1772, this army consisted of the following units:[6]

1. militia, made up of planters and other white citizens, with an average strength of about 1,000 men;
2. company troops, consisting of European soldiers serving the Chartered Company of Suriname, with an average strength of 1,385 men;
3. colonial troops, consisting of the Corps of Free Men and Corps of Black Chausseurs, with on average 235 and 165 men

respectively. The Corps of Free Men was made up of free, non-white citizens and the Corps of Black Chausseurs of slaves that had been bought by the Chartered Company of Suriname; and

4. governmental troops, made up of mercenary troops that arrived in Suriname in 1750 and 1773, counting 500 and 1,200 men respectively. They fought against the Saramakas and Alukus (Bonis) respectively and were sent and paid for by the United Provinces.

The colonial army had an extensive network of stations and military posts scattered over the entire plantation area. The stations included, among other things, the three forts, the hospitals and ammunition stores. In 1772, there were eight stations and thirty-six posts. In 1791, there were even as many as sixty-eight posts, twenty of which were situated on the Kordonpad.[7] The Kordonpad was a 94-km long military line of demarcation, which ran along the south and east borders of the plantation area and was built in order to prevent the Alukus from returning to the area.

In spite of its efforts this proportionately large army never succeeded in subduing the Maroons and even less in exterminating them. On the contrary, the Maroons succeeded in freeing thousands of slaves[8] and constantly fought against the colonial army. They succeeded in building up their free communities long before the abolition of slavery. They managed to achieve this by exacting through military means a peace with which they were legally declared free,[9] or by settling in places where they could not be reached by the slow colonial army. The creation of these communities at a time when slavery prevailed in Suriname is of enormous importance because it proves that a struggle for liberation can succeed even in extremely hostile surroundings.

These free communities withstood hundreds of years of repression and we know them today as the communities of the Saramakas, Aukas, Alukus, Paramakas, Matawais and Kwintis.[10]

THEORETICAL MODEL

The Saramakas, Aukas (Djukas) and Alukus (Bonis), in particular, developed into large communities in the eighteenth century. Peace was concluded with the first two communities in 1762 and 1760 respectively. In 1767, peace was made with the Matawais, a group that detached itself from the Saramakas. The Alukus were eventually forced to retreat to the hinterland in 1776 after more than five years of regular warfare against the colonial army and 1,200 merce-

5 The rise of Maroon communities in Suriname

naries. Most historians regard the rise of these three communities over 100 years before the abolition of slavery and their successful military struggle against the colonial army as impressive and of immense importance. Many, from de Kom[11] up to and including Hira,[12] have listed the numerous heroic episodes in this struggle and, in doing so, have contributed to a better understanding of the tradition of struggle of our people and of our national consciousness. Others, like de Groot[13] and Herskovits,[14] have stressed in their accounts the socio-cultural and anthropological aspects of these communities. Up to now, however, no theoretical model has been developed showing the relation between all these heroic episodes and the ultimate form, content, size and political position of these three large Maroon communities, which came into being virtually at the same time yet independently of one another. Richard Price in 1973 pointed out the lack of such a theoretical model, which he called "one of the most challenging problems for future research". He also mentioned a number of factors that played a part in the origin of the various Maroon communities in Latin America and the Caribbean. Unfortunately, he did not himself provide a model in his later works published between 1976 and 1983.[15]

In this article an attempt is made to provide a basis for the development of such a theoretical model which does establish this relation and can be applied to the three large Maroon communities mentioned above. In doing so, we start from a hypothesis which presupposes three fundamental phases in the development of these communities. The characteristics of these phases are mainly determined by the Maroons' urge for freedom and their opportunities for military organization on the one hand and the desire of the colonial authorities to annihilate or subjugate the Maroons or neutralize them politically by means of a policy of peace on the other hand. The hypothesis assumes three successive processes according to which the above-mentioned groups came into being. These processes consisted of several stages in which the transition from one phase to the next gradually took place. The three processes were: formation, consolidation and offensive attacks.

Formation began with small and occasionally large groups of slaves running away from plantations situated in a particular part of the plantation area. These small groups or *los* subsequently settled in a particular area of the colony.[16] In the first stage of formation, the preference of the first *los* from the same section of the plantation area for a particular part of the colony was determined almost exclusively by geographical factors. As a rule the slaves fled to areas facing the plantation area, separated from the plantation area by natural obstacles, such as rivers and swamps, chosen so as to impede pursuit and because it was easily accessible and capable of providing a long start ahead of possible pursuers. At this stage there was no contact between the various *los* because they were simply not aware of one another's existence. As a rule the *los* settled not too far from the plantation area – still maintaining furtive contacts with the slaves on the plantations they used to belong to in order to obtain food, tools and possible new additions to the *los*. From a military point of view the *los* were very vulnerable at this stage of formation to the numerous civil patrols sent out by the planters to recover 'their property'. As the years went by the *los* in a particular area learnt about each other's existence. From information obtained through contacts with plantations they knew that several groups had escaped to the same area. Through direct searches of accidental meetings while looking for suitable hiding places or arable land more and more *los* came together. In this way they formed clans.[17]

This second stage of the formation marked the transition to the next stage in the cycle.

Consolidation set in with the formation of clans which at that stage numbered from several dozen to about 100 members or more and were therefore able to organise themselves more efficiently from an economic, military and social point of view. Consequently, the clans depended less on daily contacts with the plantations and were able to move further into the interior. As a result, it became more difficult for the civil patrols and the ever-increasing number of expeditions to track down the clans. In the hinterland, a clan was able to develop its internal organisation in comparative peace, which led to the second stage of consolidation. At this stage the clan's military experience enabled it to attack any plantation whatsoever. This was necessary in order to get tools, kitchen utensils, weapons and ammunition. The desire to free slaves still on the plantations played an important part too. Moreover, some clans were short of women. It, therefore, happened quite often that women were taken from the plantations against their wish because they were vital to the clan's survival. It is not true, however, that the first *los* consisted only of men. Several *los* were even founded by women.[18] By means of economic cooperation such a clan in its second stage succeeded in adequately organising its supply of food. Women played a central role in this too. That is why they developed specific qualities such as knowledge of medicinal herbs.[19] One of the Saramaka clans even created villages and plots of arable land for slaves yet to be freed.[20] The Alukus had more than

5 The rise of Maroon communities in Suriname

200 plots of land.[21]

The second process was therefore the consolidation of the clans which eventually marked the transition to the phase of offensive attack.

The consolidation of the clans, counting 100-200 members or more in the second stage, naturally did not escape the attention of the colonial authorities. To the slave-owners, the raids on plantations, the liberation of hundreds of slaves and the attacks on military posts and expeditions meant considerable economic loss but even more a loss of authority. Stricter discipline and severer punishments could not check the growing desire for freedom among the slaves the more so, as thousands of their brothers and sisters were living in the forests as free men and women. The colonial rulers, therefore, used all possible means to achieve what they called "the extermination of the rabble". In spite of the extremely great expense, on average 100,000 guilders per expedition,[22] scores of military expeditions were organised to try and destroy the clans, their villages and plots. Thus, a regular war developed between the clans and the colonial army.

With respect to the third process, the clans soon came to realise that they could lose the war in the end. After all, the colonial troops had unlimited reinforcements at their disposition because they were supported by the wealth acquired from slavery and the capital of the rising mercantile class in the mother country. The clans, however, had to rely exclusively on their own strength and weapons and ammunition captured in raids. The clans' response to the resultant situation marked the final stage of the offensive which involved:

- cooperation between the various clans in economic, social and organisational matters but especially in the military field; and
- the launching of a military offensive, which forced the colonial authorities to conclude peace.

Through this cooperation the various clans eventually formed a tribe or rather a Maroon community led by a *Graman* (chief). In order to carry out the military offensive joint guerilla units of 100-200 well trained fighters were formed.[23] These units were made up of groups of 10 fighters led by a captain who issued his orders by means of a hunter's horn.[24] A network of spies and advance posts was set up and reserve food supplies were created.[25] Finally, the various villages were fortified.[26] The Alukus even had separate villages for women and children, well hidden and away from areas of conflict. All these military measures paved the way for the offensive in which the attacks both on military posts and plantations were intensified. This made the colonial rulers realise that the Maroon communities could not be beaten militarily and forced them to conclude peace treaties.

THE SARAMAKAS

A theoretical approach to the history of the origin of the Saramakas should not leave Price's book *First-Time*, published in 1983, out of consideration. It is the most recent and most comprehensive work on the history of the Saramakas. It is based on over 200 oral fragments related by contemporary Saramaka historians. The question is: how far does *First-Time* reflect a theoretical approach? In this work the emphasis is on the fragments and the three periods in which they have been divided.

With regard to the fragments it may be observed that they are of a highly contemplative nature. Price lets the Saramaka historians give their accounts. They have extraordinary memories and unique techniques to get across centuries old facts but they represent their history in a subjective way. This is the result of their highly emotional approach to their 'fesi ten' (past), which is almost synonymous with slavery 'never again'. By analysing these fragments on the basis of literature and records, Price succeeds in setting them in a more general historical perspective. But Price does not arrive at a military strategic interpretation of these fragments within the context of the slave society to which they refer.

Unfortunately, Price does not link the military necessity of forming los into clans and clans into the ultimate community, on the one hand, to the desire of the colonial authorities to annihilate this community by military means on the other hand. Price divides the early history of the Saramakas into three periods:
- the heroic years: 1685-1748
- toward freedom: 1749-1759
- free at last: 1760-1762

This division into periods clearly shows the lack of a military strategic interpretation of the historical facts. From that point of view, the period 1685-1748 can never be regarded as one period. From the numerous facts in *First-Time* it is quite clear that in the first two decades of the eighteenth century the *los* were pursued all the time by relatively small expeditions, whereas in the '30s and '40s the villages of the clans that had been formed by then could only be taken with great difficulty by large expeditions.[28]

It is the years 1749-1759 that Price regards as the period in which the military strength of the Saramakas caused the colonial rulers

5 The rise of Maroon communities in Suriname

to seek peace. The military strength of the Saramakas was at that time undoubtedly greater than before but as early as 1747 Governor Mauricius was convinced that the Saramakas could in fact not be beaten militarily and that peace was the only solution to neutralise them politically.[29] That conviction was so strong that he carried his plans through and agreed on a truce in 1749. This brought him into serious conflict with a section of the plantocracy, the 'Cabale', which eventually led to his downfall. Before 1749 a peace treaty was already a real possibility.

Finally, the years of 1760-1762 can hardly be regarded as a period. Two years of negotiations should rather be taken as a moment in a 75-year struggle. So the question whether *First-Time* demonstrates the connection between the phased development of the Saramaka community and the military balance of power between the Saramaka and the colonial army should be answered in the negative. This is no reproach but a simple observation, for *First-Time* is a true mine of historical facts which will be put to good use in checking the early history of the Saramakas against the hypothesis mentioned earlier.

According to the most reliable records the ancestors of the Saramakas almost all came from plantations on the Suriname River and one of its left tributaries, the Para River.[30] From 1685 the first *los* settled on the left bank of the Suriname River not far from the plantation area and even close to Paramaribo.[31] Attacks of the civil patrols in the first two decades of the eighteenth century forced them to move on in a south-westerly direction. From about 1730 several *los* had formed clans and inhabited large villages such as Kumako, the Klaaskreek villages and a village on the Yawe Creek.[32] The Klaaskreek villages included those that had been put up for the slaves that had yet to be freed.[33] At that time, three other Klaaskreek villages counted 440 houses only.[34] So the Saramaka clans had reached the phase of consolidation by 1730. It may therefore be assumed that their formation lasted until about 1725. In 1743 and 1749 battles were fought over Kumako and Bakakum respectively. The battle over Kumako was clearly a victory for the colonial troops but in the battle over the fortified Bakakum they suffered heavy losses.[35] The battle over Bakakum formed part of Mauricius' tactics of creating a favourable position to enter into peace negotiations after a single military success.[36]

The truce agreed upon in 1749 was violated by a prominent leader of the Saramakas, Zam Zam. He intercepted the expedition bringing gifts to strengthen the peace and its members disappeared.[37] The Saramakas then resumed their joint offensive and by telling the colonial authorities one lie after another they prevented Zam Zam from being identified as the real breaker of the truce.[38] From the way they protected one another it may be concluded that at that time the clans had already formed a close community with distinct leadership and had reached the phase of offensive attack. This phase must have begun about 1745 and was continued in unison after Zam Zam's act. Between 1751 and 1753 at least 5 plantations were attacked.[39] In 1755 and 1756 the colonial troops organised another two large expeditions against the Saramakas which ended in failure.[40]

In 1762, a final peace was concluded between the Saramakas and the colonial authorities, with the Aukas acting as mediators. This meant the end of the offensive and the start of the Saramaka community, the members of which were legally recognized as free citizens of the colony of Suriname. At that time, they lived in about a dozen villages with approximately 1,600-1,800 inhabitants and were led by Graman Abini.[41] The early history that preceded this stage was one of continual military struggle. Between 1710 and 1760 more than 100 Saramaka rebellions and attacks on plantations took place and more than 50 expeditions were sent out against them.[42] The three processes in the history of the origin of the Saramaka community can, therefore, be outlined as follows:
- formation: from 1685 to about 1725;
- consolidation: from about 1725 to about 1745
- offensive: from about 1745 to1762

THE AUKAS (DJUKAS)

On the early history of the Aukas, compared with the Saramakas, no detailed information is available. In spite of this, their history can be traced on the basis of generally available data. The first *los* came principally from plantations on the upper reaches of the Commewijne River, the Cottica River and the right bank of the Suriname River. They settled on the Marowijne River and its tributary, the Djuka Creek.[43] It is generally assumed that this happened about 1700.[44] When the French admiral Cassard invaded Suriname in 1712 many planters sent their slaves into the forests to avoid their being taken by Cassard and held for payment of a large ransom. Many did not return, however, and joined the Aukas or other communities.[45] From that time onwards the number of Aukas steadily increased.

During the tenure of Governor Cheusses (1728-1734), several plantations on the Tempati and Peninica, small tributaries of the Commewijne River, were attacked.[46] In the '30s and '40s, they again received some reinforcements.[47] On the basis of these facts it may be

5 The rise of Maroon communities in Suriname

assumed that they entered upon the phase of consolidation about the middle of the 1730s. In 1749[48] and 1750,[49] some more rebellions took place, which led to a further reinforcement of the Aukas. It is very likely that the *los* had already formed into clans by then.[50]

In 1757, the Aukas attacked several plantations[51] leaving behind notes in which they offered to make peace with the colonial authorities.[52] So the Aukas must have entered the phase of their offensive about the middle of the 1750s. The colonial authorities, who at that time were faced with the offensives of both the Aukas and the Saramakas, did not need to be told twice, and so peace was concluded with the Aukas in 1760. By that time the Aukas formed a distinct community consisting of 8 villages with 1,600 inhabitants in all, led by Arabie.[53]

On the basis of what has just been said, three processes in the early history of the Aukus may be outlined as follows:
- formation: from about 1700 to about 1735
- consolidation: from about 1735 to about 1755
- offensive: from about 1755 to 1762

THE AKULUS (BONIS)

With regard to the Alukus both general and very detailed information is available, particularly, on the last period of their early history. The first *los* came principally from plantations on the Commewijne River and the Cottica River. They settled between the coast and the Cottica River and between the Cottica River and the upper reaches of the Commewijne River.[54] Their formation began between 1715[55] and 1720.[56] In 1733, an expedition was organised against them, which destroyed the village of Pennenburg. Because of its name and its position, it is very likely that it was one of the Aluku villages.[57] Nothing was heard of the Alukus until 1765. The question is: what happened in all those years?

It is very likely that the *los* had joined to form clans by the end of the 1740s. An Aluku taken prisoner in 1769 stated that three clans had for some time been trying to establish close cooperation under the leadership of Boni.[58] According to Price, there are strong indications that these clans have a common historical background.[59] The captured Aluku also said that his comrades in arms were creating fortified villages and establishing extra plots of land because Boni was preparing a large scale attack. From these data it may be concluded that the Alukus entered upon the phase of the offensive about the end of the 1760s. It appears that their consolidation took place unnoticed, and for good reason. The Aluku *los* always remained close to the plantation area. Few expeditions were organised against them because of the inhospitableness of the area and the numerous swamps and morasses. This enabled the Alukus to keep in touch with the plantations. In this way they obtained weapons and tools and other slaves were able to join them. These recruits joined the Alukus gradually and never in large numbers. Of course, individual planters were aware of what was going on but they did not panic because small numbers of slaves were involved. Often they did not inform the colonial authorities so as not to get a bad reputation. Consequently, the *los* were able to develop gradually and form clans without being disturbed. As stated before, the Alukus were not heard of until they launched a series of major attacks on the plantations in 1765.[60] By that time it appears that they were living in 12 villages[61] counting 600-800 inhabitants in all.[62]

In 1770, the Aluku offensive broke out in full force. It is sufficiently known from J.G. Stedman's standard work that this offensive was unprecedentedly fierce and was carried out with great military skill. Boni became the terror of the whites and the name alone created a panic. The offensive lasted until 1776. Between 1770 and 1776, the Alukus attacked over 30 plantations[63] and were involved in at least 27 clashes[64] with authorities for the following reasons:

- The colonial authorities did not want to make peace because, if they did, the plantation area would be entirely surrounded by pacified Maroons. In the event of a general slave rebellion the Maroons might turn against them and literally drive them into the sea
- It was thought that the escape route, French Guyana in the east, should remain open for purely military strategic reasons
- The Alukus did not want peace either. Boni and his allies had declared several times that they wanted to expel the whites from the colony altogether.

For the colonial authorities, therefore, nothing remained but a military response to the Aluku offensive.

A mercenary force of 1,200 men was called in. Together with the Company troops and colonial troops totalling 1,700 men in all, which had been founded for the war against the Alukus, they went to war. This war, which lasted five years, eventually yielded two losers. Several Aluku villages were burnt down and 200 of their plots were destroyed[65] which forced them to leave for French territory. But they only lost some dozen of fighters and the same small numbers were

5 The rise of Maroon communities in Suriname

taken prisoner.[66] Of the 1,200 mercenaries only 100 survived the war.[67] The losses of the Company troops and colonial troops are not known but several hundred men must have been killed. The financial losses were estimated at 10 million guilders.[68]

In 1788, the Alukus returned to Suriname and tried to launch a second offensive. But the colonial authorities stationed a strong detachment on the Marowijne River, which was supplied from Paramaribo by sea. With the help of the Aukus, with whom the Alukus had come into conflict, this detachment finally succeeded in killing Boni in 1793 and dispersing the Alukus.[69] A number of their descendants live in Suriname, another branch lives in French Guyana. The Alukus did not achieve their ultimate goal, the expulsion of the whites from the colony of Suriname, but the colonial rulers did not succeed in exterminating the Alukus either.

The three processes in the early history of the Alukus should therefore be outlined as follows:
- formation: from about 1715 to about 1740
- consolidation: from about 1740 to about 1770
- offensive: from about 1770 to 1776

Conclusions

1. A theoretical model for the rise of the large Maroon communities in Suriname as a direct reaction to the system of slavery is primarily determined by the military/strategic interpretation of the military struggle between these communities and the colonial authorities. In working out such a theoretical model, the following secondary factors will have to be taken into account:

    i. geographical: the accessibility of the country and the existence of forests, swamps and rivers
    ii. demographic: the number of women and the slaves' ethnic background
    iii. economic: the opportunities for agriculture and the possession of tools
    iv. social: kinship relations and cultural traditions
    v. organisational: religion and leadership
    vi. political: alliances with other Maroon communities and Indians
    vii. military, tactical: knowledge of and experience in guerilla techniques and the shortage of men and military supplies as compared with the colonial army.

2. The large Maroon communities in Suriname have arisen in virtually the same way, independently of one another. The

slight differences in dates of origin should be explained by the different periods in which the areas from which they came were turned into plantation areas.

3. The classic standard works which contain information on the history of the origin of the three Maroon communities in Suriname and incorporate nearly all the extant records show significant gaps. These can only be filled by studying the oral history. The opportunity for doing this diminishes by the day because the Maroon communities of today are disintegrating gradually.

4. History only becomes history if it is understood by non-historians. The purpose of the model outlined above is to make the history of resistance to slavery in Suriname intelligible not only to the people of this country but to the people of the Caribbean region and the world.

Notes

[1] J.J. Hartsinck, *Beschrijving van Guiana of de wilde kust in Zuid-America* (1777, reprint; S. Emmering, Amsterdam, 1974), vol.2, p.649; Hartsinck does not mention an exact date. M.D. Schaafsma, "Suriname, militair geschiedkundig overzicht tot 1795" in *Jaarboek van de Koninklijke Landmacht (Annals of the Dutch Armed Forces), 1966 and 1967* (1967), p.253; Schaafsma gives January 10 – February 23, 1668.

[2] J.M. van de Linde, *Suriname suiker-heren en hun kerk* (Wageningen, 1966), p.95.

[3] J.M. van Lier, *Samenleving in een grensgebied*, 3rd edn (Amsterdam, 1977), p.103.

[4] Manuscript of the report of the commander of the expedition that put down the rebellion. Koninklijk Instituut voor de Tropen, Amsterdam.

[5] W.S.M. Hoogbergen, *De Surinamse veglopers van de 19e eeuw*, Bronnen voor de studie van Bosneger samenlevingen (Centrum voor Caraïbische Studies, Instituut voor Culturele Antropologie, Rijksuniversiteit te Utrecht, 1978), p.15.

[6] H.A.M. Essed, "De struktuur van het Koloniaal leger," *'Makandra'/ Journal of the National Army of Suriname*, 2/28 (February 1984). Sources used on numbers: F.G.J. Bosschart, *Troepenmacht in Suriname* (Breda, 1900); M.D. Schaafsma, op. cit.; J. Nepveu, *Generaal-Reglement bestemd voor alle burger-officier-en en onder-offieren* (1777); J. Wolbers, *Geschiedenis van Suriname* (1861, reprint; S. Emmering, Amsterdam, 1970); J.G. Stedman, *Reizen naar Suriname en door de binnentste gedeelten van Guiana* (1799, reprint; S. Emmering, Amsterdam, 1971).

[7] Essed, "De struktuur", op. cit.

[8] In the 1720s the number of maroons was estimated at 5,000-6,000. Hartsinck, *Beschrijving van Guiana*, vol. 2, op. cit., p.757. In the 1750s

5 The rise of Maroon communities in Suriname

it was estimated at 8,000-9,000. See Society of Learned Jewish Men, *Geschiedenis van Suriname* (Paramaribo, 1788, reprint; S. Emmering, Amsterdam, 1974), p.140.

9 In all the colonial authorities concluded peace with four groups of maroons, who were legally declared free:
With the Conde Negroes in 1684 (J. Wolbers, op. cit., p.64; he does not give a date. M.D. Schaafsma, op. cit., 1967, p.252; he mentions the year 1684). With the *Aukas* in October 1760. On the need for that peace Wolbers (op. cit., p.154) wrote, "Experience had shown that little could be achieved against the bush negroes..." The Learned Jewish Men (op. cit., p.140) wrote that "the constant anxiety in which the inhabitants lived as a result of the persistent attacks of the fugitives forced the authorities to make peace with them". With the *Saramakas* in September 1762 (J. Wolbers, op. cit., p.158). With the *Matawais* in 1767 (W.S.M. Hoogbergen, op. cit., p.5).

10 Hoogbergen, op. cit., p.1.

11 A. de Kom, *Wij slaven van Suriname* (Amsterdam, 1934, reprint; Bussum, 1981) tranalated and reprinted as *We Slaves of Surinam* (New York, 1987).

12 S. Hira, *Van Priary tot en met de Kom* (Rotterdam, 1982).

13 S.W. de Groot, *Van isolatie naar integratie: de Surinaamse Maroons en hun afstammelingen's-Gravenhage* (1963). S.W. de Groot, "Migratiebewegingen der Djoeka's in Suriname van 1845 tot 1863," *Nieuwe West-Indische Gids*, 's-Gravenhage, no. 44 (1965), pp.133-51. S.W. de Groot, *Djuka Society and Social Change* (Assen, 1969). S.W. de Groot, "The Boni Maroon War 1765-1794, Suriname and French Guiana," *Boletín de estudios Latinoamericanos y del Caribe*, no. 18 (1975), pp. 30-48. This article contains a lot of military information on the struggle of the Alukus but no analysis of the struggle.

14 M.J. Herskovits and F.S. Herskovits, *Rebel Destiny among the Bush Negroes of Dutch Guiana* (1934, reprint; S. Emmering, Amsterdam, 1974).

15 R. Price, *Maroon Societies: Rebel Slave Communities in the Americas* (New York, 1973); R. Price, *The Guiana Maroons: a Historical and Bibliographical Introduction* (Baltimore and London, 1976); R. Price, '*First-time*': *The Historical Version of an Afro-American People* (Baltimore and London, 1983).

16 This concept can be found in A. Pakosie, *Het ontstaan van de bosnegerstam de lo de bee mamaosoe pikin of wosoedendoe* (Paramaribo, 1976), p.29. "Los are groups of people bound by an oath and descended from former slaves who had escaped from slavery and conducted their affairs under a collective name, usually that of the former master of plantation." This work is mainly based on oral history. S.W. de Groot, "Migratiebewegingen der Djoeka's in Suriname," op. cit., p. 137. "These los originally consisted of small groups of runaways who came from plantation or owner."

17 Price, '*First-time*', op. cit., p.27. Clans are groups of "several hundred to several thousand people." de Groot, *Djuka Society*, op. cit., p.13. The "... formed clans composed according to the plantations from which the fugitives came". Neither Price nor de Groot (see note 16) make a fundamental distinction between clans and los.

18 Both Pakosie (*Het ontstaan*), op. cit., p.18, and Hira (*Van Priary*), op. cit., pp.172-73, give several examples.

19 Hira, ibid., p.174.

20 Hartsinck, *Beschrijving*, op. cit., p.761.

133

21. Stedman, *Reizen naar Suriname*, op. cit., vol.4, p.8.
22. Wolbers, op. cit., p.147.
23. M.D. Schaafsma, op. cit., pp.267, 278.
24. Stedman, op. cit., vol.3, p.16.
25. M.F. Abbenhuis, "Bonni," in *Emancipatie 1863-1963* (Paramaribo, 1964), p.26.
26. Both Price, '*First-time*', op. cit., and Stedman, op. cit., give many examples.
27. Abbenhuis, op. cit., p.26.
28. Price, '*First-time*', op. cit., pp.75, 83, 84, 117.
29. Wolbers, op. cit., p.121.
30. Price, '*First-time*', op. cit., p.16. A. Pakosie, op. cit., p.10.
31. Price, '*First-time*', op. cit., pp.71, 75.
32. Price, ibid., pp.75, 83, 89.
33. Hartsinck, *Beschrijving*, vol. 2, p.761.
34. Price, '*First-time*', op. cit., p.83.
35. Price, '*First-time*', op. cit., pp.117, 135.
36. Wolbers, op. cit., p.147.
37. Price, '*First-time*', op. cit., pp.140.
38. Price, ibid., pp.140-43.
39. Price, ibid., pp.140, 141, 157.
40. Price, ibid., pp.157, 158.
41. Wolbers, op. cit., p.149. Price, '*First-time*', op. cit., p.180.
42. Price, '*First-time*', op. cit., pp.39.
43. Pakosie, op. cit., pp.8, 9. de Groot, "Migratiebewegingen der Djoeka's in Suriname," op. cit., p.133. de Groot, *Djuka Society*, op. cit., p.13.
44. S.W, de Groot, "Confliksituaties; De Maroons in Suriname (sedert de 18e eeuw). Overeenkomsten met andere Caraibische gegieden," in *Suriname van slavernij naar onafhankelijkheid* (Amsterdam, 1975), p. 31.
45. Price, *The Guiana Maroons*, op. cit., p.30. E. Wong, "Hoofdenverkirzing, stamverdeling en stamverspreiding der boschengers van Suriname in de 18e en 19e eeuw," *Bijdvagen tot de Taal en volkenkunde van Nederlandsch, Indie*, Vol. 97 's-Gravenhage (1938), p.302.
46. Hartsinck, op. cit., vol.2, p.757.
47. Price, *The Guiana Maroons*, op. cit., p.31.
48. Hartsinck, op. cit., vol.2, p.779.
49. W.F. van Lier, *Lets over de Boschenegers in de Boven-Marowijne* (Paramaribo, 1919), p.7.
50. Wolbers, op. cit., p.153. At that time every village already had its separate leader.
51. Hartsinck, op. cit. vol.2, p.779. Price, *The Guiana Maroons*, op. cit., p.31.
52. Wolbers, op. cit., p.154.
53. Hartsinck, op. cit., vol. 2, p.779. Wolbers, op. cit., p.153.
54. de Groot, "The Boni maroon war etc.," op. cit., p.33. S.W. de Groot, "Boni's dood en Boni's hoofd. Een proeve van een orale geschiedenis," *De Gids*, Year 143, no.1 (1980), p.8. Price, *The Guiana Maroons*, op. cit., p.31.
55. Price, *The Guiana Maroons*, op. cit., p.31.
56. Abbenhuis, op. cit., p. 25. de Groot, "The Boni maroon war," op. cit., p.32.
57. Hartsinck, op. cit., vol.2, p.767. The names of the Aluku villages were derived among other things from the way in which they were defended. In this village wooden pins had been struck into the ground as a means of defence. On the "Algemene Kaart van de Colonie of Provintie van Suriname," A. de Leth (c. 1770), the village "Pinnenburg" is situated in the area where the Alukus lived.
58. Abbenhuis, op. cit., p.25. de Groot, "The Boni maroon war," op. cit., pp.32, 33.
59. Price, *The Guiana Maroons*, op. cit., p.31.
60. de Groot, "The Boni maroon war," op. cit., p.31.
61. Stedman, op. cit., vol.3, p.19.
62. de Groot, "Boni's dood en Boni's hoofd", op. cit., p. 8. de Groot estimates their number at 600. This estimate seems too low.
63. Ibid., pp.32-42.

5 The rise of Maroon communities in Suriname

[64] Abbenhuis, "Bonni," op. cit., pp.26, 29.
[65] Stedman, op. cit., vols.2-4.
[66] Abbenhuis, "Bonni," op. cit., p.29, According to Abbenhuis ten Aluku fighters were killed and seven were taken prisoner between 1772 and 1776. Although the losses of the Alukus were in fact negligible (J.G. Stedman) this number is probably too low.
[67] Abbenhuis, ibid., p.29. Also, J.H. de Ridder, *Een levensteken op een doodenveld* (Schoonhoven, 1857).
[68] This estimate was arrived at on the basis of information in J. Wolbers, op. cit., and F.G.J. Bosschart, op. cit.

a. 20-30 expeditions	2,000,000 guilders
b. 5 years maintenance mercenaries and passage	2,000,000 "
c. 5 years maintenance Society troops and military works	2,000,000 "
d. cost of formation and 5 years maintenance Corps of Free Man and Corps of Black Chausseurs	1,500,000 "
e. construction Kordonpad	500,000 "
f. damage to plantations and military posts	2,000,000 "
TOTAL	10,000,000 guilders

[69] de Groot, "Boni's dood en Boni's hoofd", op. cit., pp.46, 47.

135

CHAPTER SIX

Slavery and Literature in Cuba
Lloyd King

The continuance of slavery and the slave trade was such a burning issue in Cuba throughout the nineteenth century that it could not fail to affect the literary intellectuals of that colony, since slavery and with it the prospects of Cuba's plantation economy determined in a fundamental way the history of Cuba's political relations with Spain. For some time, many of the best known literary intellectuals have been represented as somewhat quixotic campaigners against the 'peculiar' institution in spite of their presumed social and economic interests. But Cuba's post-revolutionary historians have been helping to provide a context for the writing of Cuban cultural history, which suggests that these disinterested motives must be regarded with some suspicion. In an article in 1968, "Azúcar, esclavos, revolucion" (Sugar, Slaves, Revolution),[1] Manuel Moreno Fraginals pinpoints the period 1820-1857 as a time of the greatest propagandist effort concerning slavery by Cuban intellectuals and offers a sound economic reason for their postures. This was a period, says Fraginals, when the Creole sugar interest was losing out to Spanish mercantile operators engaged in the illegal slave-running trade.

The British had in 1762 occupied Havana and stimulated the mercantile spirit there but had forced Spain into signing a treaty in 1817 whereby no new slaves should be allowed into Cuba, a treaty due to take effect in 1821. Self-interest and moral indignation had in Britain found common ground to stop slave trafficking to Cuba because the Creole planters and Spanish merchants sought to replace Haiti, after its revolutionary uprising from 1789 onwards, as the principal supplier of sugar. Their expansive urge posed an obvious threat to the British West Indian plantation system. To enforce the provisions of the Treaty, a Mixed Court of Justice was set up in Havana and its first British Commissioner was Richard Madden. What Madden discovered was that the Spanish authorities scarcely hid the fact that they co-operated with the slave-runners, but also that there was a small group of intellectuals who felt that the British

6 Slavery and literature in Cuba

desire to stop the slave trade coincided with their view of what was good for Cuba.

The most notable of Madden's Cuban associates was Domingo Delmonte, a man who held a singular place in Havana's cultural life as a patron of young writers, and a man who, like his friend the historian José Antonio Saco, was convinced, with the example of Haiti before him, that an increase in the number of slaves in Cuba could spell disaster for the white population. Madden himself had first taken the post as special magistrate in Jamaica in 1833 to administer the statute abolishing slavery in the colonies. However, he was unable to cope with a campaign of hostility organised by the corporation of Kingston and returned to Britain in 1835. In 1836 he was sent to Cuba, as a result of his association with the noted abolitionist, Sir Thomas Buxton. Associating himself with Madden, Delmonte answered questionnaires prepared by him openly stating that the Spanish Government was making no attempt to suppress the slave trade and accusing General Tacón, the Captain-General, of selling off freed slaves, that is Africans freed from slave ships and landed in Cuba, instead of protecting their interest.[2] Delmonte also organised a contribution to buy the freedom of the slave poet, Juan Francisco Manzano, and encouraged the writing of a novel about plantation slavery, *Francisco el ingenio* (1838) by the youthful Anselmo Suárez y Romero. Critics who have focused on Delmonte at this period without any further consideration of his role in Cuban history, have been led to project him as a great liberal figure. Thus, Mario Cabrera Saqui, in an introductory note in a 1950 edition of *Francisco* writes: "Imbued with philanthropic and liberal ideas, Domingo Delmonte and a select group of his friends dedicated themselves enthusiastically to the dangerous task of combating the degraded and abject secular institution."[3] Except that at the time Delmonte owned one thousand slaves and his friends, that other great liberal, José de la Luz y Caballero, owned five hundred. And except that some years later, in 1844, we find the following statement in a letter to Delmonte written by his brother-in-law, Miguel de Aldama: "Don't believe, dear brother, that because of this we are losing sight of your instructions concerning the education of your son; on this point Mother follows your letter word for word and keeps him away from any form of contact with Negroes."[4] In Delmonte we see most dramatically the contradictions to which the liberal conscience in Cuba became susceptible.

If we look at the records we find in Delmonte a familiar type, a man seeking to play a historic role but a man who gradually became more and more terrified of the inevitable violence which lurked in a regime based on slavery and colonial repression. Even as he satisfied his pride in being a civilised man through his contact with Madden, Delmonte showed that at best he was a timid liberal. As we noted he had urged on his young protégé, Anselmo Suárez Romero, the writing of a novel on the situation of the slaves, which he eventually passed on to Madden. Suárez sent him the manuscript chapter by chapter not only because he wished to check its literary effectiveness but also because, as he made clear to another young friend, José Zacharias González del Valle, he wished Suárez's novel to promote humane feelings in slave-owners, not to alienate them by implying in any way that he was objecting to the institution of slavery as such. As González del Valle wrote to Suárez:

> For that reason, Domingo suggested to you that you suppress what is subversive in it... since... it could not be circulated among those who may have an interest in some slight modification of the effects of domestic slavery... This is the recourse which is left open to us – to speak, to convince by talking about the subject, to circulate good works, to write and to be prudent with regard to those who are suffering in their interest and ours (*Centón*, p.28).

Suárez' novel was translated into English by Madden but was not published till 1880 in New York, although the manuscript was known to literary intellectuals in Cuba. Suárez seems eventually to have adjusted to the realities of time after this, for one reads his *Colección de artículos* (1859) in vain for any further attack on the institution of slavery, although in the odd article he wrote sympathetically of the slaves, their songs and their music.[5]

Juan Francisco Manzano's autobiography and a number of poems he had written were also handed over to Madden who translated them into English. Manzano inspires both pity and disgust in the reader as he gives accounts of his early years. His is a kind of Cinderella story in reverse. Although born a slave, as a child he was treated by his first mistress almost as if he were white, and he never quite recovered from this childhood experience: "Doña Joaquina herself treated me like a little child, dressed me, combed my hair and kept me from contact with other little blacks."[6] In addition, his godmother often took him to mass and taught him Christian doctrine and as he had an excellent memory, he could recite long sermons by the famous Spanish preacher Fray Luis de Granada by heart. His first mistress died when he was eleven years old and his second treated him worse than Cinderella's stepmother. If one reads between the lines, it is clear that Manzano was harshly ejected from a kind of fool's paradise

6 Slavery and literature in Cuba

which had not fitted him with the art of survival a slave needed to learn. For the most trivial mistakes, he was locked in the coal shed without water or food, in the dark, with rats running over him. But however much of his spirit was cowed, he never let up his aspiration to acquire the few accomplishments of the Creole whites around him, to learn to read, to write and compose verse, and to draw. He was a compulsive storyteller, till his mistress coming upon him with an audience, was so enraged that she had him gagged and tied up in the middle of a room and his companions were forbidden to go in and say a word to him. But even as we begin to sympathise with him, we find this kind of statement: "Kind treatment, he says, makes him forget the past and love his mistress like a mother to the point that I could not stand to hear the servants criticise her and I would have reported many to her but that I was aware that anyone who went to her with tales annoyed her greatly" (*Obras*, p.41). From this unhappy situation, he was rescued by Delmonte, who raised money to pay for his freedom. And he learnt, with bitterness, that his mistress had been preparing him for the realities of his society in which he had obviously hoped to find a place. As Israel Moliner tells us:

> He confessed that he had dreamt of seeing a moral and material improvement in his situation, when he ceased to be a slave but found that he had become a pariah, victim of a colonial society which hated him because he was a black intellectual (*Obras*, p.26)

Francisco Calcango in *Poetas de colour* (1878) tells us that Manzano would never sit in Delmonte's presence and goes on to say that Delmonte preferred Manzano to the mulatto poet, Plàcido, because Plàcido unlike Manzano was cocky and self-assured.

In any case some of the reactions both to Suárez' novel and to Manzano's *Autobiografía* must have worried Delmonte. Madden on receiving the *Autobiografía* had written to Delmonte criticising his friend José Antonio Saco for playing down the horrors of domestic slavery in Cuba: "How in Heaven's name could Saco maintain that slavery in Cuba was a mild servitude… Why does a man like Saco say something he cannot believe merely to disarm the planter's hostility to his enlightened opinions?"[7] As we have already seen, Delmonte's own aims included not only organising propaganda to persuade the slave-owners to make "servitude light" but in the process not to arose their hostility either. But Madden's letter of the 23rd September, 1839 must have confirmed his feelings that all was not going according to plan, if one considers an earlier letter from Félix Tanco to him dated 5th November, 1838. Tanco, a rather neglected figure in Cuban cultural history, had some of the sharpest things to say about slavery of any figure of the period. He frequented Delmonte's literary circle, wrote him innumerable letters and must have been something of an embarrassment to him. For example, he wrote the following of Suárez' *Francisco*: "Let us set aside the ridiculous mania or terror of painting a selected group in society, that is white society, alone, isolated, because the blacks discolour and soil this society... Tell Mr Suárez that his novel has the support of all who have read it and are not coarsely insensitive...that the overseer is beautifully portrayed as the devilish and foul character he is and as all overseers are." (*Centón*, p.120).

The truth is that Tanco was repelled not only by the overseers but by the masters. In a short, wicked, and dramatic sketch, *Escenas de la vida privada en la isla de Cuba* also called *Petrona y Rosalia*, last published in the general *Cuban Contemporánea* in 1925, Tanco shows the masters to be overbearing, cowardly, hypocritical and indeed contemptible. In a foreword Tanco says that, for him, those who flattered Cuban society are rather enemies of its best interest: "Accustomed as Cubans are to hearing from birth perfidious flattery and insidious praise paid to our poor country by the veritable enemies of its happiness, we are greatly annoyed by criticism and censure coming from anyone who invokes the forceful accents of patriotism in order to castigate our vices, absurdities and crimes."[8] Tanco's story, published in 1838, contained an ironic base later utilised by Cirilo Villaverde in his novel *Cecilia Valdés*. It is the story of the Malpica family and its relations with two house slaves, mother and daughter. The mother, Petrona, is made pregnant by the master of the house, Don Antonio Malpica y Lozano and the mistress not knowing her husband to be the culprit, dispatches her to the plantation where she gives birth and brings up the child, Rosalia. Years later the daughter Rosalia is brought to the house as a companion-servant for the mistress and she is in turn taken advantage of and made pregnant by the son, Fernando Malpica, a self-willed, boorish young man. When the father overhears the mother and son arguing about the latter's relationship with Rosalia, the shock of hearing of the incestuous relations between Rosalia and Fernando, his daughter and son, brings him down with a heart attack and he dies shortly after. His wife, searching through his papers, comes across a note which allows her to put two and two together but her reaction comes as a surprise to the reader. She finds the whole thing grimly humorous because there was something that Don Antonio had never found out, namely, that his son Fernando was not his son at all but the result of an affair with a family friend.

6 Slavery and literature in Cuba

The story outline antedates one of Lord Melody's calypsos by more than a hundred years: "Your daddy ain't your daddy but your daddy don't know."

Tanco y Bosmeniel is also credited with a *Memorial to the Queen of Spain for the Abolition of Slavery* published in New York around 1860. He used the opportunity of making a case for Spain to abolish slavery by reflecting on the possible consequences of the civil war between the northern and southern states of the United States. Tanco applauds Lincoln for setting out to resolve the "antagonism of the two principles of liberty and slavery, right and interest, civilisation and barbarism",[9] and then urges upon the Queen of Spain that she ought to proceed in like fashion. He goes on to reproach the Spanish authorities in Cuba for not honouring the treaty with Great Britain whereby Spain had agreed to stop trafficking in slaves, and further suggests that the abolition of slavery was a matter of prudence:

> Your Majesty should hasten to satisfy the exigencies of the times, and avoid, by prudential measures what the forces of the circumstances and the irresistible march of time may impose on you, in a manner both decisive and contrary to the safety of the white race in the two islands, or at least the conservation of their actual richness (p.20).

Tanco then goes on to propose a series of measures which would protect "the safety of the white race", suggesting (a) that the liberation of the slaves should be accompanied by a measure granting political power in the island to the Creole whites which he felt would allow them to "exercise the public power with advantage to themselves and without injustice to the civil rights of the black population" (p.24); (b) that white immigration should be encouraged with no religious qualification in order to balance out the numbers of the two races; and (c) Spain's participation in the project of the repatriating Africans which had led to the creation of Liberia. Moreover, he noted, the immediate abolition of slavery would forestall the designs entertained by the southern states of America of taking over Cuba. The thing to do, therefore, was to follow Britain's example and declare the abolition of slavery. Tanco y Bosmeniel was a progressive and liberal man for this time, far saner and more principled than Domingo Delmonte, yet he is one of the curiously neglected figures of Cuban nineteenth century letters, possibly due to the fact that he never associated himself with those who wished independence.

In fact Delmonte was playing a dangerous game. Madden had certainly incurred the hostility of the Spanish administration and was regarded as a man who would disseminate seditious ideas. Delmonte's friend, José Antonio Saco, was eventually sent into exile in 1834 because he was known to favour the abolition of the slave trade. Yet with the departure of Madden in 1839, Delmonte now associated himself with his replacement, David Turnbull. Turnbull was a stubborn and impetuous crusader who rather frightened Delmonte. Many years later, Turnbull would express his conviction that there existed "aspirations of the Creole population of Cuba for that sort of independence which the other Spanish provinces of America have already achieved".[10] It was a conviction which Madden evidently also held, for in his *Memoirs* he had stated:

> If England could have been induced in 1837 to guarantee the island of Cuba free from the intervention of any foreign power, the white inhabitants were prepared to throw off the Spanish yoke, to undertake the bona fide abolition of the slave trade and to have passed some measures for the amelioration of slavery.[11]

But Turnbull obviously convinced Delmonte that he was likely to organise an uprising. In fact the evidence is that he felt himself to be involved in a situation which was getting out of hand. Like his friend José Antonio Saco, he was quite opposed to the elements which looked to the United States to free Cuba from Spain. He rejected the idea of independence, for like many other Cubans his imagination was haunted by the spectre of Haiti. In a letter he wrote to a friend in 1848, his confused and terrified feelings are manifested. Revolution would only lay waste the countryside and destroy the planters' investments. Imperial rule, though despotic, is bringing about progress in Cuba slowly but surely. The solution to all Cuba's problems lies in putting an end to slavery and removing all Africans from the island for Africans cannot fit in "with the forward march of European culture... the task, the only objective, the constant aim of every Cuban truly and sincerely motivated by patriotism must consist in the complete removal of the African race from Cuba" (*La falsa cubanidad*, p.21).

No doubt this notion of a total repatriation was entertained by Delmonte as a result of the moves by the United States government to repatriate ex-slaves to Africa in the 1820s and after. It may also explain in part the fact that, while hostile to the annexionists, Delmonte was quite friendly with Mr Alexander Everett, the American agent, who had an interest in Hispanic letters. While the view that Cuba could be better off without blacks is of itself not vicious, in the case of Delmonte, it would appear that it conceals the

6 Slavery and literature in Cuba

dreadful role he apparently played in the so-called *Conspiración de la escalera* (The Ladder Conspiracy), the supposed conspiracy which led to the torture and death of many mulattoes and slaves, including the poet, Plácido,. There has been considerable debate as to whether there was such a conspiracy or whether it was an invention of the Spanish authorities. Research undertaken by Leonardo Griñan Peralta has pointed to Delmonte being at the centre of the witch-hunt.[12] Griñan Peralta shows that Delmonte passed on information to Everett of a conspiracy supposedly being hatched by Turnbull. Everett sent the news to Washington, which alerted the Spanish Government, which in turn alerted the local authorities. Ironically, Delmonte came under suspicion and was forced to flee into exile in France. Aspiring to play a historic role as a patriot, Delmonte compromises any liberal image offered by his generation. His history warns us of the need to approach with rather more caution the idea that his protégés were unambiguous proponents of an anti-slavery literature.

The two early stories on slavery, Tanco y Bosmeniel's *Petrona y Rosalia* and Suárez y Romero's *Francisco, el ingenio*, were of limited literary interest but in their plot patterns, they established a format followed by later writers. Suárez makes slavery literary by offering the reader the image of the slave–in-love more or less in the romantic sentimental tradition. The limits of his vision of the slaves is indicated by the fact that his slave-in-love is a sensitive house slave, Francisco, whom the reader is adjured to pity because as a punishment he has been sent off to the country to become a field slave. Secondly, his loved one is a mulatto, Dorotea, who gives herself to the son of the house in order to save her lover from his suffering. Suicide in the end proves to be the only way out. This pattern is repeated in a more complex rewrite of the novel, *El Negro Francisco* by Antonio Zambrana, another interesting figure in Cuban nineteenth century history. Tanco's story took over another romantic convention, whereby incest rears its head as the son of the house and the mulatto turn out to be brother and sister. This is a shaping fact in the most famous of Cuba's nineteenth century novels *Cecilia Valdés* by Cirilo Villaverde and is given a twist in a play called *El mulato* by Alfredo Torroella where the mulatto is half-brother to the planter's daughter. Both Zambrana and Villaverde deserve attention because their writing was related to their political interests and should be read in relation to them.

El Negro Francisco was written by Zambrana in 1875 in Chile while he was there canvassing support for the Cuban Independence effort during the Ten Years War (1868-1878) in which the patriots were led by Manuel de Céspedes. Zambrana has stated that while attending a literary soirée in Havana in 1862 at the house of another patron of the arts, Nicolàs Azcàrate, he heard the manuscript of Suárez' *Francisco, el ingenio* read and was deeply moved at the plight of the slaves. He was sixteen at the time. But he was a man with a flair for politics rather than literature and got involved in the struggle for independence, for he had taken "the irrevocable resolution not to be an accomplice in any way to it (that is, slavery), and to devote at the earliest opportunity his heart and soul to wiping that dreadful stain from Cuba's brow".[13] Zambrana became celebrated as an orator, and was part of the 'Asamblea de Representantes del Centro' which in February 1869 declared all Cuban slaves free, and he was also heavily involved in the same year in drafting Cuba's first republican constitution, the Constitución de Guáimaro. Zambrana spent most of his time travelling in Latin America and Europe raising both financial and political support for the rebels but during the period of truce following on the Ten Years War, put himself out of the mainstream of Cuban opposition forces by accepting and campaigning for associate statehood (autonomía colonial) for Cuba. This ruined his career in Cuban politics, and he retired to exile in Costa Rica.

El Negro Francisco was Zambrana's first and only literary work and suggests that he had literary talent which he did not exploit. Published in Chile in 1875, it could have had no effect on the fate of the slaves in Cuba and is worth reading much more because of the insight it offers into more progressive attitudes among some white Cubans in the latter half of the nineteenth century. What Zambrana did, making his novel resemble Suárez' novel superficially, was to take over the outline of his plot: two young house slaves, a mulatto girl and a black African, fall in love but have their desires thwarted by an indulgent mother and her spoilt self-willed son. This leads to Francisco being sent out to plantation labour and ill-treated at the hands of that stereotyped figure, the brutal and insensitive overseer. There the likeness ends. For one thing Zambrana obviously did not have the same kind of first hand experience of plantation slavery as Suárez did, which is probably why his indignation at slavery was aroused after hearing Suárez' story. He, therefore, made no attempt to match Suárez in his descriptions of plantation life and its punishments. Instead, in his swiftly written little tale, he concentrated on introducing some subtlety into his characterisations, a quality decidedly lacking in Suárez' effort. First of all, Zambrana took a much more realistic view of the developing love affair between the two slaves, Camila and Francisco. Since it would scarcely be normal for a Creole mulatto girl to fall in love with an African born slave,

6 Slavery and literature in Cuba

Zambrana shows how Camila gradually comes to respect and admire him for his dignity, his self-confidence and his bravery. And on the other hand, Camila learns by overhearing a conversation, that Doña Josefa de Orellano, her mistress, who had brought her up almost as a daughter and kept her as a kind of lady-in-waiting, regarded any aspirations that she Camila, might have to marry a white man as both unthinkable and scandalous. This leads her to start 'thinking black' so to speak:

> And on turning towards the black race, she could not but be attracted to the moral stature of that man, its most perfect representative, so strong, so heroic, and so austere who carried his servitude with the same dignity with which one might wear a crown, and who for the love of his own kind had just defied a horrible and repugnant death; there, at his side she would surely be better protected than by the contemptuous pity of the white.[14]

Francisco had defied death by personally nursing a black servant who had a dangerous communicable disease. Camila, out of love for Francisco, goes far beyond what one would have expected from a Creole Cuban mulatto. She seeks to come to terms with Francisco's 'African' belief:

> The sombre traditions of his race, his love for the dark symbols of his homeland manifested in strange rites, in a still savage poetry, all these things which might scarcely have been expected to attract or hold the young woman's attention, took on an extraordinary value in her eyes when described, explained and defended by Francisco (pp.64-65).

Zambrana is the first Cuban writer to see 'African beliefs' as a challenge to Westernised mulattoes and blacks, something with which they would have come to terms or seek to suppress. Certainly, he had a largeness of view which was sorely needed in Cuba's early Republican years and it is a pity that this time he had ceased to be a force in Cuban life.

In his characterisation of Francisco he was less successful in that, although he is able to present him as a man of dignity and courage, he is never able to imagine him as a rebel, although blacks had staged revolts so often in the nineteenth century. Perhaps the image of Francisco as victim fitted in better with the design of winning sympathy for the oppressed slave. The author is much more successful with Carlos de Orellana. As in the earlier work by Suárez, Carlos is the spoilt only son who cannot bear to be denied the mulatto girl's favours and who besieges and punishes her lover till they are both driven to suicide. But Zambrana introduces a significant change by having Carlos recognise the enormity of his own moral depravity and join the patriots to fight not only for an end to Spanish domination but for black liberation. In fact, Carlos, writing to a friend, takes the position unheard of at the time that black liberation was more important than an end to colonial status:

> Be less taken with struggling against Spanish domination, with obtaining this or that form of government, this or that freedom, this or that guarantee. *Rather be concerned about the blacks.* Instead of worrying about being exploited, worry that you are exploiters... You all say: 'Ah, if only Cubans were not slaves! Ah, if only Cubans didn't own slaves is what I exclaim' (p.165).

These are remarkable words for their time and perhaps throw considerable light on Zambrana's subsequent career. They might indeed explain why Zambrana must have decided to campaign for acceptance of associate statehood status since in his view the first task was to rescue the black masses from exploitation by the Cuban Creole settler class. It is a pity that Zambrana's biography is still so patchy and vague. What is certain is that Zambrana's views were not widely held.

Of the writers mentioned so far, Cirilo Villaverde is the only one who was a professional writer. Even so, his novel evolved over a long period of time. Originally a short story, it was expanded to offer a picture of Havana life in the early decades of the nineteenth century and was published in serial form in 1839. Its second part was not published till more than forty years later in New York. In between the two parts, Villaverde had in 1848 taken part in a conspiracy, been arrested, sentenced to death and had been reprieved. In 1849 he escaped jail and went into exile in the United States. There, he became secretary to Narciso López , the military leader of a group who wished to see Cuba associated with the slave-owning states of the Union. Yet even as Delmonte has been considered the classic anti-slavery liberal, Villaverde has been held up as the author of the classic Cuban anti-slavery novel.

In part one of the novel, it became clear that Villaverde's narrator saw Cuban life as comedy, and further that the essence of the comedy of Cuban life lay in the tangled sexual relations between whites and mulattoes. While Tanco wished to use race relations ironically, Villaverde seems to have seen one kind of tragic possibility. The basic situation is the following. A Spanish planter, Don Candido Gamboa, married to a Cuban Creole, by whom he has a

6 Slavery and literature in Cuba

son, has also fathered a daughter, Cecilia Valdés, by a young mulatto woman who subsequently went mad. The girl grows up, encouraged by her grandmother, also mulatto, with the aspiration to marry a white Creole. Within the terms of romantic fate, she and her half-brother are drawn together, even as the father desperately works to avert their unconscious incestuous entanglement. Gamboa, so sensitive in regard to his daughter's welfare, is shown to be totally callous to the African slave. Undoubtedly related to the movement to stop the further importation of slaves, the book offers a scene in which Gamboa, the Spaniard, justifies the practice of their slaving captains throwing their "cargo" overboard rather than risk arrest by British naval vessels:

> When the world becomes convinced that blacks are animals and not men that will be the end of one of the reasons put forward by the English for being hostile to the African trade. The same thing happened in Spain with tobacco; trade in it is prohibited and those who live by it jettison their cargo and ride swiftly off to save their skins when in danger of capture by the police. Do you think that tobacco has a soul? What you must understand is that there's no difference between a bale of tobacco and a Black at least as far as feeling is concerned.[15]

Further because this is a nationalist novel, Gamboa's Spanish hostility to his son leads his wife, Doña Rosa, to discover a measure of sympathy for the slaves, at least in a general and rather abstract fashion. This is the extent to which the text engages the issue of slavery.

More central to the narrator's concern is what one might call a gradual 'deconstruction' of the figure of the beautiful *mulata*. Later in the century, Martin Morúa Delgado, a mulatto, a rather indifferent novelist and a politician, saw in the text's portrayal of mulattoes Villaverde's hostility to that group in the society. Morúa referred in particular to a scene in which a conversation takes place between two mulattoes, one of whom says the following:

> What's to be done, José Dolores? Dissimulate; be patient; behave like a dog with hornets; show your teeth so that they think you're laughing? Don't you see that they're the hammer and we're the anvil? The whites came first and took the choice cuts; we men of colour came after and must be pleased to gnaw the bones. Let things proceed, my boy, our turn must come. Things can't go on like this forever. Do as I do. Don't you see me kiss hands that I would rather see cut off? Do you think that I'm sincere? Don't be silly for the living truth is that whites can go to hell as far as I'm concerned (v. l, p.102).

The character speaking here is a master tailor called Uribe and, according to Morúa, the words put in his mouth are pure slander in so far as they are supposedly the views of a historical personage. Indeed Morúa points to the depiction of this character as an act of malice which had the worse possible consequences as far as the flesh and blood of man was concerned:

> His imprisonment and suffering, inflicted by the prejudiced government of his time, had no other origin than the declared and systematic persecution by all representative elements of the Colony against the black and mulatto class whose only crime was that of possessing great wealth won by the sweat of their brow.[16]

Morúa is therefore saying that this Uribe was among the victims of the infamous *Conspiración de la escalera* to which reference has already been made. Villaverede's text, therefore, seems to reflect the hostility towards mulattoes which prevailed and which was reflected in Delmonte's attitudes. In the case of the character Cecilia Valdés, she is shown to be ambitious, cold-hearted towards her mulatto lover José Dolores Pimienta whom she incites to committing murder, and is a woman who uses her sexuality purely to gain access to the world of whiteness. If we look at the novel less as a partisan document than as revelatory of the drift of feeling and opinion of its time, we can see it as the most adequate literary expression of Delmonte's views, helping us to understand his seemingly tranquil conscience in the face of the terrorism unleashed against mulattoes and blacks in 1844.

The second part of Villaverde's novel and a revised version of part one was published forty years later in 1882. In this interval, the tide of historical events had certainly changed. Villaverde's erstwhile chief, Narciso López, had failed in his annexationist plans, and anti-slavery sentiment in the United States had been crystallised in *Uncle Tom's Cabin* (1852), to be followed by the civil war which put an end to slavery in the American Union. In 1868, Manuel de Céspedes offered freedom to Cuban slaves who joined in the rebellion against Spain and in 1880, the Spanish government abolished slavery in Cuba. And most important of all, there was the activity both political and ethical of the great patriot, José Martí, whose impact on the approach to Cuban independence is so well known and appreciated. It is, therefore, not at all surprising that the cruelties of life on the plantation are played up in part two. The symbol of this progressive and humane attitude to slaves is Leonardo Gamboa's fiancée Isabel Ilincheta, the Creole mistress of a tobacco plantation. Here is the scene in which her liberalism is displayed:

6 Slavery and literature in Cuba

I shall tell Papa to let them play the drums on the two days of Christmas and at Epiphany.

– But if Missy not here, niggers don't enjoy themselves.

– What nonsense. Just go on and dance, enjoy yourselves and make Missy happy when she comes back from her trip. There! That's enough Pedro.

Pedro withdrew slowly and unwillingly and Isabel who remained leaning pensively on the balustrade of the porch called back saying

– There, you see Pedro! You're such a nuisance with your interruptions that you almost made me forget one of the most important things I was going to say. I have one more word to say to you, my final command. Pedro, whatever you may think, it will be best for you to keep the whip inside your hut until after Christmas. Yes, yes, it will be best. Because as long as you have it in your hand, you'll want to use it and I don't want the whip used on anyone, you hear me, Pedro? Let the whip be silent while I'm away.

– Niggers die with love for you, Missy, said Pedro with a grin (v.2, p.91).

Slaves here are shown to be really just big children, lovable orphans who respond well if treated well. Yet Isabel is not all benevolence, she is also shrewd, progressive, self-interest. In another scene she is shown reflecting: "Was it not in the interest of the master to conserve and prolong the life of the slave, his living capital?" (v.2, p.185)

By prolonging the note of hostility towards the mulatto, by striking a note of compassion towards the slaves' cruel experiences, and by noting their value as "living capital", *Cecilia Valdés* prefigures some of the contradictions of the early years of the Cuban Republic, deprived of Martí's vision and subjected to the supervision of an expansive American capitalist thrust. The racism in Cuba fostered by Americans from the South was so intense in post-independence Cuba that Juan Gualberto Gómez urged his followers to accept second class citizenship for the sake of survival: "What do I say to my people! Let us invent nothing, let us develop no taste for originality in any sphere of activity, let us accept the minor role."[17] In a story written in 1917, the mulatto protagonist seeking to study for the priesthood learns that "a black saint was possible but nobody could imagine a black priest".[18]

It is strictly speaking irrelevant to refer to an abolitionist literature in respect of Cuba if, by abolitionist literature, one means writing which at the level of praxis promoted the emancipation of the slaves.

Cuba in no sense had an *Uncle Tom's Cabin*. The environment in Cuba and indeed in Spanish America and Spain was so illiberal that there could be no equivalent of Nat Turner, or John Brown, or Frederick Douglass. And nothing in literature like Huckleberry Finn. The memoirs of Esteban Montejo would have to wait for the twentieth century and since what he said was edited by a transcriber, we have no idea what was left out.

Yet the activities and writings of the handful of Cuban literati enable us to feel the actualities and the contradictions which beset the liberal conscience in Cuba when confronted with the phenomenon of slavery and the hierarchies of race and colour. The studied ambiguities of Domingo Delmonte in so far as they were representative of the attitudes of a white nationalist bourgeoisie point forward to the era of the Republic. For Ramiro Guerrra y Sanchez in *Azúcar y población en las Antillas*, the imperial powers missed the opportunity to build colonies based on a European immigrant peasantry by accelerating the flow of African slave to the Caribbean. The early Fernando Oritz, under the influence of a positivist ideology argued in his introduction to *Los negros brujos* (1906) that from the moment Africans landed in Cuba they became criminals not in the sense of falling from a plane of higher morality but simply as people incapable of understanding moral notions. Neither of these scholars were racists but in these particular instances they gave expression to attitudes that reflect the temper of the times and of a Republic which in some ways smacked of the American South in its racial practices. Yet in the aftermath of slavery, the spirit of Martí also prevailed, embodied in the work of Fernando Ortiz, the poetry of Nicolas Guillén, the early fiction of Alejo Carpentier and in the political area, the impact of Fidel Castro and the Cuban Revolution.

6 Slavery and literature in Cuba

Notes

1. *Casa de las Americas*, n.50 (1968).
2. José Antonio Saco, *Historia de la esclavitud de la Raza Africana en el Nuevo Mundo*, v.14 (La Habana, 1938), p.22.
3. *Francisco, el ingenio* (La Habana, 1953), p.19.
4. *Centón epistolario de Domigo Delmonte*, v.7 (La Habana, 1938), p.128. Referred to hereafter as *Centón*.
5. Suárez y Romero, *Colección de artículos* (La Habana, 1963), p.343: "La musica de estos negros llega al alma, habla al corazón; principalmente aquellas canciones que entonan en memoria de los difuntos con el cadáver en medio sobre la tarima y ellos en torna sollozando."
6. Juan Francisco Manzano, *Obras* (La Habana: Biblioteca básica de autores cubanos, 1972), p.8. Referred to hereafter as *Obras*.
7. Rafael Soto Paz, *La falsa cubanidad de Saco, Luz y Delmonte* (La Habana, 1941), p.120. Referred to hereafter as *La falsa cubanidad*.
8. *Cuba contemporanea*, v.39, n.156 (1925), p.256.
9. Felix Tanco y Bosmeniel, *Memorial to the Queen of Spain for the Abolition of Slavery in the Islands of Cuba and Puerto Rico* (New York, 1860), p.15.
10. David Turnbull, *The Jamaican Movement for Promoting Slave Trade Treaties* (London, 1850), p.25.
11. Quoted in *The Life and Poems of a Cuban Slave: Juan Francisco Manzano, 1797-1854*, ed. Edward Mullen et al. (Connecticut, 1981), p.8.
12. Leonardo Grinan Peralta, *Ensayos y conferencias* (Santiago de Cuba, 1964).
13. *Colección los Zambrana*, v.6 (La Habana, 1953), p.5.
14. *El negro Francisco* (La Habana, 1953), pp.27-28.
15. *Cecilia Valdés*, v.1 (La Habana, 1972), p.377.
16. Martín Morúa Delgado, *Los novelas de Cirilo Villaverde* (La Habana, 1892), p.36.
17. Edreira de Caballero, *Vida y obra de Juan Gualberto Gómez* (La Habana, 1955), p.64.
18. Alfonso Hernández-Catá, *Los frutos acidos y otros cuentos* (Madrid, 1953), p.124.

CHAPTER SEVEN

Women and Slavery in the Caribbean: A Feminist Perspective

Rhoda E. Reddock

Much has been written on the subject of New World slavery, and indeed it may appear that the time has come for all such considerations to cease. For the Caribbean people, however, slavery is a crucial aspect of their historical experience and its existence and legacy are not confined to the distant past. In Cuba, for example, slavery still existed less than a hundred years ago. The study of history is important not for its own sake, but in order to acquire an understanding of the workings of society that we can apply to our present experience. In the women's movement throughout the world, women have had to re-examine and re-interpret history and often to rewrite it in order to make women visible. In this article I shall attempt to reinterpret the history of slavery in the Caribbean from a woman's perspective. I hope by doing so to expose some of the ideology which conceals material oppression.[1]

Caribbean slavery has been attributed varying positions in Marxist 'mode of production' analysis. To some it was a particular form of production within the worldwide capitalist system.[2] To others, however, it is seen rather as a distinct mode of production, though it was incorporated into the sphere of exchange of the capitalist one. This view is justified by the fact that most, if not all, surplus value was derived from slave labour. According to Post, "It was based upon a particular combination of capital, land and labour-power, and as Marx showed, the mere presence of capital, even in conjunction with 'free' labour, let alone chattel slaves, does not make a social formation capitalist."[3]

I take the position that New World slavery in general, and Caribbean slavery in particular, can be seen as the capitalist harnessing of an archaic form of economy. Whatever one's position, the relationship between New World slavery and the emergence of capitalism is clear, and Williams has shown that slave production

7 Women and slavery in the Caribbean

provided much of the basis for European industrialisation.[4]

African-Caribbean slavery might be said to have begun in 1518, when Charles V of Spain, on the advice of Bartolomé de Las Casas, "protector of the Indians", formally granted permission for the importation of 4,000 African slaves to relieve the labour shortage in the Antillean mines. Portugal, Spain, Britain, France, The Netherlands, Denmark and Sweden, all took part in the slave trade that ensued and, with the exception of Sweden, in the slavery which was established in their colonies.[5]

Conditions varied somewhat from one area to the next and the debate over the relative cruelty of the systems continues. What is important, though, is that at a particular time in history, the slave mode (or form) of production proved to be the most efficient means of capital accumulation for Western Europe in the sugar plantation colonies of the Caribbean. Whatever tears are shed at the thought of past brutality, economically, for Western Europe, there can be no regrets.

It is against this background, therefore, that we can approach the study of women in Caribbean slave society, where there was no necessity to conceal oppression or the profit motive. The facts revealed in this analysis though they are derived from to very particular situation, are relevant to the study of the oppression of women internationally today.

WOMEN IN SOCIAL PRODUCTION

Among the slaves the housewife did not exist. From the age of four, slave girls as well as boys worked on the estate. According to Orlando Patterson, "In Rosehall Estate (Jamaica) girls started work at four and remained in the Hogmeat Gang (which consisted of young children employed in minor tasks such as collecting food for the hogs, weeding and the like) until the age of nine. Between the ages of 12 and 19 occupations varied."[6] In one particular group, one girl aged twelve and two others aged 19 were in the field, two were attending stock, one was "with Mrs Palmer" and another was a domestic. The majority of women in Jamaica between the ages of 19 and 54 worked in the fields. By the late eighteenth and early nineteenth century, women outnumbered the men in the field, because of their lower mortality rates.[7] By 1838, when slavery in the British colonies was abolished, the proportion of men in the field had fallen below 40 per cent.[8] This is interesting when one notes that job discrimination on the basis of sex is often justified on the ground that women have lower physical strength and endurance.

In fact, according to Craton, slave women participating in field work similar to men's lived up to five years longer than men. In slavery, therefore, women were often as important as productive field labourers as men. In the words of Gwendolyn Midlo Hall, "Slave manpower has been compared to plant equipment. The purchase price of the slave was the investment, and the maintenance of the slave was a fixed cost that had to be paid whether or not the slave was working."[9] Therefore, says Patterson,

> Slavery abolished any real social distribution between males and females. The woman was expected to work just as hard, she was as indecently exposed and was punished just as severely. In the eyes of the master she was equal to the man as long as her strength was the same as his.[10]

What was work like on these estates? In mid-nineteenth century Cuba the working day in the grinding season was as long as twenty hours. Four or five hours' sleep was considered adequate. Women cut cane even during the ninth month of pregnancy.[11] According to Hall, by the end of the grinding season in Cuba even the oxen were reduced to mere skeletons, many of them dying from over-work. In Brazil, also, a booming plantation society in the nineteenth century, one coffee planter calculated on using a slave for only one year (few on his estate could survive longer than that), during which he could get enough work out of the slave not only to "repay the initial investment, but even to show a good profit".[12]

Despite their use in hard field labour, says Craton, women were always excluded from the more prestigious and skilled jobs, including, for example, work with the boilers, carpentry and masonry. Patterson also noted that male slaves had a much wider range of occupations than female slaves who were confined to being field hands, domestics and washerwomen. The most prestigious jobs for women appear to have been those related to health, in particular, nursing. Tables for 1823 in Jamaica list two midwives and one doctress (woman doctor) as being among the staff of one estate. This situation can be seen as the introduction of the sexual division of labour that had been instituted in Europe into one sector of slave society, while not extending it to areas in which it was not economically advantageous.

A minority of women (and men) became 'house slaves' participating mainly in domestic activities such as cooking, cleaning. In the hierarchy of slave societies, house slaves were a breed apart, and the

7 Women and slavery in the Caribbean

class division between women who did household labour and those who did not may have started here. It is possible (although this is pure conjecture) that field slaves, envied the position of the house-slave, not so much because of a love of housework as from a desire for a less strenuous existence and the higher status that went with proximity to white people. Patterson points out, however, that not all field slaves envied the household slaves' position. To many, the field offered more stability and relative 'freedom' for there they were not constantly at the mercy of the masters and mistresses. These views would, of course, have varied from one plantation to another and over time.

WOMEN AND REPRODUCTION

The main factor differentiating men from women is the capacity of women to produce human life. Throughout history the subordination of women has been centred around the necessity to control this important capacity. This question of reproduction, hitherto ignored in the social sciences, is now receiving increased attention with the emergence of academic studies on the subject of women, brought about by the women's movements of the 1970s.

Because of the crudeness of the social relations of production in slave society, the study of slave women and reproduction reveals much about the ability of the ruling classes to control the reproductive capacity of women to suit the economic necessity of the moment. Craton in his socio-demographic study of Worthy Park Estate in Jamaica identifies a 'Christmas tree effect' in population pyramids constructed from plantation records; the number of children was very small whereas the middle aged population was much greater, then gradually tapering off into old age. He rejects the view that this situation reflects the planters' preference for "buying rather than breeding". Instead, he suggests that it is because of the long period of lactation among African women during which sexual intercourse was taboo; high infant mortality rates due to disease and diet deficiencies; the biological and psychological effects of dislocation, stress and overcrowding, analogous to Nazi concentration camps; and the abortions performed by slave women who did not want to bring children into slave labour.[13] These are the factors he believes are responsible for the high frequency of sterility among slave women at Worthy Park and the fact that more than half of them never gave birth at all.

Other writers, however, have seen this also as the result of definite preferences on the part of the planters. Noel Deerr, in his *History of Sugar*, noted that: "Natural reproduction of the slave population was not encouraged in sugar colonies; it was held to be cheaper to buy than to breed, since a child was an expense for its first twelve years of life."[14] Similarly, Hall notes that:

> Sources from Ste Domingue indicate masters calculated the work of *a negresse* during an eighteen month period (that is the last three months of pregnancy and the months during which she breast-fed her infant) was worth 600 livres, and that during this time she was able to do only half of her normal work. The master therefore lost 300 livres. A fifteen month old slave was not worth this sum.[15]

Patterson attempts a more systematic discussion of the question, discussing the attitudes of slave-owners towards reproduction in different periods of slave history. Using examples from Jamaica, he notes that during the early period, from 1655 until the beginning of the eighteenth century estates were small and had few slaves. As a result, the treatment of slaves was better than it would become later and 'natural' reproduction was encouraged. During the eighteenth century, however, the rising planter class shifted to the large scale monocrop production of sugar and 'natural' reproduction was abandoned. Thus, by mid century, Dr Harrison of Jamaica could state that no encouragement was given to slaves to raise families, the general opinion being that it was cheaper to buy new ones than to rear children. As late as the 1830s Henry Coor, a Jamaican millwright estimated in *The West Indian Reporter* of March 1831 that the cost of rearing a slave to age 14 was £112 in Jamaica; £165 in Trinidad; £109 in Barbados; and £122 in Antigua.[16] At this time the comparative market price of a field slave was £45 in Cuba.[17] Patterson further states that it was considered "a misfortune to have pregnant women or even young slaves". He also observed that "the attitudes of the owners were reflected in those of the slaves". All the data then available indicated that slave women disliked having children. At first this was limited to 'creole' slaves, that is, slaves who were born in the region; but as the population of creole slaves increased, this attitude became more widespread. As a result of this, abortion and, to a lesser extent infanticide, were widely practiced.[18]

The conditions of life and work physically discouraged reproduction. Gynaecological disorders were rife because of the absence of facilities for pregnancy and childbirth, the poor sanitary conditions, the mistreatment of pregnant women, and heavy labour for long hours. One of the most common disorders was amenorrhea (absence

7 Women and slavery in the Caribbean

of menstrual periods); this was usually due to severe malnutrition, injury to the ovaries or problems in the endocrinal glandular system caused by severe beatings. The other major complaint was menorrhagia (excessive flow at the period). These menstrual problems often resulted in early menopause and therefore a reduced fertile time span. Thus the practices of the ruling class during the sugar era, determined by its production needs and international market opportunities led to the emergence of a dominant ideology in which both masters and slaves found the costs of bearing and rearing children greater than the benefits. This ideology led to a practice by slave women that served the interests of the ruling class even though they were derived from different considerations.

In the Spanish Caribbean colonies, the same position was held by the planters, but it was manifested in different ways. Prior to the early nineteenth century, there were very few women on slaveholding estates; in 1771 in Cuba the ratio was 1:1.9. A female slave, because of her risk of childbearing was seen as a poor investment. As Francisco De Arango y Parreño, the father of the slave plantation system in Cuba, put it:

> During and after pregnancy, the slave is useless for several months, and her nourishment should be more abundant and better chosen. This loss of work and added expense comes out of the master's pocket. It is he who pays for the often ineffective and always lengthy care of the newborn.[19]

As a result, female slaves cost one-third the price of male slaves.[20] Nineteenth-century Spanish moralists justified this situation in terms of the undesirability of the coexistence of the sexes on the estates without marriage. Thus male slaves were condemned to celibacy (or homosexuality).

The nuclear family was actively discouraged by planters in all Caribbean colonies. Where such families did develop they could be easily destroyed through sale of members to creditors and/or to other plantations. In Jamaica, children were taken from their mothers after weaning and placed during the work day with a driveress first in the grass gang, then in other gangs as they grew older.[21] Similarly, in Cuba, slave mothers returned to work about six weeks after childbirth, at which time the child was turned over to the plantation nursery.[22] Patterson notes with some regret that "the male head could not assert his authority as husband and father as his 'wife' was the property of another".[23] This illustration lays bare the realities of marriage and the nuclear family. In this period in Caribbean history, this form of social organisation did not meet the needs of capital. Therefore, there was no need to construct the ideological support for the nuclear family that conceals its fundamental nature today.

In response to the attitudes of the masters, contempt for marriage was great among slaves, especially young ones (both female and male), in the towns. Women in particular disliked marriage because, according to Patterson, it meant extra work and being confined to only one man. Regular sexual activity began very early in life, especially for girls, and both men and women maintained multiple associations. One writer observed in 1823 that "the husband has commonly two or three wives, and the wives as many husbands which they mutually change for each other".[24] As old age approached, however, couples usually settled down into stable monogamous unions. It has been suggested that in the later years of slavery, when women were allowed to keep their children, the women may have assumed a 'matriarchal' position in the household, all the children more than likely, being hers and not the man's.

AMELIORATION AND REFORM: NEW LAWS AND WOMEN

As the last two decades of the eighteenth century drew near, the slave trade, that had up to this point efficiently supplied the Caribbean slave-owners with labour, began to face difficulties. One source of these was the rise of industrial capitalism in Europe. It was at this time, after years of campaigning, that more attention was beginning to be paid to the abolitionists. In a controversial interpretation, Eric Williams identified a contradictory relationship between monopoly, slave-grown sugar production and new industrial production. The former, in giving rise to the latter had sown the seeds of its own destruction, because it was the capital accumulated from slavery that fuelled industrialisation. In addition to this, the increasing competition from 'free' grown sugar from India and the East Indies and the demand of British sugar producers in that region for equal treatment provided another source of support for the campaign against slavery and the slave trade.

Williams' book has been subjected to numerous criticisms, and the specific details of his interpretation of abolitionism have come under question. But his general point – that the antislavery movement gained political force once it served the needs of a rising industrial capitalism – has held up well.[25] As Williams states, the humanitarians

7 Women and slavery in the Caribbean

could never have succeeded a hundred years before when every important capitalist was on the side of the colonial system. 'It was an arduous hill to climb,' sang Wordsworth in praise of Clarkson. The top would never have been reached but for the defection of capitalists from the ranks of slave-owners and slave-traders.[26]

The struggle against monopoly and in favour of free trade was the main causal factor in the 'defection of capitalists' in England from the cause of the planters. The new industrialists needed cheaper raw materials and markets for manufactured goods. A second difficulty with the slave trade was the growing shortage of slaves along with west coast of Africa, which forced slavers to go deeper inland in search of them, resulting in fewer and more expensive slaves.

For these and other reasons, the colonial governments of all slave holding territories, whether British, French or Spanish sought to address this problem around the same time. In contrast with the shortsighted planters, the metropolitan ruling classes saw the slave plantation economy within the framework of their wider colonial interests. For example, the increasing incorporation of Africa as a supplier of raw materials and producer of cash crops necessitated some control over the depletion of its labour force.[27] In addition possible slave revolts presented a continuing threat to the plantation system. In the words of Hall:

> The get-rich quick mentality of the planters and their managers generated conditions which were highly destructive to the slave population and undermined the stability of the colony. Revenues from these colonies, both direct and indirect, were vast and the metropolis had a great deal at stake as it sought to prevent interest groups within the colonies from killing the goose that lay the golden eggs. Generally the metropolis embraced a broader more long-range point of view than did the planter class.[28]

Each of these three governments responded with a body of laws and regulations aimed at appeasing the abolitionists by 'humanising' slavery and increasing local reproduction of labour through measures directed at women and family organisation. The British Amelioration Acts of 1787, the French *Ordonnances de Louis XVI* and the Spanish *Código Negro Carolino* of 1785 and the *Código Negro Español* of 1789 in general, all advocated the same reforms: the encouragement of marriage and the nuclear family and the discouragement of 'illicit' relations which tend to reduce fertility; restrictions on the work hours of female slaves, especially pregnant and nursing slaves; improvement in the nutrition of pregnant slaves; provision of facilities such as infirmaries for the new-born slave infants; the allocation of 'provision grounds' for slaves to produce their own food; and the allocation of minimum yearly clothing allowances.

In general, the response of the planters to this was negative. Although they recognised the necessity to increase the 'natural' reproduction of the local slave population, they resented any attempt to reduce their control over the life and labour of the slaves, and their immediate profit. Resistance was greatest in the Spanish colonies, in particular Cuba where the Cuban slave plantation economy was just gaining momentum. Consequently the 1789 Code, written for the entire Spanish empire, was never promulgated in any of the Spanish slave plantation areas of the Caribbean.[29] The planters of Havana justified this in terms of fears that if slaves heard about these reforms, instability would result. A *Real Cédula* of 1804 exhorting that slaves be treated humanely and that "female slaves be introduced on estates where there were only males until all desiring marriage were married" was not published.[30] A further slave code passed in 1842 reinforced some of the more oppressive aspects of slavery.

The result was similar where these reforms were developed or supported by the local planter class. The attempts to increase local slave reproduction at best yielded only modest increases. In Tobago, for example, in 1798 a committee of both houses of the legislature set up to look into the "the causes which had retarded the natural increase of the slaves", made the following proposals:

1. That the commodities and quantities which should be provided for slaves be fixed at:

    (a) 3 lbs. salted pork or 4 lbs. salted beef or 4 lbs. salted fish, or 4 lbs. good herrings per week for each working slave and pro rata for children of different ages;

    (b) 7 quarts weekly of wheat flour or oatmeal or ground provisions such as Indian corn, peas, plantains, yams, potatoes or eddoes for each working slave and pro rata for children of different ages;

    (c) *For men* a cloth jacket, hat, frock and a pair of trousers in June and another frock and pair of trousers for December. *For Women* a cloth jacket, hat and coarse handkerchief, a petticoat and a wrapper in June, and another petticoat and wrapper in December.

2. A duty on all imported slaves above 25 years and a premium on all female slaves between the age of 8 and 20.

7 Women and slavery in the Caribbean

3. The erection of a comfortable house on each estate with a boarded platform for the accommodation of slaves.

4. Slave women should be prevented by law from taking young children into the fields and every estate is obliged to establish a nursery for the care of young children.

5. The distribution of good land to the slaves, and the allocation of time to work on it.

6. The erection of a comfortable house at the expense of the slave-owner for a young woman on her marriage, plus a gift of livestock valued $16 to $20 and clothing of a superior quality.

7. That a law should be passed entitling a midwife to a fee of $1.00 for every child which she delivers alive.

8. That a law be prescribed preventing women from working up to five weeks after having a child and then work to begin only on production of a surgeon's certificate.

9. That mothers of six or more children be granted a total exemption of all labour.

10. That overseers of the six plantations with the highest natural increase be given bonuses ranging from $100 to $50.[31]

These measures, however, met with little immediate success: "Slave women of childbearing age, now largely creoles, were hardened in their anti-breeding attitudes with the result that most of the schemes for increasing the population by greater reproduction failed."[32] These rather modest changes in the material reality of slave women's existence were not enough to challenge the dominant ideological positions. Thus, even though the planters desired increased reproduction the slave women did not see it in their interests to comply.

In Cuba, in response to the failure of the new measures to increase local reproduction, some planters resorted to slave-breeding similar to that in the slave states of the United States of America. One writer identified the estate of Esteban Cruz de Oviedo at Trinidad (in Cuba) as the most shameless of these establishments. This "farm" – "served by its female blacks" yielded an estimated thirty blacks a year, whereas its loss per year was only ten.[33] G.M. Hall notes that a child of good stock was worth 500 pesos. This method nevertheless also proved unsuccessful and the slave trade which was abolished in 1819-1820 continued illegally.

The slave trade was abolished in the British colonies in 1807; and in the French in 1818. After this, methods aimed at increasing local reproduction were intensified. In most islands, more female slaves were imported during this period of illegal trade than prior to abolition. In many islands abortion and infanticide were outlawed. In Jamaica, Sabina Park, a slave woman charged with the murder of her 3-year-old child, spoke in her own defence at the Half Way Tree Slave Court, saying that "she had worked enough for bukra (master) already and that she would not be plagued to raise the child... to work for white people".[34]

To forestall the growing demand for abolition, in 1823 the British government attempted once more to impose reforms in British slave colonies. These were enforced in the crown colonies of Trinidad and British Guiana in 1824 but were attacked by the self-governing legislatures of Jamaica, Tobago and Barbados. These included new rules on punishment, including abolition of the flogging of slave women and girls; provision of the slaves with two days off work, one for the Negro market, and Sunday for religion; manumission reforms, including mandatory freedom of slave girls born after 1823; and judicial changes allowing slaves to admit evidence in court; establishment of a savings bank for slaves and establishing a 'Protector of Slaves' who would keep a legal record of slave punishments.[35]

The planters strongly objected to most of these proposals, especially the abolition of the Sunday market and the flogging for female slaves. They argued that "it was necessary to punish women. Even in civilised societies", they argued, "women were flogged."[36] A member of the Barbados legislature stated: "Our black ladies have rather a tendency to the Amazonian cast of character, and I believe that their husbands would be very sorry to hear that they were placed beyond the reach of chastisement."[37] The Tobago planters similarly "condemned the prohibition of the flogging of female slaves as 'tantamount' to unqualified emancipation at this hour".[38]

Attempts at reform and increased slave reproduction ran up against resistance of slave women themselves, and the reluctance of many planters to depart from their traditional means of exploiting and physically disciplining female slave labourers. The planter class, even when it accepted the necessity of biological reproduction of the labour force, considered harsh, physically damaging violence an indispensable weapon in its relations with slave women.

In the flurry of activity which resulted, the slaves in the British islands came to believe that emancipation had been granted in England, but withheld by the local planters. This led to a series of slave revolts, rebellions and suicides in the region and eventually,

7 Women and slavery in the Caribbean

in 1833 to abolition. To appease the planters, however, in addition to £20,000,000 in compensation which was to be divided among them, a six year transition period was established during which the new 'free wage labourers' were still tied to the estates as apprentices.

THE TRANSITION TO POST-EMANCIPATION PRODUCTION AND REPRODUCTION

As early as the beginning of the nineteenth century, signs of the decreasing productivity of the slave plantation system had begun to be evident in the British Caribbean. This was usually attributed to the decline in sugar prices because of over-production and increasing costs of production. Craton, writing on Jamaica, suggests that two alternatives might have presented themselves to the planters, both based on economies of scale: to produce more with the same workforce or to produce the same amount with a smaller workforce. In view of their fear of overproduction, the latter solution was preferable but 'trimming' the workforce implied the substitution of 'free wage labour' for slavery, a solution which the planters in general were very slow to advocate.[39] For some years between 1815 and 1838, attempts were made to increase productivity by driving the workforce harder. This period was one of increasing alienation, forced labour and rebellion. In Spanish Cuba, the 1820s saw the beginning of mechanisation in sugar production. For the majority of planters only partial mechanisation was possible, and large numbers of slaves were needed to maintain the level of production in the non-mechanised processes. These days have been described as "slavery's darkest hours", a rationalisation process which aimed at squeezing the last drop of work from the slave.[40] With mechanisation in all the colonies came increased specialisation in particular skills of production. Women were more and more relegated to the manual and agricultural tasks whereas more men moved into the more highly skilled operations.

Examination of the transitional period immediately following slavery yields some insights into the direction in which female labour force participation was likely to develop. In his study of Worthy Park Estate, Craton notes that discrimination between the sexes was established at the outset, the daily wage being determined by sex and seniority.[41] Female ex-slaves were paid only half as much as men for equivalent tasks. In order to appreciate the significance of this fact, earlier-mentioned ones have to be recalled: that at the time of abolition females represented nearly two-thirds of the slaves working on estates in the British colonies and that slave women worked as hard as men and were punished as severely.[42] Women continued to be 70 per cent of the cane-cutting gang, while men, moved up to the more skilled and prestigious jobs which were more highly paid as well. In Worthy Park, one head fieldwoman is recorded as being paid 1 shilling 6 pence per day whereas the head fieldmen were paid 2 shillings. This differentiation in wages might be seen as a change equally as important as the introduction of the wage itself. It concretised differences within the newly emerging agricultural working class. Its effects as far as men and women were concerned must also have been important, for the status of the male as the official breadwinner must have been strengthened with the differential wages and access to skilled positions.

As time went on, the participation of women in estate labour decreased as women continued to be relegated to the most menial and lowest-paid jobs. Planters and managers developed a marked preference for male labourers and justified this ideologically on the basis of the "relative unreliability of female labour". Craton reports that, "The most notable change in the composition of the 1842 workforce was the decrease once more in the proportion of women... the overall proportion of males rose from just under 40% in 1838 to over 60%, a return to the ratio of the earliest days of slavery."[43] He notes, however, that at least 75 per cent of the women at Worthy Park continued as irregular workers during the early 1840s. One factor that contributed to the decline in the participation of women in 'social production' was the continued introduction of new, 'labour saving' technology, particularly in agricultural production. Around 1841, for example, the plough was introduced to Jamaica. The stipendiary magistrate, Bell, wrote during this period:

> The constant and improved use of ploughs in this neighbourhood has and will save almost a fourth of the money formerly disbursed for the digging part of the planting operations for canes, for instance, opening and preparing 15 acres with the plough £15; digging etc., 15 acres with the hoe £60. This, of course, keeps money out of labourers' pockets, and accounts, with the dry weather, for the anxiety to get work.[44]

Of course, 'the labourers' referred to were mainly women by this time.

Concurrent with this development, Craton notes, was an increase in the frequency of marriages and stable monogamous unions, and in the rate of natural population growth, now up to fifty per cent higher than what it had been during slavery. This situation, considered in

7 Women and slavery in the Caribbean

conjunction with the earlier observations on differential wages, gives us some indication of the trends developing in ex-slave society. As far as the planters and the colonial state were concerned, the African ex-slave woman was moving into capitalist wage-labour society. Theoretically, her *primary* economic activity was now not to be the production of commodities for exchange on the world market, but the production of the labour force and the reproduction of labour power, formerly the responsibility of the slave-owner. Her position on the labour market was now only secondary in relation to her primary responsibility in the household as a dependent housewife. Her labour was now to be exploited on an irregular basis in periods of necessity and at the lowest terms.[45]

Women were defined as 'dependent housewives' whether they were married or not. The main economic activities of women that emerged, therefore, were those that could be centred around the household (often self-employment) and that were compatible with child rearing: market gardening, petty trading, laundry work, dressmaking and domestic work. This new sexual division of labour, though evident before emancipation, became more so after. Sidney Mintz, for example, reports that there is no evidence that prior to emancipation women were predominant in internal marketing in Jamaica, but this was definitely the case thereafter.[46]

Thus, by attributing lower status to women as workers, planters were able to gain additional profits by paying lower wages to what was still a large proportion of the workforce. At the same time, they ensured that their new labour force and reserve army were continuously available.

Concluding Remarks

My aim in writing this article has not been simply to elucidate an interesting case. Rather, I hope that the lessons and inferences drawn from this study of Caribbean slavery will throw light on the mechanisms of control and oppression used on women internationally today.

Historically the generative capacity of women has been the material basis for their subordination and oppression. Throughout history, men, ruling classes and states have sought to manipulate this capacity to suit their economic and political needs at various periods. This study presents one example, that of a planter class attempting to control the reproductive capacity of slave women in order to further its economic interests. The evidence is that its ability to do so, although great, was limited. Given the material conditions of slave life, women resisted these pronatalist policies. Love of motherhood was neither natural nor universal.

My study also shows that changes in the approach to control over reproduction, women's participation in wage labour and the family can occur within a relatively short time. Today this question is an international one, with many economic, political and racial connotations. Although population control measures are being introduced among non-European women throughout the world, European women throughout much of Europe and in other parts of the world (e.g. South Africa)[47] are confronting pronatalist policies. In some instances 'motherhood' and the 'fatherland' are being invoked, but in the majority of instances the incentives offered are physical and material – payments at childbirth or on the birth of a third child; one to three years' maternity leave with pay; and attempts to 'roll back' the pro-abortion laws. These measures, like those of the planter class during its pronatalist period, underscore the political and economic importance attached to female reproductive capacity.

Another question of importance here is the degree to which oppressed people's notions of 'good', 'bad', 'natural' and 'unnatural' are determined by ruling class control on the reproduction of ideology. This is seen here in the selective use of various conflicting ideological constructs in relation to marriage, the family and 'motherhood' as needs and patterns of production changed. On a deeper level, we note that the decisions of the slave women regarding childbearing were determined largely by physical and material factors and not merely by ideas. Similarly today, many of the factors which force women to accept a certain course in life are material as well as ideological even though they may be expressed only in ideological terms. Attempts to change this situation, therefore, cannot be successful at the level of ideological struggle and consciousness raising alone, but must involve material changes in the organisation of the family, the economy and the society.

In relation to the family, a number of other interesting questions arise from this study of Caribbean slave women. One of major importance today is the relationship of 'the family' to the participation of women in wage labour. In relation to this, one has to examine the reasons why it was necessary at some point to introduce the nuclear family which had earlier been discouraged. The family, one might suggest, provided the niche within which the ex-slave woman could become a housewife and mother and into which she could fit when deprived of wage labour. This problem still confronts us

7 Women and slavery in the Caribbean

today – women's participation in wage labour is predetermined by their presumed relationship to a family, making them an ever existing reserve army and an easily dispensable workforce. Despite the fact that women fieldworkers in the British colonies showed a higher survival rate than the men in estate work, and had proved themselves to be as efficient as male workers, they were from the outset paid lower wages than men on the ground of their 'relative unreliability'. Women's relative weakness has always been used as a justification for their position in the labour market, and for the prevailing sexual division of labour. The example of slavery suggests that we should reject this view.

In the Caribbean, the attempt to impose the Western nuclear family on the ex-slave population largely failed. The ideal still prevailed until at least the 1970s but the material circumstances of the majority of the people prevented this ideal, complete with its male breadwinner from becoming a reality. It is on this question of family organisation that I would like to conclude. Studies of the Caribbean family have variously viewed it as deviant or as an aspect of Afro-Caribbean culture.[48] On the basis of the analysis presented above, I would suggest that slavery or at least the system of slavery that developed in the Caribbean indirectly – by destroying African family systems; removing power and control over individual women from individual men; making men and women relatively equal producers; and by removing the obligation of daily and generational reproduction of labour power from individual women – caused a 200-year break in the transfer of African patriarchal control to the Caribbean. Attempts in the postslavery period to reinstate it either in a supposedly traditional African form or in a Western nuclear form have never been completely successful.

Notes

1. I am grateful to Sonia Cuales, Andy Vickerman and Steve Stern for comments on earlier drafts of this paper. I am however totally responsible for any errors caused by my stubborn adherence to certain positions. R.R.
2. See Robert A. Padgug, "Problems in the Theory of Slavery and Slave Society," *Science and Society*, Vol. 40, No. 1 (1976-1977), pp.3-27 and Eugene Genovese, *The Political Economy of Slavery* (New York, 1965).
3. Ken Post, *Arise Ye Starvelings: The Jamaica Labour Rebellion of 1938 and Its Aftermath* (The Hague, 1978), pp.22-23.
4. Eric Williams, *Capitalism and Slavery* (Chapel Hill, 1944).
5. Franklin W. Knight, *The Caribbean: Genesis of a Fragmented Nationalism* (Madison, 1978), p.214.
6. According to Orlando Patterson, *The Sociology of Slavery* (London and New Jersey, 1967), p.59, the 'Hogmeat Gang' consisted of "young children between the ages of four or five to nine or ten. They were employed in minor tasks such as collecting food for the hogs, weeding and the like."
7. See Patterson, op. cit., p.157. Also, Michael Craton, *Searching for the Invisible Man: Slaves and Plantation Life in Jamaica* (Cambridge, Mass., 1978); and R.S. Dunn, *Sugar and Slaves* (Chapel Hill, 1972).
8. Craton, op. cit.
9. G. Midlo Hall, *Social Control in Slave Plantation Societies*, John Hopkins University Studies in Historical and Political Science, 1971, p.17.
10. Patterson, op. cit., p.167.
11. Franklin W. Knight, *Slave Societies in Cuba during the Nineteenth Century* (Wisconsin, Madison, 1970), p.76.
12. G.M. Hall, op. cit., p.19.
13. Craton, op. cit., pp.97-98.
14. Noel Deerr, *A History of Sugar*, 2 vols (London, 1950), p.227.
15. G.M. Hall, op. cit., p.24.
16. Patterson, op. cit., p.105.
17. Douglas Hall, "Slaves and Slavery in the British West Indies", *Social and Economic Studies* (1962), pp.305-18.
18. Patterson, op. cit., pp.106-107.
19. G. M. Hall, op. cit., p.24.
20. Ibid., p.26.
21. By 'driveress' is meant a female head of a gang, the highest position among the field slaves, who directs the work process by force if necessary (R.R.). The 'grass gang' was a group of slaves responsible for cutting grass on the plantations (R.R.).
22. Knight, op. cit., *Slave Society*, p.76.
23. Patterson, op. cit., p.167.
24. Ibid., p.164.
25. Eric Williams, *Capitalism*, op. cit.; see also David Brion Davis, *The Problem of Slavery in the Age of Revolution, 1770-1823* (Ithaca, 1975), pp.347-50.
26. Williams, ibid., p.136.
27. I. Wallerstein, *The Capitalist World Economy* (Cambridge, 1979), pp.28-29.
28. G.M. Hall, op. cit., p.112.
29. Ibid., p.103.
30. Ibid., p.107.
31. Eric Williams, *A History of the People of Trinidad and Tobago* (London, 1964), pp.60-62.
32. Patterson, op. cit., p.112.
33. Manuel Moreno Fraginals, *The Sugarmill: the Socio-economic Complex of Sugar in Cuba, 1769-1860* (New York and London, 1976), p.143.
34. Patterson, op. cit., p.106.
35. Williams, *Capitalism*, op. cit., pp.197-98.
36. Ibid., p.198.

7 Women and slavery in the Caribbean

[37] Ibid., p.198.
[38] Williams, *A History*, op. cit., p.130.
[39] Craton, op. cit., p.172.
[40] Fraginals, op. cit.
[41] Craton, op. cit., p.286.
[42] Patterson, op. cit.
[43] Craton, op. cit., pp.286-87.
[44] Douglas Hall, *Free Jamaica* (New Haven, 1959), pp.49-50.
[45] R. Augier, S. Gordon, D. Hall and M. Reckord, *The Making of the West Indies* (London, 1961), p.188.
[46] Sydney Mintz, *Caribbean Transformations* (Chicago, 1974), pp.216-17.
[47] When this article was originally published, South Africa was still under apartheid rule.
[48] See, for example, M.G. Smith, *West Indian Family Structure* (Seattle, 1962); R.T. Smith, *The Negro Family in British Guiana* (London, 1956); Edith Clarke, *My Mother Who Fathered Me* (London, 1957).

CHAPTER EIGHT

Economic Determinism vs Humanitarianism: Examining the Williams Hypothesis

Selwyn H. H. Carrington

It is a rare achievement for an author when his scholarly work, like the event with which it deals, remains the focus of attention of scholars for almost half a century. The publication of *Capitalism and Slavery* in 1944 changed the conservative, traditionalist viewpoint regarding the relationship between European countries and their Caribbean colonies. The appearance of the book occurred at a time when the Marxist interpretation of historical events was in its nascent stage of development. As a result, Marxist theoreticians readily embraced its findings, although the study itself cannot be considered Marxist. It therefore escaped any thorough criticism from this school of historical thought and its main critics have belonged to the conservative, traditional circle.

The work is divided into two main sections each founded on the concept of economic determinism, and contains several distinct theses. The first deals with the origins of slavery; the second postulates the idea that the African slave trade and the sugar industry based on black slavery led to the formation of capital in Britain, which helped to finance the industrial revolution; another argues that the West Indian plantation system was only possible because of the existence of the American colonies whose independence "marked the beginning of the uninterrupted decline" of the sugar colonies. Finally, the growth of industrial capitalism at the end of the eighteenth century brought about the demise of the slave trade and of slavery itself.

CONTEMPORARY VIEWS

The immediate response to the publication of *Capitalism and Slavery* was mixed. Most critics accepted the economic argument preferring to concentrate their attack on Williams' treatment of the role of the

8 Economic determinism vs. humanitarianism

abolitionists. These summary reviews stressed his emphasis on the economic changes which underlay European attitudes to slavery and the slave trade to the detriment of the legal, political and intellectual changes which were taking place in Europe after the middle of the eighteenth century. Writing in *Commonweal*, John Monaghan postulates the generally accepted belief that the first half of the book which contends that "Britain created the slave trade because it was profitable to her expanding empire and emancipated the slaves when their enslavement became unprofitable... is elaborately proven." He goes on to point out that a contrary opinion can be maintained "hereafter only in prejudice to a high-heaven massing of facts".

Despite his general acceptance of the presence of economic factors in the decision to emancipate the slaves, Monaghan despises Williams' economic determinism which he allegedly employs in measuring all "human relations". Monaghan writes: "The factors we call moral factors the author simply equates with an enlightened self-interest and so they too come within the pattern of economic determinism." As an example of the bias which Monaghan cites that Williams demonstrated towards the church, he stresses that the economic factors which gave rise to abolition would have remained static had it not been for the "humanitarians" whose moral convictions and agitation made them dynamic.[1]

Keith Hutchison follows a similar line of argument in his review. He too contends that Williams had pushed "his economic determinism too far at times" because he refused to recognise any "virtue in the Abolitionist movement beyond its recognition that the game was up". Hutchison agrees in part with the viewpoint that the abolitionists were able to make meaningful headway in the struggle for the end of the slave trade precisely because the economic climate was adverse; but he notes, however, that credit must be given to the abolitionists as a group because their efforts hastened the end of slavery. In support of one of Williams' statements, he writes: "However, we can agree about Wilberforce, one of the disagreeable 'dogooders' in history whom Professor Williams finds 'small' and 'smug' and, as a leader, adhered to moderation, compromise and delay."[2]

The reviewer in the *Times Literary Supplement* accepts uncritically Williams' thesis that black slavery was rooted in the labour needs of the West Indies with their low man/land ratio. This writer stresses that black slavery grew out of the forced labour system which was in place in the colonies because it was considered more efficient/cheaper. He goes on to emphasise his disquiet over the fact that Williams failed to establish whether or not "the cheapness of the

Negro was a result of political fact", making it possible to impose on blacks "lifelong hereditary servitude while the White labourer was only a temporary slave". On the other hand, he agrees that massive fortunes were garnered from the "highly profitable slave labour" and contributed significantly to the accumulation of capital "for the nascent industrial society that was to kill slavery in the nineteenth century far more effectively than any rhetoric or moral indignation could have done, or would have done, had it been left to itself".[3]

Supportive of Williams' observation, the writer reiterates that in London, Liverpool, Bristol, and Glasgow, even in inland towns like Birmingham and Sheffield, profits from the West Indian trade "fertilised the economic soil as well as produced such fantastic ephemeral growths as the two Fonthills of so typical a West Indian dynasty as the Beckfords". He went on to emphasise that Liverpool, in particular, was intertwined with the slave trade and the resultant slave economy of the seventeenth and eighteenth centuries. Only men of exceptional moral strength such as William Rathbone escaped the lures of the profits of the trade. Most of the other members of the local dynasties were involved in it.

There were many factors which, in that reviewer's opinion, contributed to the abolition of the slave trade and slavery. Among these were "the profits and losses of the declining West Indian trade; the genuine moral passion of Clarkson and the less consistent activities of Wilberforce; the possibilities of development in Cuba; the strength of the new East India interest; the cause – and effect – of the squadrons kept to suppress the African slave trade".

In her review, Elizabeth Donnan stresses that Eric Williams had successfully established the relationship "between the slave trade and the commerce of the day". She notes however that he was on shaky ground in his analysis of the destruction of the mercantilist system and slavery, an outworn economic institution which was created by the very forces which destroyed it in the end. As in the case of the other reviewers, Donnan chides Williams for simplifying the issue because "the lines are far less defined; motives are mixed; economic influences are less simple". She further notes that in Williams' haste to establish the primacy of the economic forces, he "diminished the contribution of the humanitarians whose voices were raised against the slave trade and later against slavery". She writes:

> A man is not of necessity a hypocrite because his economic interests and his moral convictions coincide. Humanitarianism may be 'lucrative' and still be humanitarianism. Nor is it necessary to

8 Economic determinism vs. humanitarianism

conclude that the zealots who struggled to abolish the slave trade at the end of the eighteenth century were insincere because they countenanced the institution of slavery, or because they accepted the slave-raised cotton of the Southern United States.[4]

It is understandable that Donnan, influenced by metropolitan concepts of the abolitionists' role in slavery, should seek to defend the 'humanitarianism' of late eighteenth century Britain. However, as an objection to Williams' thesis, it does not reduce its effectiveness. In fact, humanitarianism alone is a simplistic explanation for the abolition of the slave trade at a time when personal liberty did not increase; at a time when politicians did not depend on public opinion for votes; at a time when the 'rotten and pocket boroughs' still existed and at a time when large numbers of English women and children were brutalised and dehumanised in British factories.

William Gee, writing in the *American Sociological Review*, supports the economic argument of *Capitalism and Slavery* and confirms that the wealth of the West Indies "had undoubtedly formed a substantial part of the store of capital in English banks which sought investments in the factories and related enterprises of the beginning years of the Industrial Revolution". He also contends that with the expansion of the ideas of *laissez-faire* capitalism and free trade, the industrialists wanted cheap labour, which "meant necessarily lower costs of food than high productive duties made possible". This invariably led to a campaign for the abolition of West Indian monopoly and before it the end of the slave trade (1807), slavery (1833) and duties (1846) along with the famous Corn Laws (1846). He is critical of what he sees as Williams' exaggerated attempt to "make slavery almost the indispensable foundation stone [for] the establishment of modern capitalism...."[5]

Writing in 1947, J.F. Rees in a review of *Capitalism and Slavery*[6] does not dissent from the opinions of his predecessors. However, he notes that Williams' work was "inclined to stress the economic motive to the exclusion of all other motives". Yet, despite this bias, as Rees calls Williams' economic determinism, "his thesis of the rise and fall of the West India interest (and with it of slavery) is in its general bearing irrefutable". He is critical of Williams' handling of the abolitionists, whom he seeks to defend by arguing that they did not have the benefit of hindsight and were involved in the fray from the beginning. He notes that opposition to the slave trade and West Indian slavery was voiced in England from as early as the 1750s and he concludes that "economic advantage by no means dictates unanimity of opinion".

The contemporary reviewers of *Capitalism and Slavery* were of the same historical mould as Williams. They were of the traditional school of historical thought and their knowledge of quantitative history was minimal. Consequently, they accepted the basic tenets of the Williams thesis as far as the economics of mercantilism and the relationship between the slave trade and British slavery and capital formation are concerned. A few of the reviewers have nevertheless claimed to have detected certain 'biases' in the marshalling of the information as far as the study is concerned. In fact, this is not a serious criticism since the historian's art forces him to zero in on the information that supports his thesis. Others have contended that Williams' economic determinism has caused him "to be less than fair to the humanitarians whose voices were raised against the slave trade and later against slavery". This is also an unfair criticism of the book since the author stated clearly that his work is "an attempt to place in historical perspective the relationship between early capitalism as exemplified by Britain and the Negro slave trade, Negro slavery and the general colonial trade of the seventeenth and eighteenth centuries". It is therefore a study which seeks to show the contribution of slavery to the Industrial Revolution and how the mature forces of industrialism destroyed West Indian monopoly and with it slavery. One reviewer wrote of the book: "*Capitalism and Slavery* is more than a thesis in the usual American academic sense. It is a thesis in the old sense, the affirmation and defence of a doctrine."[7] In short, it was not Williams' aim to detail the role of the abolitionists. This had already been done by historians such as Reginald Coupland; what had never been done was to explain how and to what extent the slave trade between Africa, the West Indies and the Americas stimulated industrial development in Britain and, arguably, other parts of Europe.

THE SCIENTIFIC APPROACH: MODERN HISTORIANS VS WILLIAMS

The renewed assessment of Williams' work began as a result of two reprints between 1961 and 1964, with two conference papers presented by Roger Anstey and C. Duncan Rice. Anstey's aim was not to undertake an examination of the first part of the book "where the role of the slave trade and slavery, and of mercantilism, in the British economy up to the closing years of the eighteenth century" are considered. Instead, Anstey, following the lead of the earlier generation of reviewers, chose to re-examine the second section of the book where Williams contended that "Britain's changing attitude to

8 Economic determinism vs. humanitarianism

slavery and the slave trade was essentially a function of her changing economic situation and interest", with a concentration on Williams' "interpretation of Pitt's conduct of the abolition of the British slave trade in 1807, and of Palmerston and the suppression of the foreign slave trade".

Writing in 1965, Anstey notes that "much of Williams' general evidence is persuasive". In the published article[9] Anstey modifies his earlier statement and writes: "Williams' argument is to an extent persuasive." In spite of this change, he accepts Williams' application of the decline thesis and concludes:

> It is difficult not to think that the radical change in the position of the British West Indies in the later eighteenth century did not affect English attitudes to the slave trade and slavery, whilst some of the figures Williams quotes are significant. For example, he shows that... the West Indies became relatively less important as a mart for British exports and that British sugar imports from Brazil, Cuba and Mauritius increased considerably whilst British Caribbean production remained stationary. Again... by 1807 the slave trade had become much less important to Liverpool, the British port most engaged in it...

Although unconvinced that these declining changes in the fortunes of the West Indies led to the abolition of the slave trade, Anstey is willing to concede that "in relation to the abolition of slavery in 1833, the economic argument seems, *prima facie*, much more convincing". He too agrees that British West Indian sugar could not be sold in European markets as cheaply as foreign sugar and therefore the West Indians were being subsidised to compete with some of Britain's chief customers. On the question of the 1846 measure, Anstey notes that Williams was the first writer to make the connection between the equalisation of the duties and the abolition movement and that he "has made a case which the exponents of the 'traditional' view have yet to answer".[10]

C. Duncan Rice who has examined the question of the abolitionist movement and the sugar duties contends that even though it is a "truism to stress that there can be no going back on Williams' conclusions that the abolitionists, broadly speaking, were free traders", they favoured West Indian monopoly mainly as a means of voicing their opposition to the "horrifying amount of labour" extorted from the Cuban and Brazilian slaves. The position of the abolitionists on this issue thus suggests that "their earlier attacks on the planters over slavery had not been entirely the product of their distrust of protection". Thus the abolitionists showed in the debate over the Sugar Duties

Act that, given a choice over monopoly or slavery, the majority were prepared "to jettison their free trade principles – at the risk of accusations of having become lackeys of the West Indian slave-drivers, or ex-slave-drivers".[11] Rice has not convincingly established his case against Williams' thesis. His essay depends too much on circumstantial evidence. On the other hand, Anstey supports Williams' charges that the abolitionists had favoured the abolition of the sugar duties, a position which would have undoubtedly encouraged "the Brazilian and Cuban slave trades". In support of this point of view, Anstey quotes Cobden who mused:

> I am the representative of a country which was eminent in the slavery movement... Now I unhesitatingly assert that nearly all the men who led the agitation for the emancipation of the slaves, and who by their influence on public opinion aided in producing that result, are against those hon. Gentlemen in this House who advocate a differential duty on foreign sugar with a view to put down slavery abroad.[12]

Since 1968 there has been a more concerted effort by economists and economic historians trained in research methodology to test many of the assertions to be found in *Capitalism and Slavery*. One of the first areas to come under close scrutiny is Williams' thesis that the slave trade and the resultant sugar industry based on slavery led to the formation of capital in Britain which helped to finance the Industrial Revolution. The appearance of these new critical works by a generation of new scholars initiated a switch from a concentration on the earlier historians' concern over Williams' failure to look more seriously at the contribution of the humanitarians to the economic questions.

Leading this new wave was Robert Paul Thomas. His work was aimed at an assessment of Richard Sheridan's claim that the concerted growth of the Jamaican economy in the eighteenth century produced surplus wealth which was centred in Britain. Employing cost-benefit analysis of much of the very statistical information provided by Sheridan, Thomas concluded that the reverse was true of the economic relationship between Britain and her colonies. On the contrary, he believed that the West Indies retarded the growth of the national economy and the sugar colonies were a net loss to Britain. Thomas was in fact reiterating the claims of Adam Smith in his *Wealth of Nations* and his hypothesis is founded on two unproved claims: the first states that the islands benefited from preferential duties to the sum of approximately £446,000 annually; the second

8 Economic determinism vs. humanitarianism

argues that the cost of maintaining the islands both militarily and administratively should be deducted from the profits gained from them. In conclusion, Thomas postulated that the £37 million invested in the West Indies would have gained more if invested at home.[13]

Thomas criticism of Sheridan was seen as an attack on Williams and was adopted by others such as Stanley L. Engerman who set out to test Williams' thesis that Negro slavery and the slave trade contributed significantly to capital formation in Britain, which then helped to finance the Industrial Revolution. Engerman's main thrust was to determine the degree to which profits from the West Indies helped raise the investment levels in Britain. Employing the available published statistical information, he concludes that less than 10 per cent of the national income in any year of the eighteenth century came from the slave trade and the West Indian plantations. Although this represented a minor amount in his opinion, Engerman nevertheless sees the British West Indian role as a positive one since it undoubtedly gave rise to some investments in industrial activities. About his own methodology, based heavily on cost-benefit analysis, Engerman dismisses it as unsuitable to the task of testing the Williams thesis and he suggests that better results may be achieved by employing the 'export base' model which has been relatively successfully used in the United States and Canada.[14]

Also following Thomas' themes of West Indian loss to Britain because of her monopolistic structures, colonial administrative and defence costs, Coelho bases his assessment on the period 1768-1772 and concludes that the West Indies cost the British Government an estimated £1.1 million annually. Similarly, Coelho's review is basically a naïve restatement of Adam Smith's criticisms of the British West Indian sugar planters. Like Smith, Coelho has misunderstood the nature of capital accumulation in the colonies. In fact, he also does not seem to have comprehended the financing and credit structure of the plantation system. Perhaps the most noticeable flaw in Coelho's work is his statement that the eighteenth century was one of substantial capital formation in the West Indies and that the net capital transfer was in favour of the colonies. Judging from the official values of the imports into Britain from and exports to the West Indies for the entire eighteenth century, the net trade balance was always in favour of the sugar colonies. However, no capital transfers took place from the metropolitan centre to the periphery. The relationship between the planters and the merchant houses and factories in Britain was based on a credit-debit system. It is undoubtedly this financial arrangement which had led Richard Pares to write:

The profits of the plantation were the source which fed the indebtedness charged upon the plantations themselves... The wealth of the British West Indies did not all proceed from the mother country; after some initial loans in the earliest period, which merely primed the pump, the wealth of the West Indies was created out of the profits of the West Indies themselves.[15]

Although not directly an attack on *Capitalism and Slavery*, R.K. Aufhauser has looked at the Ragatz/Williams contention, accepted by most historians that by 1820 sugar production in the British West Indies was unprofitable. He has rejected this view and by utilising a neoclassical economic analysis of a limited set of Barbados plantation records, he has postulated that the West Indian plantation system was profitable down to the emancipation of the slaves. He concludes that the minimum rate of return was probably 4 per cent while the mean was as high as 7 per cent. Transferring his findings to the rest of the West Indies, Aufhauser has contended that given the high unit cost of production in Barbados because of the infertility of the soil, the rate of return on slave labour would have been higher in the rest of the West Indies.[16]

This has found support in W.A. Green's "The Planter Class and British West Indian Sugar Production, before and after Emancipation".[17] Green's work reinforces the argument that British West Indian slavery did not impede technological change which was most likely to improve the production capacity of the colonies. He too concludes from his research of a limited set of plantation records that sugar production was profitable down to the time of emancipation. Writing in very much the same vein, J.R. Ward has succeeded in initiating a calculated attack against the Ragatz/Williams decline thesis. After somewhat more detailed research and a tighter methodological analysis, Ward establishes that sugar production in the British West Indies "was profitable throughout the years of slavery". He carefully points out, however, that profits of 40-50% were unusual and were the results of special circumstances. These exceptionally high profits declined throughout the eighteenth century to modest levels of approximately 10% in the period 1744-1755; 14% for the years 1756-1762; 9.3% from 1763 to 1775; 3.4% during the years of the American War, 1776-1783; but recovered to around 8.5% in the decade 1783-1791. Assessing the period 1775-1883, Ward writes:

> Certainly the years of the American War were miserable. For the first and only time in the eighteenth century Britain lost command of the sea to her commercial rivals, supplies from North America were cut off, and the slaves starved. But profits recovered well in the next

8 Economic determinism vs. humanitarianism

decade and were maintained through the vicissitudes of the French wars; production costs may have risen, but sugar prices rose also. Depression came only in the 1820s. Then prices fell with the end of wartime scarcities, and with the growth of production in the newly acquired territories the older colonies lost their monopoly power in the British market. Also the burden of sugar duties levied at specific rates, increased the post war depression.[18]

Departing from his acceptance of Williams' argument that the British West Indies were in some state of decline at the end of the eighteenth century, which he examines in his article "Capitalism and Slavery: A Critique", Anstey sets out to explore Williams' economic determinism in his major publication *The Atlantic Slave Trade and British Abolition*. Here, he claims that the economy of the West Indies was prospering during the years of the abolitionist campaign. He also shows that the slave trade produced modest profits of approximately 9.5 per cent in the period 1760 to 1807. "Anstey's use of a moving 'rate' rather than a fixed percentage profit or loss" led him to conclude that "between 1763 and 1772, the Liverpool slave trade was running at a loss". This seemed to have been reversed during the last years of the century.[19]

The most detailed contribution to the debate over Eric Williams' economic arguments in *Capitalism and Slavery* is Seymour Drescher's *Econocide: British Slavery in the Era of Abolition* (Pittsburgh, 1977). Here, Drescher has set out to dismantle the 'decline thesis' by countering with a number of assumptions/hypotheses. First, in opposition to the generally accepted belief that the islands were in decline from as early as 1763, Drescher adopts Anstey's position that the economies of the sugar colonies were growing both in absolute and relative values after 1783 reaching levels well above those of any putative 'golden age' before the American Revolution. Secondly, he deviates somewhat from Anstey's conclusion and contends that "in terms of... capital value of overseas trade, the slave system was expanding, not declining, at the turn of the nineteenth century". In order to add weight to his view, Drescher stresses that Britain's shipping and capital were widely involved in the slave trade of other European nations. Adopting a global view, he goes on to show that British slave trade and slavery maintained levels of performance in the period 1783 to 1820 equal or superior to those in the decades prior to the American Revolution.

Adding a new dimension to the criticism of Eric Williams is Drescher's contention that the American Revolution had little or no effect on the economy of the West Indies. This position was adopted in order to dispel the generally held view of the decline theorists that this event was "both a political and economic blow to the sugar colonies, weakening slavery's ability to resist assaults after 1783". His position is that "the American separation did not alter the balance of economic forces against British slavery and, above all, against the British slave trade". On the contrary, it was not until constricted by abolition that the economies of the islands went into a state of decline. Furthermore, in order to establish this point, Drescher argues first that there was still a sugar frontier in the British West Indies, chiefly in Jamaica, Dominica and St Vincent. However, "taken as a whole, the slave colonies had exhausted neither their soil nor their potential". Secondly, it was cardinal to his study that he should show that the British government's decision to impose its mercantilist policies with regard to American trade with the sugar colonies created only a temporary transportation and supply problem. Having thus made these two critical points, Drescher can now speculate that if the abolitionists had not convincingly influenced British public opinion and thus secured abolition, British slave trade and slavery, given time, would have readjusted to the burgeoning *laissez-faire* capitalism in Britain, leading to the continuation and further entrenchment of slavery.

SUPPORTERS OF THE WILLIAMS HYPOTHESIS

From critic to supporter – this is probably the most accurate evaluation of Sheridan's role in the present debate. It was from being a critic of the 'decline thesis' that Sheridan emerged as one of the main supporters of the Williams position that African slave trade and British slavery generated vast sums of money which flowed into Britain, accelerating the rate of capital accumulation, and thus increasing the amount of working capital available for industrial development in the eighteenth century. In fact, Sheridan was the initiator of the renewed assessment of Eric Williams. Following the lead of Pares, Sheridan contended that initially the West Indies consumed a quantity of capital from England to establish the plantations. However, they quickly became self-financing and provided their merchant creditors with significant amounts of capital returns for over 100 years. The capital formation/accumulation performance of the West Indian plantations was better than any other single sector of the domestic economy. Consequently, the surplus to the British economy emanating from the British West Indies in the latter years of the eighteenth century was conservatively estimated at 8-10 per

8 Economic determinism vs. humanitarianism

cent. This was smaller than during the years preceding the War of American Independence.[20] Sheridan thus concluded that in spite of the decline in the later eighteenth century, the surplus from the West Indian trade was instrumental in the growth of the economy of the metropolitan powers.

In a discussion paper, Barbara L. Solow has undertaken probably the most detailed scientific analysis of one of the several themes in *Capitalism and Slavery*.[21] Solow begins by restating Williams' thesis that the institution of Caribbean slavery resulted from economic factors and was not born of racism. She contends that when Black African slavery was instituted, the Caribbean colonies were in the indentured stage of staple production and most farmers were engaged in a losing battle to raise minor crops such as tobacco, ginger, indigo and cotton. Their performance was weak and only small quantities were exported to Europe. However, the introduction of the sugar plantation system manned by African slaves changed this trend. The monocultural production of sugar brought wealth and power to the planters. This raised the level of exchange in tropical products and manufactured goods between Britain and the West Indies. Similarly, the emergence of the plantation system and with it the rapid expansion of slavery also increased the external trade of the sugar colonies with their American counterparts, enabling the latter to cover their trade deficit with the mother country. The introduction of slavery and the plantation economy also initiated a significant change in the flow of capital to Britain. During the first stage, the capital invested was small and the returns for the merchant factors were miniscule. But with the introduction of slavery, larger amounts of capital were invested. Returns to the merchant factors became significantly greater because land was now more profitably utilised; production was larger; "the opportunities for the division of labour increased" and so did total trade within the Empire.

The eighteenth century view of the West Indies formulated by contemporaries rested mainly on their role in agricultural production and on the belief that the colonies contributed significantly to the economic importance of Britain. The chief proponents of this view were contemporary planter historians such as Edward Long, Bryan Edwards and Abbé Raynal. Long was one of the first to link West Indian economic development to British growth. In demonstrating the immense value of West Indian trade to Britain, Long cited the numerous 'linkages' it created in the imperial economy. In addition, he stressed that a multifaceted network of manufacturers resulted from the trade between the Caribbean colonies and Britain illustrating "the prodigious value" of the sugar colonies and "their immense importance to the grandeur and prosperity of their mother country".[22] Bryan Edwards, planter, colonial official and historian, supported Long's view.[23] Similarly, Raynal, writing about the same time as Edwards, points out that the colonies of the American archipelago were immensely valuable to their European possessors. He estimated the total annual value of tropical products reaching all European countries at approximately £11,000,000. The added economic value of this sum lay in the fact that it provided a base for the agricultural products and manufactures of the metropolitan centres. In addition, he wrote:

> The labours of the people settled in the islands are the sole basis of the African trade; they extend the fisheries and cultures of North America, afford a good market for the manufactures of Asia and double, perhaps treble, the activity of all Europe. They may be considered as the principal cause of the rapid motion which now activates the universe.[24]

The publication of Adam Smith's *Wealth of Nations* raised doubts as to the profitability of British slavery. As the chief proponent of free trade, Smith was interested in proving that investors would have made greater profits in ventures other than the slave trade or in the West Indies plantation system. It remains doubtful whether or not Smith was correct. As has been discussed earlier, his influence has remained important in the assessment of the questions of West Indian profitability and the islands' contribution to capital accumulation in Britain. Smith undoubtedly mis-stated the role of the sugar islands when he wrote: "The prosperity of the English sugar colonies has been, in a great measure, owing to the great riches of England, of which a part has overflowed, if one may say so, upon those colonies." He thus offered a different assessment from that of the eighteenth century mercantilists and planter-historians when he suggested that "Great Britain derives nothing but loss from the dominion which she assumes over her colonie [sic]".[25]

Although Smith's statements have remained the foundation stone of the argument postulated by the revisionists of the Williams theses, they have been revised to show that the slave trade and slavery were profitable. The financing of West Indian plantations, after the initial capital input, was based on a system of long-term credit which went to support the trade in plantation supplies and staple production. An interest rate of 5 or 6 per cent was charged on both capital and credit. It was mainly this system of credit which led to the accumulation of

8 Economic determinism vs. humanitarianism

large amounts of debt which, in turn, forced up the charges correspondingly. The profiteers were the merchant houses that furnished the credit which increased their profits which thy then reinvested in the sugar industry and other domestic ventures. Elsa Goveia states that the profits from the West Indian plantations went to repay interest on loans, both capital and credit. At times, the profits could not repay the interest let alone the annual payment of the capital. Thus, the system of financing, while it contributed significantly to the establishment of the great plantations of the eighteenth century, led to chronic indebtedness among the planters.[26]

This system of financing, despite its limitations, expanded and maintained British Caribbean slavery and propped up the plantation system. It allowed the elastic flow of African slaves to the plantations and also maintained the triangular trade, all of which gave an added impetus to British industrial growth. Basing his arguments on contemporary statements and official statistics, Williams linked the profitability of the sugar colonies to the expansion of British slavery, increased staple production and trade, and he postulated that the profits of the sugar islands "provided one of the main streams of that accumulation of capital in England which financed the Industrial Revolution".[27] Solow contends that this linkage by Williams of "the profitability of the colonies with slavery" is an innovative and important insight which has not been adequately addressed by his critics, since their evaluation of "the importance of the colonies to metropolitan growth deduces significance from size" and is therefore "vulnerable to the simple economic observation that significance must be measured by the opportunity costs of the factors involved". Thus, she has set out to assess the value of the colonies to Britain "by comparing the returns on the capital invested there with the return on the next best alternative". Her work is based on an evaluation of Engerman's quantitative analysis. Using a Cobb-Douglas production function model,[28] Solow establishes that "the Williams hypothesis can be... shown to result in plausibly significant effects on British economic growth; that it can neither be disproved because the magnitudes are too small... nor because the colonies can be shown to be a net loss to Britain".[29]

Solow's findings are indeed interesting. She has shown that the profits of the slave trade and agricultural production in "the West Indian colonies were quantitatively large compared with total British investment and with commercial and industrial investment, at the beginning of the Industrial Revolution". Furthermore, using the £37 million value of investments in the sugar colonies quoted by most

183

historians, including Engerman and Thomas, she has concluded that that sum returned a profit four to six times greater than if it were invested in the domestic market. Likewise, "if total investment at home ran at 6 per cent of a national income of £130 million, the difference due to the greater profits in the colonies would have... amounted to 12 or 14 per cent of total British investment". From these findings, Solow restates the Williams thesis that the capital/credit invested in the British sugar islands created a significant profit/saving which was invested in the industrial sector in Britain. Thus, the enslaved in the West Indies contributed markedly to British economic growth and to industrialisation in the eighteenth century. "Taken as a whole," she emphasises, "slavery made more profits for investment, a larger national income for empire and a pattern of trade which strengthened the comparative advantage of the home country in industrial commodities."[30]

Other research into investment patterns in Scottish industrial development in the eighteenth and early nineteenth centuries, mainly in the manufacturing sectors of textiles, iron, mining, distilleries and breweries, support the Solow findings. For example, T.M. Devine has found that no less than 17 of the estimated 25 merchants who joined the cotton partnerships were primarily involved in the sea-island cotton trade on which the new industry flourished. Some merchants, involved in both the tobacco and sugar trades, no doubt invested in Scottish industrial development and this poses a problem for researchers. It is also possible that there was an indirect relationship between West Indian profits and industrial development. For example, one possible source of funding came from the profits of the West India trade deposited in British banks.[31]

CAPITALISM AND SLAVERY: SOME COMMENTS

Most critics of Williams have concentrated their attack on different aspects of his thesis as we have seen. There are those who argue that the West Indies were not as profitable as Williams has stated and therefore argue that their contribution to capital accumulation was minimal; others have criticised him for understating the contribution of the humanitarians, while some have revived the eighteenth century view of the West Indian supporters and contend that the islands were profitable until the outbreak of the War of American Independence. Finally, others have rejected this latter statement adopting the position that the islands were not affected by the American Revolution and were profitable until the abolition of the

8 Economic determinism vs. humanitarianism

slave trade and the emancipation of the slaves. Despite these varying viewpoints and lack of unanimity among the critics, there is nevertheless a common theme which surfaces in the criticisms. Williams is accused of placing too much emphasis on establishing the primacy of the economic forces to the exclusion of all other factors and that this economic determinism was carried too far. While they were prepared to criticise his underestimation of the humanitarian influence on the movement for abolition of the slave trade, they nevertheless accept, without question, his first thesis that the origin of African slavery in the Caribbean was economic, not racial.

In order for Williams to argue his main thesis along the economic determinist lines, he first had to establish that slavery was born of economic forces. Had he based his argument on political or racial factors, it would have been more difficult for him to establish the primacy of the economic forces in the abolition of slavery. In fact, a close reading of Williams' first chapter, "Origin of Negro Slavery", does not support his thesis. His evidence, for the most part, seeks to establish only the reasons for the introduction of African labour. Similarly, his contention that black slavery was the logical sequence to the forced labour systems in the West Indies previously is also not convincingly established. It is probably more accurate to place the forced labour systems under which the Amerindians and indentured White servants were employed within the category of 'serfdom'. Enslavement of the native Indians failed for a variety of well-known reasons and indentured white servants were subject to contractual agreements, which were not enslavement. Furthermore, European migration to the Caribbean and the Americas was for the most part voluntary. Even when convicts were exported to the islands, their conditions of service were regulated. Furthermore, the social status of both British indentured servants and Amerindians endured only during the life time of their members. Why, then, was black slavery from its establishment lifelong, hereditary and matrifocal, if there were no political or social reasons involved in its creation? Metropolitan historians have neglected this aspect of Williams' work accepting his thesis without question because it clears the conscience of their society. Yet, it is apparent that of the three theses enunciated in his book, this is probably the weakest and most vulnerable to indepth and critical examination by serious scholars.

The linking of Caribbean slavery to the development of capitalism has emerged in the literature and provides the key to an understanding of the expansion and growth of European colonies in the region. However, certain questions remain unanswered and, despite the fact that African migration was forced, it has not been satisfactorily established that there was any necessity for the right of ownership in humans or for the hereditary status of Black slavery or the dehumanising classification of slaves as chattel. It is necessary for one to make the distinction between African labour and African slavery. The question of the need for more labour input in the New World to meet the low man/land ratio in the Caribbean in the seventeenth and eighteenth centuries is undisputed. Africa seemed an inexhaustibly elastic source of supply. Thus, while African labour imports into the West Indies might have been born of economic necessity, the badge of slavery was a racial decision. Since blacks were from the beginning initiated into a system of slavery, one has to conclude that the reasons for this social status was more than economic and definitely had racial implications and overtones. The explanation that the enslavement of the African resulted from factors of climate because they were better able to work under hot humid conditions has been dispelled by most authors, including Williams. They have rejected as a myth the belief that white labour could not work efficiently or effectively under the tropical or sub-tropical conditions of the New World.

Even before slavery was established in the Caribbean, racial thought had emerged in Europe and was used to explain differences between economic and social classes especially between the nobility and the peasantry. Furthermore, ethnocentrism was a part of the cultural heritage of those Europeans who became early colonists, and racial concepts provided the rationale for the slave trade and slavery. Added to this, Africans were considered outsiders whose blackness was from the earliest contact seen as a sign of inferiority; racial prejudice was indeed a factor in their classification as "slaves". As slavery became more entrenched, racism became more widespread.

PROFITABILITY: THE WEST INDIES AND BRITAIN

Were the sugar colonies profitable to Britain and did they contribute significantly to large amounts of capital formation in the mother country? These questions, as we have seen, have not been answered with convincing unanimity by the historians. Eric Williams was the first to respond positively and thus change the trend among historians to adopt the Adams Smith view of the West Indies and regard the islands as burdens on their European mother countries. Apart from a couple of critics of Williams, for example Thomas who basically restated Smith's view in his critique of Sheridan's work, the literature

8 Economic determinism vs. humanitarianism

since *Capitalism and Slavery* has invoked the Long/Edwards/Raynal position in demonstrating that the Caribbean islands were invaluable to European economic growth and were exploited during the eighteenth and early nineteenth centuries. In fact, many have adopted the Pares contention that "the wealth of the West Indies was created out of the profits of the West Indies themselves" and have used it in their argument that European economic growth, in particular the English Industrial Revolution, was fuelled from the profits of the slave trade and slavery.

This position has been challenged, as has already been stated, by those historians who contend that the size of the capital accumulation was too small to contribute significantly to British industrialisation. In fact, they make two claims: first, that the eighteenth century was a period of substantial capital accumulation in the colonies, which was the result of net capital transfer to the periphery from the centre. Secondly, that the military, defence and administrative costs of the islands, plus the tariff preferences allowed on their sugar, made the colonies a net loss to Britain. But specie was seldom ever sent to the islands. I could remember only two occasions throughout the eighteenth century, both during the War of American Independence, when severe currency shortages in the islands forced the British Government to send out money to pay the soldiers. Whenever the West Indian planters and merchants had a balance in their favour, the accounting system with their merchant factors allowed them a credit, but money itself hardly ever moved. Instead, the commission system ensured the flow of capital from the West Indies to Britain.

Capital from the Caribbean reached Britain from three distinct sources. First, there was the direct trade, including the slave trade; secondly, there was the illegal trade in manufactures, slaves and rum between the Caribbean colonies and the Spanish colonies which sent to England an annual sum ranging from £150,000 to £300,000 sterling; this trade also provided the islands with their circulating specie/currency supplies. In 1776 the illegal trade was incorporated into the Free Port trading system. Thirdly, there were also vast sums of money, mainly in bills of exchange drawn on merchant houses in Britain, which were often given to the New England traders to cover the imbalance in West Indian/American trade. These were in turn sent to England to offset debts arising from the imbalance in trade between Britain and the American colonies. Historians tend to lose sight of the complex trade network in which the Caribbean merchants and planters were involved and the various sources through which they contributed to capital formation in Britain when they look only at the direct trade between Britain and the Caribbean.

Even Adam Smith recognised the importance and value of the British West Indies and African slavery to the prosperity of the islands and Britain when he wrote: "The profits of a sugar plantation in any of our West Indian colonies are generally much greater than those of any other cultivation that is known either in Europe or America."[32] It was this prosperity of the islands that made them one of the best markets for British manufactured goods such as wrought iron, copper, sugar mills, earthenware and large quantities of consumer goods both for the domestic market and foreign trade. To meet the demands of this trade, an inordinate amount of shipping was required. This led to the growth of the ship-building industry and to the rise of the western ports both in England and France. As the trade developed, expansion of facilities at these ports was undertaken to meet the growing size of the vessels and to expand the global capabilities of the British merchant marine. New research, discussed earlier in this paper, shows that West Indian slavery contributed markedly to the large savings invested in the industrial sector in Britain. Research into investment patterns in Scottish industry also demonstrates that merchants involved in the West Indian trade were heavily involved in some industries, such as cotton.

Another theme in *Capitalism and Slavery* which has been gaining the attention of historians concerns the question of the state of the Caribbean economy in the post 1775 period. In his decline thesis, Williams contends that American independence led to the "uninterrupted decline" of the British West Indies. This of course is really the corollary of another more significant and interesting thesis which has received only limited examination: the development of the plantation system was not possible without unlimited access to American markets for foodstuffs and lumber.

A recent study[33] which I have undertaken shows that after the outbreak of the War of American Independence, the economy of the British West Indies went into decline from which very little recovery was made as late as the early years of the last decade of the eighteenth century. This downturn was aided by British post-war commercial policy imposing strict mercantilist and monopoly principles in the trade between the United States and the West Indies. The years of the French revolutionary and Napoleonic Wars witnessed a period of upturn in the economy of the islands but the die was cast in the decades before 1775. The separation of the American colonies also shifted the balance against British Caribbean slavery. British policy forced the islands into the North Atlantic commercial system to which

8 Economic determinism vs. humanitarianism

they were unable to adjust. Although the sugar colonies remained of importance to the commerce of Britain at the end of the eighteenth century, they had peaked in the decades immediately preceding 1775 and British interests were directed to the possibilities of profiting from the development of Cuba, to enlarging trade with South America, especially Brazil; to controlling United States economic development and to reducing the high costs of maintaining the suppression of the African slave trade.

Capitalism and Slavery has survived almost two generations of critics, with minimal damage to its three main theses. As I have demonstrated, the book has the unique quality of the historical Phoenix. For example, it was attacked and seemingly destroyed in the work *Econocide*, only to be rejuvenated, reemerging with its theses reinforced in Solow's paper. The complexity of the study defeats its critics because no work has sought to examine all three of its major theses at the same time. Modern technology which has aided the methodology of the reviewers has enabled the serious scholars to test many of Williams' findings and to put them under the careful scrutiny of the computer using scientific methods. In many ways, it is unfair for historians to require a work written in the 1930s/1940s to undergo such stringent reexamination. But the fact that it can survive after such intense analysis is enough testimony to the scholarship of the author.

Notes

1. 16 February 1945, p.452.
2. 24 February 1945, p.226.
3. 26 May 1945, p.250.
4. *American Historical Review* (July 1945), pp.782-83, 786.
5. August 1945, p.566.
6. *Economic History Review*, Vol. XVII, nos. 1&2 (1947), pp.77-79.
7. *Times Literary Supplement* (26 May, 1945), p.250.
8. Roger Anstey, "Capitalism and Slavery: a Critique", in *The Trans-Atlantic Slave Trade from West Africa* (Centre for African Studies, University of Edinburgh, 1965); C. Duncan Rice, "Critique of the Eric Williams Thesis: the Anti-Slavery Interest and the Sugar Duties, 1841-1853", in *The Trans-Atlantic Slave Trade*, ibid.
9. Roger Anstey, "Capitalism and Slavery: a Critique," *Economic History Review*, 2nd ser. Vol XXI (1968).
10. Anstey, "Capitalism and Slavery", op. cit. (1965), pp.17-18.
11. Rice, "Critique", op. cit., p.48.
12. Anstey, "Capitalism and Slavery", op. cit. (1965), p.18.
13. Robert Paul Thomas, "The Sugar Colonies of the Old Empire: Profit or Loss for Great Britain," *Economic History Review*, 2nd ser. Vol. XXI (1968).
14. Stanley L. Engerman, "The Slave Trade and British Capital Formation in the Eighteenth Century: a Comment on the Williams Thesis," *Business History*, Vol. XLVI, no. 4 (Winter 1972).
15. Richard Pares, *Merchants and Planters* (Cambridge, 1960).
16. R. Keith Aufhauser, "Profitability of Slavery in the British Caribbean," *Journal of Interdisciplinary History*, Vol. V, no. 1 (Summer 1974).
17. *The Economic History Review*, Vol. XXVI (1973).
18. J.R. Ward, "The Profitability of Sugar Planting in the British West Indies 1765-1834," *Economic History Review*, Vol. 31, no. 2 (1978), pp.197-213.
19. Roger Anstey, *The Atlantic Slave Trade and British Abolition 1760-1810* (London, 1975); see Hilary Beckles, "Down But Not Out: Eric Williams' *Capitalism and Slavery* After Nearly Forty Years of Criticism," *Bulletin of Eastern Caribbean Affairs*, Vol. 8, no. 2 (May/June 1982).
20. R.B. Sheridan, "The Wealth of Jamaica in the Eighteenth Century," *Economic History Review*, 2nd ser. Vol. XVIII (1965); R.B. Sheridan, "The Wealth of Jamaica: a Rejoinder," *Economic History Review*, Vol XXI (1968); R.B. Sheridan, "The Caribbean Plantation Revolution, 1625-1775," *Caribbean Studies*, Vol. IX (1969); R.B. Sheridan, *Sugar and Slavery: An Economic History of the British West Indies, 1623-1775* (Baltimore, 1973).
21. Barbara L. Solow, "Caribbean Slavery and British Growth: the Eric Williams Hypothesis," unpublished paper, no. 86 (Dept. of Economics, Boston University, 1982).
22. Edward Long, *History of Jamaica*, 3 vols. (London, 1974), vol. I, pp.491, 493.
23. Bryan Edwards, *The History, Civil and Commercial of the British Colonies in the West Indies* (London, 1805), vol. I, p.362.
24. Abbé Raynal, *A Philosophical and Political History of the Settlement and Trade of the Europeans in the East and West Indies* (London, 1798), vol.5, pp.106-107.
25. Adam Smith, *An Inquiry into the Nature and Causes of the Wealth of Nations*, ed. E. Cannan (London, 1961).
26. Elsa Goveia, *Slave Society in the*

8 Economic determinism vs. humanitarianism

British Leeward Islands at the End of the Eighteenth Century (New haven and London, 1965), pp.106-107.
[27] Eric Williams, *Capitalism and Slavery* (London, 1964).
[28] Solow, "Caribbean Slavery and British Growth", paper, no. 86
[29] Ibid.
[30] Ibid.
[31] T.M. Devine, "The Colonial Trades and Industrial Investment in Scotland, c.1700-1815," *The Economic History Review*, 2nd ser. Vol. XXIX, no. 1 (February 1976), p.11.
[32] Adam Smith, *Wealth of Nations*, op. cit., vol. I, p.412.
[33] Selwyn H.H. Carrington, "The Economy of the British West Indies, 1775-1791: the Makings of the Williams/Drescher Controversy", unpublished paper, January 1984.

CHAPTER NINE

Caribbean History in the Schools: A Critical Assessment of Recent Writing for Secondary Schools in the Anglophone Caribbean

Bridget Brereton

Students of West Indian historiography are well aware that the major thrust in serious writings on the Caribbean over the last thirty years or so has been to escape from the dominant Eurocentrism of earlier works. Ever since the foundation of the University of the West Indies after the war, but more particularly since the 1960s, historians have studied the West Indian experience primarily from the perspective of the Caribbean peoples rather than the Europeans who came, conquered, planted and departed, focusing on enslaved Africans, free coloureds, immigrants, peasants and workers rather than pirates, governors and planters. The Caribbean has been seen as a region whose unique history is worth studying in its own right rather than as an extension of European history, a field for European endeavour and achievement. Nor is there anything unique in this: it is part of a much wider historiographical trend towards "people's history" or "history from below" which seeks to restore to the vast anonymous majority of every human society a degree of visibility in the historical record. It is also part of a movement common to the whole postcolonial world to attempt to redress the distortions created by historical studies which saw these societies as merely the creation of European colonists and their peoples, as inert masses whose fate was wholly determined by the European settlers and officials.

The new trend – if indeed it can be called new in 1984 – has been to place the peoples of the Caribbean at the centre of the stage, to explore the 'inner plantation' in E.K. Brathwaite's phrase. Increasingly historians see the need to study the founding cultures of the Caribbean, the Amerindian, the African, the European and the Asian, and to view

9 Caribbean history in the schools

West Indian history as the interaction of these four great cultures rather than as the impact of Europe on other (and by implication, weaker) peoples. The majority, who were not of course Europeans, must be made visible, they must be seen to have played an active role in producing wealth and creating societies rather than merely responding to stimuli from across the Atlantic. G.B. Nash's *Red, White and Black: The People of Early America*[1] provides a good example of these approaches at the textbook level. He views the history of colonial North America as "not primarily the history of European settlers but the complex interaction of three major culture groups – white, red and black": a minority of Britons reacting with a majority of very different Indian and African nations, the interaction of many peoples from a wide range of cultural backgrounds over a long period. Nash seeks to show that Africans were not merely enslaved, Indians were not merely driven off their lands, but both participated actively in the creation of a new society. "Our task is to discover what happens when peoples from different continents, diverse among themselves, came into contact with each other at a particular point in history."

These new perspectives have been applied to West Indian history with increasing sophistication since the 1960s and a substantial body of scholarly writing has been the result. But, as often happens, little of this work has influenced teaching in the region's secondary schools or the production of texts or syllabi on Caribbean history. Until the end of the 1970s students in the secondary schools of the Anglophone Caribbean wrote the General Certificate of Education (GCE) O level examination in West Indian history. There is little doubt that the syllabi and examination papers used in the metropolitan organised O level programme were both conventional and Eurocentred, failing to take account of the new approaches and the new research of the historians. By contrast, the Caribbean Examination Council (CXC) West Indian History syllabus (Caribbean students first sat the CXC History paper in 1979 and it has now largely replaced the GCE O level examination throughout the region) was explicitly designed to reflect the new historiographical trends and to break away from the Eurocentred focus of the GCE syllabus. In addition, CXC sought to emphasise research skills and the use of sources to a far greater degree than the GCE programme.

With the announcement of the new CXC syllabus, a number of new books on West Indian history appeared from 1979 onwards, all seeking to exploit a perceived market for new, CXC oriented school texts, all published by British firms (some with Caribbean subsidiaries). They challenged the two major texts for the GCE examina-

193

tion which held sway in the schools: Augier et al.'s *The Making of the West Indies*[2] and Dookhan's two-volume *Pre- and Post-Emancipation History of the West Indies*.[3] New CXC inspired texts were put on the market by John Murray,[4] Heinemann,[5] Macmillan,[6] Nelson[7] and Longman.[8] Ironically, despite CXC's strong orientation towards student use of sources, no book of readings or documentary extracts has yet appeared to challenge Augier and Gordon's *Sources of West Indian History*,[9] though the CXC authorities themselves have begun to commission theme books which are expected to be heavily biased towards source materials, and Longman has produced a book of maps intended to be a companion volume to its new text.[10]

This paper offers a critical assessment of the post-1979, CXC oriented texts. How far do they reflect current approaches of historical scholarship? Have they succeeded in breaking away from Eurocentrism, and are they focused on the people of the Caribbean? To what extent have they incorporated recent published research and new insights? Do the texts encourage research skills and the use of source? How adequately do they cover the 16 themes and the overview provided for in the CXC syllabus?[11] In short, are these books acceptable texts for West Indian secondary school students in the 1980s?

It seems to me that the degree of Eurocentrism, and the extent to which the West Indian peoples are presented as visible and active, are two key criteria for assessment. The worst offender in this respect is undoubtedly Watson's *West Indian Heritage*. Watson begins his book at 1492 in a chapter entitled "The European Discovery of the Caribbean" and relegates pre-Columbian society to a skimpy discussion at the end of the chapter. By contrast, his treatment of the privateers, pirates, buccaneers, etc. is excessively detailed (they get 14 pages in all while pre-Columbian civilisation gets under three). Watson's treatment of the sugar revolution and sugar production in the eighteenth century is entirely Eurocentred. A whole chapter (8) is devoted to the Anglo-French wars of the eighteenth century – entirely from the perspective of European quarrels and their consequences for the planters – while the Haitian Revolution, the abolition of the slave trade, amelioration and emancipation are all squeezed into a single chapter (9). In this last chapter, save for a brief account of the Haitian Revolution consisting of seven paragraphs, there is absolutely no recognition of the slaves' role in emancipation: it is an account of what Europeans said and did about slavery. The account of post-emancipation changes in chapter 10 tries to explain what happened to the planters and the plantation economy rather than to

9 Caribbean history in the schools

the ex-slaves and their descendants and the newcomers. And when Watson comes to look at the 1930s, he is preoccupied with external stimuli (the world Depression, outside influences) and external responses (Moyne, Imperial Preferences, Colonial Development and Welfare) rather than the inner dynamics behind the "riots". He even sees fit to tack onto chapter 14, on the decolonisation of the British Caribbean, a section of West Indian emigration to Britain discussed as a problem for the British government and people.

There is no doubt that Watson's effort represents Eurocentrism in an exaggerated form, but he is not alone. In a text which is generally free from this bias, Hall devotes an entire chapter (2) to a detailed description of Columbus' voyages. His treatment of nineteenth century immigration (ch.12) devotes too much space to the views of the Government of India, the Colonial Office and the planters, not enough to the Indians themselves and their experiences in their new societies. More serious, the organisation of Book 1 of the Claypole and Robottom text reflects a Eurocentric bias, with entire chapters devoted to eighteenth century European wars and their impact on the planters (1, chs.15, 16, 17). For instance, the chapter on slave resistance (1, ch.20) consists of only two pages of text while eight pages in chapter 15 were devoted to an exclusively European oriented account of wars between 1713 and 1763. Their coverage of abolition (1, ch.22) is exclusively on British events. The Greenwood and Hamber text is distinctly Eurocentred in its organisation and approach throughout Books 1 and 2; but the Honychurch 3-volume work has been largely successful in breaking free of this bias.

How far do these texts present the West Indian peoples as active participants in Caribbean history, as the focus of that history? The Amerindians are generally seen as passive victims, being enslaved and dying off (cf. Watson, pp.22-27). As for the Africans, Watson's view is quite explicit: "What is perhaps most remarkable is how passive vast numbers of the slaves remained" (p.83). Greenwood and Hamber would agree: "In contrast to the Caribs, the Africans could be made servile – many accepted slavery as their lot" (1, p.93). Naturally, these authors do not give the slaves any role in the events leading to emancipation (2, ch.7) and stress the total passivity of the Afro-West Indians after the end of slavery: "The blacks had no other life than that of the plantation, and had no other ideas than those instilled into them by their former owners" (3, p.121). Honychurch makes a far greater effort to see the Africans as active participants in West Indian history; for instance, his Book 2 has two chapters devoted almost entirely to the Africans as autonomous beings and as rebels and another (12) on the slave trade which tries to depict the experiences of the enslaved men and women themselves. And it is refreshing to read, in Claypole and Robottom's text, this unequivocal declaration: "At the centre of the history of the 18th century colonies is the life of the plantation slaves. What they endured there has been the most important influence on the development of the free Caribbean societies of today" (1, p.102). This is not just rhetoric either, for these authors do attempt (not with complete success) to show the slaves as autonomous people with their own culture and lifestyle (1, ch.14).

After emancipation the tendency to present West Indians as inert masses with no active role is on the whole less pronounced. Claypole and Robottom, for instance, offer a reasonable account (2, ch.2) of the development of the blacks' social and religious life after 1838, stressing the movement away from European culture and control. Honychurch has an interesting and rather innovative section on coloured politicians in the postslavery decades (3, ch.8) which emphasises the role of an indigenous political leadership in political and constitutional changes, men like Jordan, Osborn, Prescod, Reeves, Gordon and Bogle. Several texts give biographical data on 20th century leaders like Critchlow, Cipriani, Marryshow, Butler, Manley, Bustamante, Adams and others: this is important, and goes some way to correct the distortions in the coverage of the earlier periods where biographical information was presented only on personages like Columbus, Las Casas, Hawkins, Drake, Warner, Morgan and their ilk. Even so, both Watson and Greenwood and Hamber tend to downplay the role of the nationalists in the decolonisation process. Both texts state that Britain was "anxious" to cede self-government as early as 1938-39 and certainly 1945 (Watson, p.164; Greenwood and Hamber, 3, pp.48-51) and Greenwood and Hamber seem to think that the impact of nationalist agitation and 'unrest' on constitutional decolonisation was exclusively negative; unrest *delayed* progress (3, p.58). These authors do not think much of the work of the Puerto Rican nationalists either, for they confidently state (3, p.75): "Most pressure for Puerto Rican independence comes from outside, chiefly led by Fidel Castro of Cuba."

The Asian immigrants who entered the Caribbean from the 1830s are not always adequately portrayed as active participants in building new societies. Watson, as we may expect, gives the most perfunctory attention to the immigrants' contribution to society and culture in the West Indies (ch.10: one paragraph and one small illustration) and dismisses the Indians' painful rites of passage with the cheerful remark: "No doubt Indians were well satisfied with the deal they

9 Caribbean history in the schools

obtained, for they were rewarded far beyond what they could have hoped for in India itself" (p.94). Hall offers only three brief paragraphs on the "contribution of the Indians" (ch. 12), one of which deals with present-day race tensions in Trinidad and Guyana, but at least he allows Bechu of Guyana to speak for the immigrants (p.94). Although Honychurch devotes an entire chapter to Indian civilisation in Book 1, his account of the Indians' socio cultural contributions in Trinidad and Guyana is very perfunctory (3, p.106); on the whole, Claypole and Robottom offer the best perspective on the Asians' role in Caribbean societies in the nineteenth and twentieth centuries (1, ch.25).

Everywhere in these texts, whatever the quality of treatment received by Amerindians, Africans, Asians or post-slavery West Indians, Caribbean women are invisible, voiceless. Not one of the authors of the major texts now under review is a woman, and none of them is informed with even the most rudimentary feminist consciousness. It is perhaps only fair to note that the CXC syllabus is itself notably devoid of any such consciousness.

If we agree that the West Indian past should best be viewed as the interaction of four great world cultures over a long historical period, we need to examine our texts' treatment of the founding cultures, and especially Africa since the majority of the people in the Anglophone Caribbean are predominantly of African descent, and since the Eurocentric bias of earlier texts and syllabi had resulted in the denial or submergence of the African heritage. The track record of our texts is not impressive. Watson dismisses African civilisation in just over three pages (68-71) which do nothing more than trot out the old planter clichés about the "characteristics" of the different "tribes": the Ibos are suicidal, the Ashanti warlike, etc. etc. African 'culture' is represented by 'Obeah' and 'vodun'. Hall offers absolutely no account of the African background. Greenwood and Hamber dismiss Africans as "pagans" (1, p.94) and provide no account of African civilisation or culture, except to state with truly impressive confidence that: "West Africa [sic] did not resist the Slave Trade but actively fostered it" (1. p.95). It is a relief to observe that Honychurch devotes a whole chapter (1, ch.9) to African civilisation – and the chapter on Africa precedes those on Europe and Asia – which he begins with the unequivocal statement: "Most of the people of the Caribbean today are the descendants of Africans who were brought across the Atlantic Ocean from West Africa (1, p.82). Claypole and Robottom also – after much prodding from critics of their first draft, including this writer – have devoted a chapter to West Africa

(1, ch.11) which gives a reasonably balanced account of West African civilisation and society.

What of the other world cultures that interacted in the Caribbean? It is probably redundant to state that all our texts give ample coverage to European civilisation and achievements in the Age of Discovery. The Amerindian civilisations are generally well covered too. Only Watson's treatment of the indigenous civilisations is completely inadequate (pp.8-10), though Greenwood and Hamber are not much better (1, ch.1); they opine that the Arawaks were "totally unsuited to physical labour" (1, p.29) without explaining how they had managed to survive up to 1492, and both texts state categorically that the Caribs, and only the Caribs, were ferocious cannibals. Honychurch devotes the whole of Part 1 of Book 1 to Amerindian civilisations, with separate chapters on the Maya, Aztecs, Incas, Arawaks and Caribs. Hall has a reasonable survey of Amerindian civilisations (ch.1) while Claypole and Robottom assign two chapters to the indigenes (1, chs.1, 2). Asia, not unexpectedly, receives sketchy treatment, if any at all. Honychurch is the exception in devoting two chapters in Book 1 to Indian and Chinese civilisations, and he stresses the cultural superiority of medieval India and China to contemporary Europe. Of the other texts, only Claypole and Robottom offer a reasonable account of the Indian historical and cultural background in their chapter "The Indians" (1, ch.25).

No doubt our authors could justify their failure to examine Asian civilisation adequately by reference to the relatively small proportion of persons of Asian descent in present-day Caribbean populations. But this defence will not do when we come to consider their treatment of slavery and the slaves, Africans and Afro-Creoles, which I believe is a crucial area for any assessment of these books. Are enslaved Africans *visible* in the texts? Are they seen as the true producers of wealth and as autonomous human beings? It should already be only too clear that our texts are far from uniformly acceptable in this respect.

Watson's only chapter on plantation slavery (7), which is chiefly about sugar and slave control, is totally inadequate as an account of the slaves' lives or of the dynamics of West Indian slavery. There is nothing about the life of the slave community nor the slaves' culture; *two* paragraphs are devoted to slave resistance; nowhere in this chapter do enslaved Africans appear as people or as actors. His brief account of the Haitian Revolution and the French Antilles during the Revolution (pp.102-104) down plays African resistance and fighting strength: in Guadeloupe he notes the restoration of slavery in

9 Caribbean history in the schools

1802 but there is no mention of the thousands of Africans who died resisting it; in Haiti in 1802-3 we read that yellow fever decimated Leclerc's troops "until they were no match for the Africans", which implies, of course, that without disease they would have been decisively defeated by the French troops.

Perhaps the most seriously distorted account of slavery and the slaves, however, is to be found in Greenwood and Hamber. We noted that these authors believed that most Africans "accepted slavery as their lot", unlike the Caribs (1, p.93). This is only one of the ancient, long discredited ideas about enslaved Africans which they trot out. "Mentally the slaves were already broken by the Middle Passage" (1, p.114). African slaves are said to have "usually" lost "their religions and customs" after one generation in the West Indies; "they did not try to preserve their culture because the planters had succeeded in persuading them that it was inferior". The African cultural inheritance was destroyed and the slaves "usually" tried to adopt "the white man's culture" and accepted "their station in life in the white man's world" (2, p.41). The slave-owners – like "fathers of a huge family" – "ordered the whole life of the slaves, in and outside working hours, and the lives and futures of slave children", even determining the "festivals, music and dancing" which the slaves took part in (2, p.40). In other words, there is a total denial of the existence of vibrant, autonomous slave communities which helped shape the life of the slaves, as confirmed by the mass of recent published research on slavery in the New World. Greenwood and Hamber repeat the old myths about the lack of 'proper' families and family ties among the slaves (1, p.90; 2, p.81); the absence of legal or Christian marriages did *not* mean the absence of close family ties (2, p.36). Our authors are confident that "irreligion and immorality were widespread among the slaves" and that because the slaves were "denied Christianity" they developed "rituals and superstitions" (2, p.72). There is no attempt to define irreligion, immorality or superstition,[12] no recognition that African religious beliefs were brought to the Caribbean and flourished whether or not the slaves were "denied Christianity".

There is nothing nearly as bad in the other texts. Hall's chapter on society in slavery days is interestingly written, though it is not especially strong on the inner life of African and Creole slaves, their social and family organisation, their culture and community. Honychurch is better here: his chapter 12 in Book 2 deals with the slaves' daily life, food and clothes, languages, folklore, music and dance, festivals, religion and magic; he also has short sections on the domestic and the skilled slaves. His chapter 13 offers a reasonable account of slave revolts with some data on individual leaders like Coffy of Berbice and Cudjoe of the Jamaican Maroons. Claypole and Robottom, we have noted, make a serious effort to place the enslaved African at the centre of their coverage of plantation slavery. Their chapter on this topic (1, ch.14) contains sections on slave culture, family and social life, customs and beliefs, crafts and languages. And it is encouraging to read (1, p.93) that the African came to the Caribbean with "languages, beliefs, skills and a place in society as perhaps a warrior, priest or skilled craftsman... a rich store of memories, stories and dances. In time he would use all these to piece together a life in his new American surroundings which owed much to his African heritage." Simple and obvious enough; yet it needs to be said in a school text, and unequivocally.

It might be worthwhile, in addition, to look at our authors' treatment of one or two further areas; and I have decided to examine their coverage of "Black Nationalist" movements and of some sensitive near – contemporary developments. All the texts mention Garvey, but usually he is presented as the only West Indian Black Nationalist worth looking at, and his importance is not always adequately recognised. Watson gives him two paragraphs (pp.159-160) of rather hostile coverage which emphasises his prison terms in the United States and Jamaica and concludes: "He had little that was concrete to show for his life's work and he had quarrelled with many of his colleagues." Greenwood and Hamber content themselves with the flippant remark that in the 1980s "it became more fashionable to display one's blackness and African traditions" (3, p.127), dismissing the whole thing as a sort of fad. Certainly Honychurch has a more reasonable account of Garvey's work (3, pp.113-16), but he pays no attention to other early Black Nationalists and he seems unaware of the Pan-African Association. By contrast, Claypole and Robottom deserve credit for their innovative chapter (2, ch.9) which is wholly devoted to the development of black consciousness. With sections on the "scramble for Africa", Blyden, J.J. Thomas, H.S. Williams, F.E.M. Hercules, Garvey and UNIA, Padmore and African independence, this chapter contains material which (to my knowledge) no other school text on West Indian history has used, and it presents in appropriate fashion the ideas and actions of thinkers like Blyden, Thomas and Williams who are little known even to educated West Indians. The continuities between Thomas, who was active in the 1860s to 1880s, Padmore, and Rastafari and 'Black Power' of the contemporary Caribbean are well brought out, and the long West Indian tradition of Black Nationalist thought is firmly established.

9 Caribbean history in the schools

For all school texts, the correct approach to contemporary developments where key participants may still be alive, or for that matter running a regional government, is an especially difficult problem, particularly where all the publishers and most of the authors are not West Indians. Outspoken comment may be counter-productive when approval from ministries of education is an important factor in getting the texts sold. I found the chapters dealing with post-1962 events to be unsatisfactory in virtually all the texts, marked by an obvious determination not to be controversial. It is only fair to note that CXC has announced that "for the time being" no question will be set which demands a knowledge of the period beyond 1962, and this may have influenced the texts. If so, I believe it would have been wiser to omit the post-1962 chapters altogether, the solution adopted by Hall whose book is subtitled "An Historical Survey 1450-1960", rather than to include pages of bland platitudes about economic problems, regional cooperation and searches for identity (cf. Claypole and Robottom 2, ch.20; Watson ch.15; Greenwood and Hamber 3, ch.8; Honychurch, ch.15). The texts had special problems, it seems, in dealing with the stormy history of Guyana between 1950 and 1966: Jagan and Burnham being still centre stage, as it were. There is a tendency to skate very lightly over these important years. Watson declines to offer *any* explanation for the constitutional suspension in 1953 – merely calling it "an unhappy beginning to the process of bringing about self-government as the prelude to independence" – or to notice the British and American involvement in the affairs of 1961-1964 (pp.164-67). Similarly, Greenwood and Hamber are silent on the external factors in the crises and blame the whole debacle of the early 1960s on Jagan's "bold" policies (3, pp.58-59). Honychurch does hint at US involvement in 1961-1964, but his discussion is very sketchy and he fails even to mention the events of 1953 (3, pp.140-41). At least Claypole and Robottom offer a more realistic, if brief, analysis (3, pp.118-20 and 132-34) paying some attention to US-UK machinations and their impact on the Guyanese political scene.

Perhaps we may turn now from our authors' handling of particular subject areas to an analysis of organisation and scholarship: that is, the degree to which they show a familiarity with reasonably recent published research and incorporate it where possible into their texts. Since CXC attempts a fairly innovative approach to the development of a West Indian history syllabus, we need to examine whether these texts adopt a strictly conventional organisational framework or show some willingness to innovate in this respect. Some of these texts are entirely conventional in the sequence and organisation of their chapters: this is especially true, in my view, of the books by Watson and Greenwood and Hamber. Both texts concentrate on "facts", both order their chapters in the time honoured sequences, both tend to subordinate analysis, interpretation and insight to a plodding narrative approach. Reading most of Greenwood and Hamber's 3-volume text, in fact, one would not easily realise that it was intended for the CXC syllabus; until suddenly, two-thirds through Book 3, we come to five chapters arbitrarily tacked on the end of the book to "cover" CXC themes 9 (social conditions in the 20th century), 13 (religion as a social force), 14 (social life 1838-1938) and 16 (art forms), with no effort to integrate this material. On the whole, the organisational framework used by Hall and by Claypole and Robottom is conventional, but both these texts contain a few unexpected chapters on rather novel themes. Hall has an interesting chapter on the "non-sugar" territories, Belize, Curaçao, and the Bahamas, which presents information not easily come by elsewhere. Besides their innovative chapter on Black consciousness, Claypole and Robottom offer chapters on Trinidad and Guyana during the Revolutionary and Napoleonic Wars (1, ch.19), on slavery and the churches (1, ch.21), and on the "middle class challenge" to colonialism between the 1890s and 1930s (2, ch.10) as well as two useful chapters (2, chs.7 and 15) on the Dutch and French islands in the nineteenth and twentieth centuries, both of which present material difficult to find at this level.

There is no doubt that Honychurch's 3-volume text adopts a quite different organisation; but his book presents a special problem in that he never makes it clear whether it is designed for CXC candidates or for students in lower forms of secondary schools nor whether it is specifically a history of the Caribbean or a wider history of the Americas. The title suggests the former, but several aspects of the organisation and approach hint at the latter. Indeed, Honychurch's text is to some degree modeled on an earlier 3-volume work, *The People Who Came*,[13] which was quite specifically a history of the Americas written for forms 1 to 3 (i.e., the pre-O level or pre-CXC forms) of the secondary schools. This uncertainty as to exactly what kind of book Honychurch meant to write does show up in its organisation. Book 1, like Book 1 of *The People Who Came*, describes in some detail the founding civilisations of the Americas: the Amerindians (to which the whole of Part 1 is devoted), Africa, India, China and Europe, with Part 2 concluding with a chapter on the Age of Discovery. Books 2 and 3, however, contain a far higher proportion of strictly Caribbean material. Only chapters 4 and 5 of Book 2, on the conquest of Mexico and Peru, and chapters 2 and 4 of Book 3, on the American Wars

9 Caribbean history in the schools

of Independence, cover ground that might be more appropriate to a general history of the Americas than to a CXC oriented history of the Caribbean. By contrast, *The People Who Came*, explicitly a history of the Americas, has far more non-Caribbean material, particularly in Book 3. In any case, Honychurch's Book 1 does set his text apart from the rest in terms of organisation and content, and there are some novel touches in his second and third Books as well: his chapter called "Pawns and the Power Game" (3, ch.1) takes a rather original approach to eighteenth century wars, and chapter 8 of the same Book, on Crown Colony government, includes interesting material on coloured politicians and the coloured owned newspaper press of the post-1830 decades.

Some of these texts, regrettably, show little familiarity with recent scholarly work, even well known and easily accessible material. No doubt, this is not surprising where the authors are not professional historians and where neither they nor their publishers sought expert advice. This is certainly the case with Watson's text, and even more shamefully with Greenwood and Hamber's. The latter are clearly ignorant of the mass of published research on slavery in the New World. Thus they are, to put it mildly, confusing in their discussion of comparative slave treatment (2, pp.31-32) and totally wrong in their account of slave family life and religion (2, pp.36, 43, 72). They are confused about the distinction between the campaign to abolish the slave trade and the later movement to end slavery (2, pp.60-64) and this is their rather clever contribution to the debate over abolition: "Historians who want to play down the humanitarian motive for the abolitionist movement emphasise the economic reasons for it" (2, p.62); end of story. Their rosy view of Crown Colony government in practice in the nineteenth century Caribbean (3, p.46) and their conviction that "life in the British Caribbean changed little in the 19th century" (3, p.125) do not suggest much familiarity with the literature on the post-slavery Caribbean either. Claypole and Robottom's text indicates a much greater degree of acquaintance with the scholarship, particularly Book 2, but it is still surprising to note that they give very little attention to the economic forces behind abolition and emancipation in Book 1, chapters 22 and 23. Both Hall and Honychurch incorporate new research in their texts – it is interesting to see that Honychurch acknowledges the possibility of contacts between the New World and Africa before Columbus (2, p.9) – and so does Beckles in his short text on European settlement and rivalry, seeing his organising theme as the integration of the Caribbean into the "rising world economic system" in the Wallerstein formulation.

Since the CXC syllabus seeks to familiarise students with the use of original sources, we need to assess the extent to which our texts encourage this; we have already noted that no CXC oriented book of readings or documents has yet emerged. Naturally all of them include quotations of varying lengths from contemporary sources; but the text which stands out is Hall's. Nearly every chapter contains long extracts from source materials, some of them unusual or even unpublished. He includes extracts from Ottobah Cugoano and John Newton (ch.5), estate accounts from Westerhall in Grenada (ch.6), Lady Nugent's diary (ch.7), the 1842 House of Commons Committee (ch.10), Bechu's evidence to the 1897 Royal Commission (ch.12), the journal of an estate owner on Watling's Island, Bahamas, in the early 1830s (ch.13). Honychurch is good too, with extracts from Cugoano, Nugent, Esteban Montejo, and several other interesting sources. Claypole and Robottom go in for rather shorter quotations, but they do include a long, revealing dialogue between Citrine of the Moyne Commission and the Barbados Sugar Producers' Association (2, p.102).

A school text must, at the very minimum, be accurate; all teachers know the fatal tendency for errors to be handed down from textbook to textbook and become entrenched in generations of student essays. By this very basic criterion, Greenwood and Hamber's text fails miserably. It is full of distortions, inaccuracies and plain howlers. A choice selection: The authors apparently fail to understand that the planters succeeded in getting the Crown lands shut off from the ex-slaves in Guyana and Trinidad and that it was impossible for ex-slaves in these colonies to buy these lands until the late 1860s in the case of Trinidad (2, pp.83-84). Neither in Guyana nor in Trinidad did the post-1838 sugar industry "collapse" or even "suffer drastic decline" (2, p.84). The planters did not reject Chinese immigrants because they were "unsatisfactory physically" (2, p.93), whatever that may mean. It is clear that Indian labour *was* a major contributing factor to increased sugar output in Guyana and Trinidad (2, pp.99-100). It is foolish to imply that cocoa was not a successful alternative crop in Trinidad (2, p.121); for fifty years it was the backbone of that island's economy. West Indians did not leave their native islands to live and work elsewhere because "many of them wanted to get as far away as possible from their 'roots' " (2, p.237), but because of harsh economic and social conditions.

And again: Trinidad is given three totally fictitious slave revolts in 1819, 1825 and 1829 (2, p.46). The 1831 slave rising in Jamaica is first said to have spread to the eastern parishes, then to have been confined to the north-west (2, pp.53-54). Granville Sharpe was not

9 Caribbean history in the schools

a Quaker (2, p.61). Dessalines was not African born (2, pp.18, 25). The planters did not win five-year indentures for the Indian labourers in 1850 but in 1863. The ex-soldiers of the West India Regiments settled in Trinidad were hardly "runaway black soldiers" (2, p.118). Louis de Verteuil was white, not black (2, p.136). The *encomiendero* was never expected to "educate" the Indians in his grant (1, p.26). The yam is not indigenous to the New World (1, p.32); the Dutch East India Company was chartered in 1601, not 1595 (1, p.51). 'Mestizo' means a person of mixed European and Amerindian descent, not African and Amerindian (1, p.128). Although Book 3 contains fewer distortions or factual errors than the first two books, it has its share. On three different occasions Muñoz Marín is described as "President of Puerto Rico" though there is no mention of this "office" in the account of the Associated State constitution (2, pp.73-74). Tobago did not keep "its own Assembly" when it was linked to Trinidad in 1889 since it had lost its Assembly in 1874, and it did not become a "ward of Trinidad" in "1899" (3, p.45). It is interesting to learn that "health", "agriculture" and "transport" in the Commonwealth Caribbean have "come under CARICOM's control" (3, p.94). And Boscoe Holder neither "gave up painting in favor of dancing" nor "emigrated to the United States" (3, p.148); I suppose this is Geoffrey, but he hasn't given up painting either. Not all these errors are of great importance. But so many of them could have been avoided if only MacMillan had sought some specialist advice, or had got a specialist to write the text in the first place.

In comparison to Greenwood and Hamber, the other texts score well on accuracy. For all its other shortcomings, Watson is relatively error-free. Claypole and Robottom were saved from innumerable horrors by the criticism of their specialist readers. Hall and Honychurch make few mistakes, though Honychurch repeats the usual inaccuracies about Cipriani "reviving" the Trinidad Workingmen's Association and becoming its leader "shortly after his return from the war" (3, p.118). Stewart, in her short text on the United States and the Caribbean, seems to believe that Muñoz Marín was responsible for Puerto Ricans getting US citizenship in 1917 (ch.7), and her discussion of Puerto Rico's constitutional status in the same chapter is highly confusing, with terms like "self-government", "free", "independent" being bandied about without adequate definition.

Stewart's failure to define difficult words – surely highly necessary in a school text – brings me to consider the question of language: is the language appropriate to CXC level students and is the degree of difficulty (concepts and material) suitable? Generally, so far as I am competent to judge, the texts do reasonably well on these counts. Honychurch seems to be the 'easiest' of the lot, and this may relate to the uncertainty as to whether his text is geared for CXC candidates or for pre-Form 4 students. Book 1 in particular, in its language type, format and illustrations, seems targeted at younger pupils. Claypole and Robottom are probably the most "difficult", with a denser, longer text and probably fewer illustrations than the others. The language of these books seemed generally appropriate, but there were some examples of the use of words in a misleading way and of bias in language, probably unconscious. Thus Victor Hugues is described as a "bloodthirsty revolutionary" (Greenwood and Hamber, 2, p.28), an old, conservative cliché which will hardly allow readers to form an adequate judgment of the man; the 1651 "Barbados Revolt" is described as if it were a popular demand for self-government (Greenwood and Hamber, 1, pp.63-64). Several of these texts use "cult" to describe Afro-Caribbean religions (e.g. Greenwood and Hamber, 3, pp.118-19), an example of unconscious bias of language.

All these books are lavishly illustrated and their visual impact – cover, layout and design, typeface, balance between text and illustrations – is generally good. In this respect, they represent a tremendous improvement on the older texts by Augier et al. and by Dookhan. The illustrations include contemporary prints and pictures, modern sketches and full-page paintings of events or situations, maps, copies of newspaper material; teachers should be able to find suitable visual "stimulus materials" from these texts. Honychurch's text is especially good, particularly Book 1 where literally every page has at least one illustration; his work includes some very striking full-page or double-page modern paintings, such as the portrait of a nineteenth century newspaper office in a small West Indian town (3, ch.8). But one can find interesting illustrations in all these books. My only criticism here is that there were perhaps too many portraits of European notables of marginal relevance to the Caribbean – notably in Books 1 and 2 of Greenwood and Hamber – and I thought it unfortunate to illustrate indigenous religion with a nineteenth century print of a Baptist "total immersion" which was obviously intended to ridicule the faith and the Blacks depicted in it (Greenwood and Hamber, 3, p.106).

Several maps, diagrams and charts are presented in the texts, many quite useful, but Longman has published a separate book of maps by Ashdown designed as a companion volume to Claypole and Robottom. It is intended to cover all the CXC themes as well as the overview, and it features over 175 separate maps and diagrams. This

9 Caribbean history in the schools

is a well designed work and I think it could be a valuable teaching tool, especially for the period up to c.1900; the maps and diagrams which tried to illustrate aspects of twentieth century history seemed less successful. Some maps and/or diagrams put together useful statistical information in a convenient form: for instance, no.38 presenting material on comparative abolition and emancipation (dates of abolition and of emancipation; numbers emancipated; whether there was an apprenticeship and, if so, for how long). The book includes a list of "West Indian heroes", somewhat erratically chosen; and another list of persons, journals, books and terms important to culture and the arts in the Commonwealth Caribbean.

Finally, to what extent are these books adequate texts for the CXC syllabus? Do they cover CXC's themes and overview satisfactorily and further the pedagogical aims of the syllabus?

On the whole, the texts succeed in covering the syllabus rather well, with the notable exception of the difficult themes on religion as a social force, social life 1838-1938, and art forms. As we noted, Greenwood and Hambert try to deal with these themes by tacking five chapters rather arbitrarily to the end of their book, but none of the other texts really come to grips with them. The extreme Eurocentrism of Watson's offering leads him to give inadequate coverage to the CXC themes on slave resistance and revolt and the Haitian Revolution. He devotes exactly two paragraphs to slave resistance (p.83) and seven to the Haitian Revolution (pp.102-104). While the syllabus devotes a whole theme to trade unions Watson gives the topic three paragraphs (pp.160-61). Hall's coverage of slave resistance and the Haitian Revolution is also very skimpy (ch.8) but it is fair to note that this text is conceived specifically as a survey to satisfy the CXC's 'overview' of the whole period, supplemented by short books on specific themes.

Although CXC focuses primarily on the Anglophone Caribbean, the "foreign" territories comprise an integral part of the syllabus; in earlier sections dealing with the period up to 1650 or even 1750 this presents no particular problem, but in themes 6 to 16 the question arises of how and to what extent to integrate material on the Spanish, French and Dutch Caribbean. The detailed guidelines to each theme indicate that comparative topics should be studied wherever possible, for instance, in theme 6 the movements towards abolition and emancipation in the British, French and Spanish islands are to be compared and contrasted. To cover the syllabus adequately a considerable body of material on the non-British Caribbean needs to be presented, especially since information is not easily accessible in

English, except for well-known topics like the Haitian Revolution or US relations with Cuba and the Cuban Revolution. Up to the later eighteenth century, all our texts provide adequate material on the Hispanic, French and Dutch Caribbean, but with one or two exceptions coverage falls off markedly for the nineteenth and twentieth centuries.

Watson, for instance, devotes only nine paragraphs to the Haitian Revolution and the whole subsequent history of Haiti up to 1917 (pp.102-104), and his account of the sugar industry in nineteenth century Cuba and the Hispanic Caribbean in the twentieth century is so skimpy as to be almost useless (pp.124-25, 127). Puerto Rico's Operation Bootstrap gets exactly one paragraph (p.134). Hall's survey is also weak on the non-British Caribbean. In his otherwise good chapter on society in slavery days, he makes no references to slave society in Saint Domingue or in Cuba; he gives absolutely no account of abolition and emancipation in the French, Dutch or Spanish Caribbean; he offers only passing references to the nineteenth century Cuban sugar industry. His chapter 14 on the US and the Caribbean seems unduly skewed to the eighteenth and nineteenth centuries, with the result that he devotes just over one page to post-1898 US relations with the Caribbean, and nineteenth century Cuba only appears as part of the US involvement in the region. In chapter 16 the Cuban Revolution is barely touched on; Curaçao has a few paragraphs in chapter 13 but the French Antilles are virtually invisible in Hall's text. Claypole and Robottom are clearly most successful in providing substantial material on the "foreign" Caribbean after c.1800. Their Book 2 devotes seven out of 20 chapters to the non-British territories, which probably gives them better coverage than the syllabus itself. Especially useful are their three chapters (2, chs.7, 8, 15) dealing with the French and Dutch islands in the nineteenth and twentieth centuries and the three Hispanic territories up to 1898: they contain information not easy to come by at this level, and they are unique in paying some attention to Haiti between 1804 and 1915 (they recognise that Haiti was the "one country which challenged slavery, the plantation economy and colonialism" (2, p.62)) and to Puerto Rico and the Dominican Republic in the nineteenth century.

It is the explicit aim of the CXC syllabus to encourage research skills and individual enquiry by students, and it may be appropriate to consider how far these texts help to further that aim. They all include 'exercises' for each chapter to be performed by the students. In some cases these exercises are fairly standard, not to say conventional: essay questions, questions calling for responses to tables,

9 Caribbean history in the schools

graphs, illustrations, maps or quotations in the text, and multiple choice or true/false exercises. This is broadly true of both Watson's and Hall's texts, and also of Greenwood and Hamber's work, though the latter do occasionally set a more innovative task: for instance, the student is invited at the end of Book 3, chapter 11, to "visit your local library, museum and newspaper offices and collect material for a project on one of the following topics in your own territory over the past 150 years: customs; recreation; dress. Try to illustrate your project with photographs, etc."

The texts by Honychurch and Claypole and Robottom, however, suggest exercises and projects that are often quite innovative and give considerable scope for research and the use of local sources including oral history sources. Honychurch encourages "activity" projects, especially in Book 1, which seem suitable perhaps for students of the lower forms rather than for CXC candidates: "Collect pictures of pyramids in other parts of the world and paste them in your scrapbook. How do they differ from Maya pyramids?" (1, ch.2), or: "Collect five types of seed from along the seashore or river bank" (1, ch.5). But other exercises seems well suited to CXC's aims: "What African traditions do you think remain in your country?" (1, ch.9); "Ask your parents and grandparents about the type of schools they went to, how the schools were equipped and what textbooks were used..." (3, ch.7); "Write an essay on life in your country during the 1930s based on research and discussions with your older relatives and friends" (3, ch.11). Similarly, Claypole and Robottom include for most of their chapters a section headed "further work" featuring some ingenious research projects including oral history work. In Book 1, students are asked "Do your national archives, libraries or public records offices have bills of sale, auction notices or other material referring to newly arrived Africans? Would it be possible to examine any of these?" (1, p.185) and "Can you trace your family history to emancipation? What evidence have you used to answer this question?" (1, p.188). In Book 2 the scope for this kind of project is even wider as more recent periods are reached: "Do you know of any villages, roads or markets that can be traced to 19th century freemen enterprise?" (2, p.207); "Did any members of your family emigrate to seek work in the period up to 1914? What can you find out about them?" (2, p.208); "Try to find someone who can give you a firsthand account of one of the riots discussed in this chapter" (2, p.212). Such exercises, useful in themselves, should also inspire teachers to devise suitable projects of their own.

With the appearance of a number of texts within a short space of time, all geared for the same market, some duplication is inevitable, and there is no doubt that these texts to a considerable extent manipulate the same material and often in much the same ways. This is particularly marked in the early period: virtually identical information on Arawaks and Caribs, Columbus and Las Casas, *encomiendas* and missionaries, pirates and settlers, appear over and over again in each text. After around 1750 there seems a little more scope for diversity and selection, and as we have noted, some of our texts succeed in taking a novel approach at times or presenting material which is rather unusual at this level. There is little doubt that a certain amount of 'borrowing' has gone on or that the older O level texts by Augier et al. and Dookhan were carefully mined for information and for ideas on organisation and selection.

The most striking example of one text 'influencing' another perhaps requires a brief comment here: Honychurch's text bears a close resemblance to *The People Who Came*, published between 1968 and 1972 and conceived as a pre-O level history of the Americas for forms 1 to 3 of the secondary schools. The organisation, content and format of Honychurch's Book 1 are almost identical to Book 1 of *The People Who Came*. Both books are divided into two parts, and in Part 1, chapters 2 to 5 of *The People Who Came* the authors deal with the arrival of man in the Americas, the hunters, farmers and warriors, precisely the content of Honychurch's long chapter 1; then each book has chapters in sequence on the Mayas, Aztecs, Incas, Arawaks and Caribs. Part 2 consists, in each book, of virtually identical chapters in the same sequence on Africa, India, China and Europe; each book ends on an identical note, Columbus' departure from Spain in 1492. The correspondence between Books 2 and 3 of the two texts is less striking, but there is some resemblance between Parts 1 and 2 in *The People Who Came* and Honychurch's Part 1, and the former's Part 3 and the latter's Part 2. In the third books there is some correspondence between Part 1 chapters 1 to 3 and part 2 chapters 6-11 of *The People Who Came*, and Honychurch's Part 1 chapters 1 to 6. Although Honychurch's text has some strengths and is visually a most attractive production, it is difficult to see to what extent it marks an advance on *The People Who Came* – which, incidentally, the publishers hope to reissue in a revised edition.

We must conclude our assessment of these recent school texts by stating that they are not, on the whole, satisfactory texts for CXC candidates in the 1980s. Some of them illustrate in exaggerated form the dangers of metropolitan publishers commissioning individuals who are neither professional historians nor practising teachers in

9 Caribbean history in the schools

West Indian schools to write books on Caribbean history, and then compounding the error by failing to seek or take professional advice before publication. The result is likely to be a disaster and in this category I must place the texts by Watson and Greenwood and Hamber, books which in my view should not be used by any school preparing candidates for the CXC history syllabus. Claypole and Robottom's text, by contrast, has definite strengths as well as some shortcomings, and proves to be a reasonably useful text, and the same is true of Hall's survey supplemented by the short theme books which Heinemann has already published or are now in preparation.

It is obvious that commercial publishers, however well intentioned their Caribbean editors or agents and their authors, will seek to produce marketable books first and foremost, responding to specific concerns of the CXC authorities and teachers in the schools only to a secondary extent. Of course, they have the financial and technical resource to produce attractive and sturdy books[14] and to market them aggressively. But it seems clear that texts must now be produced which are directly commissioned and controlled by the CXC body, whatever the actual mechanisms of publication eventually chosen. The recent move by CXC to commission texts on specified themes in the History syllabus is therefore welcome, if belated. It will enable CXC to choose authors carefully and to direct them as to content and approach; in particular it will make possible the appearance of works which are essentially selections of readings and documents rather than the straight texts which commercial publishers usually prefer. This seems to be the priority now: to make available source materials on all the themes in forms suitable both for teachers and for students, so that CXC may wish to commission both teachers' books and students' books. If it seems desirable CXC may wish to enter into contractual relations with commercial publishers, but the crucial question is control: control over the choice of author/editor and over the final product. In the production of materials CXC will of course need to work closely with history teachers in the different territories through History Teachers' Associations where they exist; and to draw on the expertise of University of the West Indies personnel wherever appropriate. When suitable teaching materials and students' texts/readings have reached the schools, teachers will be able to be more discriminating in their choice of texts, and while the better commercial publications will hold their own, it will no longer be possible for any production, however worthless, to find a market merely because it claims to be a 'CXC text'.

Notes

1. Prentice-Hall 1974: *History of the American People Series*, ed. Leon Litwack.
2. F.R. Augier, S. Gordon, D.G. Hall, M. Reckord, *The Making of the West Indies* (Longman, 1960).
3. I. Dookhan, *A Pre-Emancipation History of the West Indies* (Collins, 1917); and *A Post-Emancipation History of the West Indies* (Collins, 1975). Both Augier et al. and Dookhan went into several editions.
4. J. Watson, *The West Indian Heritage: A History of the West Indies* (John Murray, 1979).
5. D. Hall, *The Caribbean Experience: An Historical Survey 1450-1960* (Heinemann, 1982). Theme books already published by Heinemann are: E. Halcrow, *Canes and Chains: A Study of Sugar and Slavery* (1981); R. Stewart, *The US in the Caribbean* (1982); and H. Beckles, *European Settlement and Rivalry 1492-1792* (1983).
6. R. Greenwood and S.Hamber, *Caribbean Certificate History* (Macmillan) Book 1, *Arawaks to Africans* (1979); Book 2, *Emancipation to Emigration* (1980); Book 3, *Development and Decolonisation* (1981).
7. L. Honychurch, *The Caribbean People*, 3 Books (Thomas Nelson, 1979 to 1981).
8. W. Claypole and J. Robottom, *Caribbean Story* (Longman), Book 1, *Foundations* (1980); Book 2, *The Inheritors* (1981).
9. F.R. Augier and S. Gordon, *Sources of West Indian History* (Longman, 1962).
10. P. Ashdown, *Caribbean History in Maps* (Longman, 1979).
11. The themes and overview are set out in the CXC 1980 Revised History Syllabus.
12. Sidney Mintz suggests that superstition is "the other man's religion" and immorality "the other man's sex life".
13. E. Brathwaite (ed.), *The People Who Came* (Longman), Book 1, A. Norman (1968); Book 2, P. Patterson and J. Carnegie (1970); Book 3, E. Brathwaite and A. Phillips (1972).
14. Even so, the copy of Watson (John Murray) which I purchased was missing pages 137 to 152. So much for metropolitan efficiency.

CHAPTER TEN

Labour and Capital after Emancipation, 1838-1897

James Millette

Before 1838 a working class, as that term is scientifically understood, did not exist in Trinidad or in Tobago. There was, of course, a labouring population in both islands consisting in the main of slaves, apprenticed since 1834, but comprised as well of an admixture of free workers, mainly black and coloured, engaged in a wide variety of employments. Economic activity was concentrated in sugar within which the majority of workers were employed. At emancipation the population of Trinidad amounted to 36,655, that of Tobago numbered about 12,000 to 13,000.[1] In the former, the white population numbered 3,993, the free coloured and black population totalled 12,006, and the apprentices or ex-slaves 20,656. In the latter the corresponding figures for 1833 were 304 whites, 1,266 free coloured and black, and 11,628 slaves giving a total of 13,198. Effectively the strength of the work force, allowing for children, the aged, and the infirm amounted to some 30 to 35 thousand persons in both islands. In Trinidad about 11,000 and in Tobago 7,443 workers were, at emancipation, said to be engaged in agriculture.[2] With the coming of emancipation the character of this labouring population underwent a dramatic change, the essence of that change being that what was formerly a subject slave or near slave population became free, possessing principally, among other things, the right to bargain for and earn wages, and to dispute within limits the terms and conditions on which its labour power would be sold. The impact of this metamorphosis in the condition of the labourer pervasively affected the entire sugar plantation system on which the economy of the two islands, Trinidad and Tobago, was principally based.

The most direct influence was on the organisation of production on the plantation itself. Where, before emancipation, with a labour supply assured, the plantation had been able to operate reasonably successfully on the basis of credit, after emancipation successful oper-

213

ation of the plantation demanded that the planter should have at his disposal a supply of ready cash with which to pay wages recurrently all year round, but most insistently during the period of the crop. In addition, even when the planter found the capital with which to pay wages, there was no automatic supply of labour on which to depend. Many ex-slaves, savouring their hard won freedom, simply refused to work on the plantations at any price. Such labour as was to be had needed to be not only paid but cajoled, or else coerced.

In Trinidad and Tobago, as elsewhere, cajolement and coercion were tried by turns. In the former, where the decisive difference from nearly every other West Indian territory was to be found in an admixture of soils of great fertility supported and enhanced by an abundance of available arable land, and where the relative immaturity of the sugar plantation system was a fact of life, high wages were at first nearly always paid. In the latter where the plantation system had already fallen into a state of decrepitude, wages of any sort often could not and were not paid.

In Tobago, the planter class had to resort to the system of *metayage*,[3] a kind of sharecropping made necessary by the desperate circumstances of two antagonistic classes thrown together virtually without alternative on a small, worn out plantation island. The planter occupied the land and to some extent possessed the implements of cultivation and manufacture; and the labourer possessed his labour power. Left to himself the planter would soon be the distressed overlord of nothing more than an old, abandoned, overgrown *lastro*; and the labourer had to eat. If he could be induced to work, labour was not really deficient. But the wage paid to labour had to compete with what was known to prevail in Trinidad which already was attracting away labour as well as capital from the less attractive economic environment then prevailing in Tobago. Few planters could pay competitive wages particularly in the state of depression gradually confronting the industry as free trade policies demolished the preferential position of British West Indian sugar in the United Kingdom, and most pertinently in the disastrous aftermath of the hurricane of 1847.

Within this context, *metayage* emerged by 1848 as a compromise between planter and labourer, the essence of the compromise being that the worker was given access to the land and the planter given access to labour the purpose being to create a product which could be shared. The product was not always shared equitably, for the planter retained the initiative and used it to increase his share of the output always, and sometimes notoriously, at the worker's expense.

10 Labour vs capital after emancipation, 1838-1897

Yet, in the long run, even *metayage* could not secure the future of the plantation and ultimately the sugar industry collapsed. In 1832 there were 75 estates in cultivation; in 1862 there were 62; by 1897 there were 39.[4] In so far as the labouring population was concerned, the decline of the sugar industry was an event which triggered mixed responses. On the one hand, the labourers had a fondness for sugar and "were reluctant to give it up";[5] they knew it well and the sugar cane not only provided them with an important part of their own dietary needs, it also provided them with fodder for their livestock. Yet, particularly after 1885 when a general and serious depression of the sugar industry took place, the labouring population turned more and more towards other crops for sustenance and for trade: cocoa, coconuts, peas, corn, potatoes, plantains, poultry and a variety of livestock were produced in significant quantity and provided the basis of an important export traffic to Trinidad. In 1896 the value of this trade to Tobago was estimated at £10,360 sterling, a not insignificant amount, and constituted a veritable umbilical cord to an otherwise depressed and devastated economy.[6] What was more, to the extent that there was a sugar industry to speak of, that industry was rapidly falling into the hands of the workers; it was the failure of the industry under continuing capitalist organisation to provide for the reasonable remuneration of this class, as well as the general shortage of capital within the ranks of the planters, that led to its final extinction.

If *metayage* settled the question of planter-worker relationships in Tobago during the immediate post-emancipation period, no such solution was possible in the case of Trinidad. There the objective conditions confronting labour and capital were different. In Trinidad there was and had been since 1783 a critical labour shortage. The *cédula* of population granted by the Spanish government in that year opened up the possibilities of plantation enterprise, and led to a rapid increase in population between 1783 and 1797. In the latter year the British conquered the island, bringing with them not only British industrial and commercial enterprise leading to the development of a maturer capitalist environment but also the reforming impact of a leading European power increasingly committed to the abolition of the slave trade. As early as 1802 the question of the future cultivation of the island with specific reference to the form of labour to be used was a hotly debated issue, culminating in the establishment of a Commission of Enquiry and Government[7] and a general slowing down in the official importation of slave labour. After 1807, the year of slave trade abolition, it was only by devious means, particularly

215

involving the importation of slaves on the pretence that they were 'domestics', that the labouring population inched forward from the 20,000 odd which it had attained in 1806, the year before the abolition. Between 1813 and 1821, 3,800 new recruits, most of them 'domestics' entered the island, 1,100 of them from Dominica, and about 1,200 from Grenada.[8] Even so, for reasons already noted, between 1806 and 1838 the population increased only by some 6,000 persons, from 30,043 to 36,655.

This critical labour shortage is to be appreciated in the context of yet another important factor, namely, the abundance of land. In 1838, only 43,265 of 208,379 acres were under private ownership. Even as late as 1860 only some 60,000 acres of land were under cultivation. Compared with Barbados, an island of just over 100,000 acres which was completely covered with sugar plantations by the end of the seventeenth century, Trinidad was virtually untouched. With a total acreage of 1,120,000 only about one-twentieth was under active cultivation, and by far the greatest portion of the land was publicly owned, Crown land as it was called. For an ex-slave population eager as elsewhere to move out of the shadow of the plantation, there was abundant land to which to move, a feature which was unlike that existing in the smaller West Indian islands but which was comparable with that existing in Jamaica and British Guiana. Such a situation provided many options for the labouring population which could only, and even then not always successfully, be induced to undertake plantation work by the offer of high wages. Also, the planter was not impecunious as he was in Tobago. The high productivity of land compared most favourably with the older established islands; by one calculation the rewards to sugar were two-and-a-half to three times as high as in the older islands, a reality which was recognised by the higher prices asked and obtained for slaves in Trinidad in the period before emancipation.[9]

After emancipation, and indeed even before that, in the period of apprenticeship, the initial struggles between capital and labour took place over the length of the working day, but particularly over wages. In this struggle the aim of the planter was to keep the worker closely attached to the plantation by lengthening the period over which he would be required to work on it, and at the same time to increase his dependence on the plantation by paying him the barest possible wage. During apprenticeship the planters' position was stronger than it was to be immediately thereafter, but even then the workers held the whip hand. As a consequence, in Trinidad as in Guiana, the system of task work was very generally employed, to the distinct advantage of the worker both in terms of time as well as wages.

As apprenticeship ended this ascendancy of the worker in the new industrial relations situation existing between himself and the planter was carried over into the era of freedom. Where, for example, wages in Tobago averaged 16 cents per day in 1839 the rate for Trinidad was between 40 and 50 cents and continued to be so until as late as 1846.[10] In the same period, the rate per task varied between 30 and 50 cents for first-class field workers, and some estates were even willing to go as high as 60 to 65 cents.[11] A good worker could perform at least two tasks per day, with the result that the remuneration paid to labour was higher in Trinidad than in any other British West Indian territory even including Guiana. As one upstanding pillar of the local plantocracy complained in 1842, a worker could earn in one hour what he could only earn in a day in Tortola.[12]

Yet, inducements had to be offered in the form of free housing, provision grounds, and even an allowance of salt fish and rum in order to get the workers to stay on the estates and procure for the planter the adequate and reliable labour force which was his constant aim. As in the case of wages, so too in the case of perquisites; planters competed among themselves to offer higher and higher inducements to workers in order to secure the labour that they needed.

The willingness of planters to meet the workers' demands had yet another aspect apart from their economic ability, under appropriately favourable circumstances, to do so. When times were hard wages were reduced as, for example, in 1844. But, apart from the economic vicissitudes, there were also the socio-political factors which conditioned the planter to meet the workers' demands.

In the first place, the planter class was not homogeneous as it was in Barbados or, say, in Jamaica where the collective infection of the planters seemed to be to make emancipation fail even at their own expense.[13] Though it is true that the planters were united as a class in their perception of the workers and their role in the scheme of things significant subtle differences existed between planter and planter based on nationality, race and size of ownership.

Ever since 1783 the demographic composition of Trinidad had reflected a level of diversity sufficient to make the island unique within the Caribbean context, a society *sui generis*. Within the ranks of the planter class the significant features were to be found in the large numbers of non-British or 'foreign' whites as they were called, with whites of French and Spanish descent prevailing, and in the high concentration of free coloured proprietors themselves part of a free coloured population which, at this time, alone in Trinidad of all the British West Indian islands outnumbered the whites.[14] Between 1783 and 1838 both of these factors, the one of nationality, the other of race acted against the consolidation of planter solidarity such as had developed in the other territories. The absence of this solidarity is the more marked when one considers the high incidence of resident proprietorships in the islands but it is a fact that throughout the period a high level of differentiation prevailed among the planter class.

Issues like constitutional change, the maintenance or the demolition of the Spanish legal system, the creditor-debtor relationship existing between the British mercantile and the plantation based French and Spanish community, the ramifications of the Picton-Fullarton controversy which destroyed the Commission of Enquiry and Government in 1802 and completely frustrated its objectives, and, in respect of the free coloured, the long and agonising struggle for civil equality with the whites which was only achieved in 1829: all of these and more agitated the national and racial dissimilarities among the planter class and made for a lack of class cohesion. In the second place, Trinidad was a Crown Colony, that is to say that its political institutions were not only dependent but, at this stage, rudimentary and embryonic. The Crown Colony despotism with which the planters were elsewhere able successfully to replace the old representative system after the Morant Bay rebellion of 1865, and particularly after the introduction of modified Crown Colony rule in Jamaica in 1884, had not yet developed. Consequently the planter class had little political resource with which to threaten or to browbeat the labouring population. The Trinidad experience for this reason had been that of a social laboratory where, between 1812 and 1838, metropolitan policies aimed at the amelioration and ultimate abolition of slavery were introduced by *fiat*, by Order in Council, always in the hopeful anticipation that the measures so introduced would thereafter be adopted by those islands possessing representative assemblies.

For most of this period, Trinidad did not even possess a Legislative Council, no matter how much dependent. A Council of Advice existed on the specific declaration that the governor was not bound to take its advice. And when, in 1831, a Legislative Council was introduced, it was fully nominated with not even the merest suggestion of an elected or representative element. Yet the Legislative Council, dependent though it was, did provide a rallying point for planter influence. From the early 1840s aided and led by the bigger planters, among whom William H. Burnley was outstanding, the local sugar interest deepened its links with metropolitan capital and established

10 Labour vs capital after emancipation, 1838-1897

a near monopoly of local influence by virtue of its domination of the unofficial nominated seats in the Legislative Council. By 1841-42 this greater coherence of the planter class manifested itself in collective attempts to lower wages and to withhold the inducements offered to plantation workers. These first efforts failed but later the planters were successfully able to combine to reduce wages and to keep them lower than they would otherwise have been for the period 1845 to 1850.[15] From this time forward the planter-worker conflict proceeded more and more to the advantage of the planter and less and less to that of the worker.

In explaining this reversal of the worker's position, consideration must be given to a few important factors which reflected the race and class realities in the society which was then developing. In such an analysis pride of place must be given to the delineation of the imperial objectives for the society. What, then, were these objectives?

First and foremost, there was the absolute necessity of maintaining the imperial connection, of perpetuating imperialist possession and domination of the society. Secondly, in order to do this, and at the same time to avoid an incessant drain on imperial finances, there was the concurrent objective of establishing where possible a viable colonial economy which could provide revenues with which to carry on the business of the colony and provide profits for metropolitan investors. Thirdly, in the light of the historical development of the society and of its metropolitan connections such an economy should be principally based upon the cultivation of an export crop of which sugar was the best known, the best organised, and ecologically the most suitable. It followed as a consequence of these postulates that planter society should be provided with a reliable, continuous and dependent supply of labour such as would be needed to carry on the industry and such as could no longer be supplied by the conventional means associated with the slave trade and slavery.

The implications of these considerations were neatly tied together by Lord Harris, governor of Trinidad from 1846 to 1854, an able imperialist whose work did much to secure the plantation ascendancy in the country in those difficult middle years of the nineteenth century. In 1846, writing to the secretary of state for the colonies, Harris expressed himself as "fully and cordially" agreeing with that official "that the highest interest of the negroes requires that the cultivation of sugar should not be abandoned, and that the proprietors of European race should be enabled to maintain their present place in the society of the colony, which can only be done by giving them greater command of labour."[16] In other words, the sugar industry representing itself in all its manifestations as the main enemy of the black workers was to be maintained in their "highest interest"!

It was not the first time, nor would it be the last, that an imperial administrator was to justify the most rampant discrimination against blacks by the assertion that what was being proposed was indeed in the interests of these blacks. Lord Liverpool in 1810 declared against the introduction of representative government in Trinidad in the interest, as he put it, of the free coloured majority who could not be "expected" to participate in those institutions.[17] The secretary of state of the day, the Duke of Buckingham, was to do it again in 1868 when explaining the decision to introduce Crown Colony government in the Leewards: "The population at large," he wrote, "consisted of uneducated negroes, (who) neither had nor could have any political powers; they were incapable of contributing to the formation of an intelligent public opinion; and the consequence was that the Assemblies performed their office under no real or effective responsibility".[18] Against this background of half-truth and misrepresentation it is almost refreshing to read in a Jamaica newspaper of the same period the real reason for the demolition of representative and the introduction of Crown Colony government. As the *Jamaica Guardian* of November 10th, 1865, put it, "Jamaica is not the country for either a respectable coloured or white family to live in unless the government can safely protect life and property. To do these, we must have a strong government and to have this, our present constitution must be greatly changed."[19] And so, indeed, it was; in the titanic struggle between capital and labour that ensued in the British West Indies after emancipation, it was fear, not favour, that explained the introduction of the Crown Colony system.

The political economy of sugar, however, necessitated at least two responses, the one political, the other economic. Crown Colony government was the political response; at the economic level the planter response was immigration. Given the historical circumstances – among which the accustomed exploitation of black, African labour and the British command of significant sources of such labour at international level were the two most important – it was natural that immigrant labour should first be sought among free Africans and West Indians. With respect to the former between 1838 and the end of the 1890s there was one main source of supply, liberated Africans either taken directly off the slaving ships, or shipped from St Helena and Sierra Leone, both of them depots for Africans so taken before they could otherwise be disposed of. From this source 8,390 labourers came to Trinidad out of a total of 36,160 imported into the British

West Indies in this period.[20]

As for West Indian labour, it was by no means difficult attracting workers in significant numbers into Trinidad. The Leewards proved to be a good source of supply as did the Windwards including Barbados, and for the very good reason that wages were considerably lower in these islands than in Trinidad. The top wage per day in the Leewards between 1838 and 1848 was ten pence in Nevis in 1845, but six pence was common and four pence was paid in Montserrat in 1848,[21] in that island in 1849-50, the rate even sunk to two and quarter-pence.[22] In Barbados the top wage for the decade was 1s.3d.; in Dominica, 10d; in Grenada, 1s.2d; St Vincent and St Lucia an unusual 1s.8d. and 1s.10d. respectively though in the former the norm was just about eight pence.[23]

The Trinidad planters did not however leave it to the vast, impersonal forces of private enterprise to determine the issue. They encouraged immigration from these islands. Under planter pressure legislation was passed providing bounties to persons who whether in the guise of employers or otherwise brought labourers to the country.[24] Bounty hunters fell like a plague on the rest of the Eastern Caribbean recruiting workers for the estates. In the Leewards the going rate per person was £3 sterling and in the period 1839 to July 1846 bounties did much to encourage the movement of the 6,083 who migrated from Antigua, Montserrat, Nevis and St Kitts to Trinidad in that period.[25] This traffic, mainly to Trinidad and Guiana, with Trinidad taking the lion's share, was so significant that the other territories took positive measures to stop it in the mid-1840s. In the Caribbean, securities were demanded from ships' captains and recruiting agents against their removal of labourers from the islands with Antigua, St Vincent and Barbados being among the first to take such measures. In Britain, pressures were exerted successfully to procure a Colonial Office embargo on the payment of bounties for inter-island emigration. Even so the trade continued; by the end of 1849, 10,278 West Indians had emigrated to Trinidad, the majority of them to become permanent settlers.

The international grapevine of the day, well aware of the work of the American Colonisation Society in respect of black repatriation to Africa, even suggested the United States as a possible source of supply, and agents were sent out to recruit among blacks in the northern states of the Atlantic seaboard between Maryland and New Jersey and extending inwards to Pennsylvania. All told, about 1,500 black Americans were lured to the island's shores between 1839 and 1847. In terms of what was anticipated, however, this result could hardly be described as heartening.

In their desperation for labour the Trinidad planters did not scruple either at encouraging other kinds of workers, as they had been doing for decades. A scheme for Chinese immigration had been attempted in 1802-6;[26] European labour had also been mooted, though the idea was more oriented towards the establishment of what was sometimes called a "European yeomanry".[27] After emancipation such propositions were once again made, and were sometimes acted upon. A party of British labourers and artisans in 1846,[28] 676 ill-starred French and German immigrants in late 1839,[29] another 190 of the same kind in May 1840,[30] a much more substantial Portuguese immigration mainly from Madeira between 1846 and 1847,[31] about 1,000 Chinese between 1859 and 1866: these comprised the sum total of the result of such policies.

The fact was, quite simply, that these results were only slightly better than no result at all. What was more, nearly all the immigrants were lost within a very short space of time to the people who wanted them most, namely, the planters. Neither liberated Africans, West Indians, Chinese, Europeans or nondescripts found any reason for doing otherwise than the native blacks were themselves doing, that is, abandoning the estates. By 1859, according to one estimate, less than 5,000 Trinidadian blacks were attached to sugar not because, as some would have it, they had moved off into idleness but because they had found other methods of improving themselves and maintaining their independence.[32] The Europeans, for their part, were quite quickly absorbed into those easy, remunerative occupations which the West Indians specially reserved for people of white skin, with the Portuguese, as later the Chinese, showing a decided preference for shopkeeping. The English, French, German and other whites, when they did not become destitute, melted into the middle and upper levels of the social and economic order and became part of the race and class elite. The blacks squatted on idle land, turned to huckstering, and congregated in the new villages which were springing up on the outskirts of Port of Spain, San Fernando and the north-eastern districts, preferring to keep their relationship with the plantation at arm's length, to work on it when they pleased and as far as possible on their terms.

This was, indeed, the heart of the matter, for the workers' terms were not the planters' terms. The evidence is clear that there were two rival sets of objectives in the post-emancipation society. On the one hand, there were the planters who wanted to maintain the old plantation system even though every reasonable rationale for its

10 Labour vs capital after emancipation, 1838-1897

existence, apart from race and class oppression expressed in its most imperialist form, had collapsed. For them the idea was to return, by hook or by crook, to a master and servant relationship which would put the ex-slaves once again in a state of virtual slavery. That was the planters' objective. On the other hand, the ex-slaves, the nascent working class, free for the first time in the West Indies to give or withhold their labour, to bargain for wages and, to some extent, their working conditions, had a different set of objectives. Their simplest objective was to live as they had never lived before, outside the shadow of the plantation and the whip, whether that involved the destruction of the planter and the plantation system or not.

The point was, however, that the labourers had no political apparatus with which to realise their objectives. They had no armies, they did not have access to state power, they did not even have the vote. On the other hand, the planters had access to state power though they did not quite control it, and through the manipulation of a number of means, especially the exertion of influence over the imperial government, they were able to implement such policies as they wished. Of course there were limits; imperialism had its own objectives: cheap food in the metropolis, profits, and free trade throughout the world being chief among them. Thus there was no question of turning back the clock as far as the equalisation of sugar duties was concerned. It was not a time for easy loans, and certainly not to help the planter meet his big wage bill; nor would the British capitalist continue to import expensive West Indian sugar when he could get the product more cheaply from Cuba or Brazil or the East Indies. But the British imperialist was more than willing to return with one hand what he had taken away with the other, particularly if this could be done in ways which were consistent with his principal objectives.

The point at which this consistency could be reached was on the issue of cheap labour. Metropolitan and colonial philosophy rationalised the free movement of persons and regarded immigration and the right not only to labour, but to cheap labour, as rights which ought to be protected for the West Indian planter. Thus the ascendancy of the worker over the planter which was the first fruit of the struggles of the immediate post-emancipation period was broken – definitely and comprehensively. It was, if one wishes to say so, also broken nicely, as only the British can do, but it was broken all the same. The spirit of high-mindedness, of humanitarian concern, with which the British have always been able to cloak the most repulsive policies is fully represented in the following complete text of the fateful Resolution accepted by the Select Committee on the West India

Colonies which reported in July 1842 and set the stage for the introduction of East Indian contract labour.

Resolved, that it is the opinion of this Committee,

1. THAT the great act of emancipating the Slaves in the West Indian Colonies has been productive, as regards the character and condition of the Negro Population, of the most favourable and gratifying results.

2. THAT the improvement in the character of the Negro in every Colony into the state of which this Committee has had time to extend inquiry, is proved by abundant testimony of an increased and increasing desire for religious and general instruction; a growing disposition to take upon themselves the obligations of marriage, and to fulfil the duties of domestic life; improved morals; rapid advance in civilisation, and increased sense of value of property and independent station.

3. THAT, unhappily, there has occurred, simultaneously with this amendment in the condition of the negroes, a very great diminution in the staple productions of the West Indies, to such an extent as to have caused serious, and, in some cases, ruinous injury to the proprietors of estates in those Colonies.

4. THAT while this distress has been felt to a much less extent in some of the smaller and more populous Islands, it had been so great in the larger Colonies of Jamaica, British Guiana, and Trinidad, as to have caused many estates, hitherto prosperous and productive, to be cultivated for the last two or three years at considerable loss, and others to be abandoned.

5. THAT the principal causes of this diminished production and consequent distress are, the great difficulty which has been experienced by the Planters in obtaining steady and continuous labour, and the high rate of remuneration which they give for the broken and indifferent work which they are able to procure.

6. THAT the diminished supply of labour is caused partly by the fact that some of the former Slaves have betaken themselves to other occupations more profitable than field labour; but the more general cause is, that the labourers are enabled to live in comfort and to acquire wealth without, for the most part, labouring on the estates of the planters for more than three or four days in a week, and from five to seven hours in a day; so that they have no sufficient stimulus to perform an adequate amount of work.

7. THAT this state of things arises partly from the high wages which the insufficiency of the supply of labour, and their competition with each other, naturally compel the Planters to pay; but is principally to

be attributed to the easy terms upon which the use of land has been obtainable by Negroes.

8. THAT many of the former slaves have been enabled to purchase land, and the labourers generally are allowed to occupy provision grounds subject to no rent, or to a very low one: and in these fertile countries, the land they thus hold as owners or occupiers not only yields them an ample supply of food, but in many cases a considerable overplus in money, altogether independent of, and in addition to, the high money wages which they receive.

9. THAT the cheapness of land has thus been the main cause of the difficulties which have been experienced; and that this cheapness is the natural result of the excess of fertile land beyond the wants of the existing population.

10. THAT in considering the anxious question of what practical remedies are best calculated to check the increasing depreciation of West Indian property, it therefore appears that much might be effected by judicious arrangements on the part of the Planters themselves, for their own general advantage, and by moderate and prudent changes in the system which they have hitherto adopted.

11. THAT one obvious and most desirable mode of endeavouring to compensate for this diminished supply of labour, is to promote the immigration of a fresh labouring population to such an extent as to create competition for employment.

12. THAT for the better attainment of that object as well as to secure the full rights and comforts of the immigrants as freemen, it is desirable that such immigration should be conducted under the authority, inspection, and control of responsible public officers.

13. THAT it is also a serious question, whether it is not required by a due regard for the just rights and interests of the West Indian Proprietors, and the ultimate welfare of Negroes themselves, more especially in consideration of the large addition to the labouring population which it is hoped may soon be effected by immigration, that the laws which regulate the relations between employers and labourers in the different Colonies, should undergo early and careful revision by their respective Legislatures.[33]

And so East Indian immigration into the British West Indies was set upon its way. Its object was to secure the future of the sugar plantation by cheapening labour, an end which would be obtained by providing the subject labour force which the planter wanted and, consequentially, by inducing competition among the labouring population.

From the planters' point of view a better solution could hardly be found. The labour supply from India, as the labour supply from Africa at an earlier stage, was inexhaustible. What was more, social chaos in India – in Bengal, in the United Provinces, in Madras, the main sources of Indian immigrant labour[34] – itself the result of British imperialist policies, and of British hegemonic control of that country, made it easy for the British to manipulate labour from one British colony to another British colony. As long as these conditions continued, and they continued for a very long time, the supply of immigrants was safe, and the planter class could rest secure in the knowledge that a permanent solution had at last been found to the labour problem which threatened it with destruction.

Between 1845 and 1917, a considerable number of East Indian immigrants recruited as contracted labourers were moved into the West Indies, creating what has justly been called "a new system of slavery".[35] In the British Caribbean 238,909 Indians went to British Guiana, 143,939 to Trinidad, 36,412 to Jamaica, with much smaller numbers going to Grenada, St Lucia, St Vincent and Tobago.[36]

For the Trinidad blacks, as well as for the East Indian labourers, immigration was a bad bargain. As the planters had hoped, the arrival of large quantities of new labourers saved the sugar industry and depressed wages, and so the black worker was in a manner of speaking, given his quietus. From that time onwards the black worker became once again dependent on the capitalist and forced to work on his terms. The consequence was a long run and continuing depression of wages so much so that the daily wage for labour in agriculture was better in 1838 than it was in 1938: the post-emancipation wage rate per task of 40 to 65 cents compares very favourably indeed, one hundred years later, with the weekly wage which then ranged between $1.20 and $3.00. Unskilled labour in sugar could expect to earn only 35 cents per day, and even the oil industry was not offering more than 72 cents per day.[37] It was a rare and favoured worker who could take home $5.00 at the end of a week's hard labour. Also, immigration coincided with the perpetuation and with the tightening of the policies relating to landholding. A proclamation of June 22nd, 1847 gave squatters six months in which to prove their title to the land they occupied on payments ranging between six shillings and £1 sterling per acre, plus costs. Ordinances passed in 1848 and 1852 decreed summary eviction and jail of six months' hard labour for squatting. And Lord Harris, that most efficient of imperialist governors, increased the price per acre to £2 sterling, partly to pay for the costs of immigration. In the event, these policies were to prove no more agreeable to the labourer than that which, during the period of

10 Labour vs capital after emancipation, 1838-1897

acute labour shortage, had earlier placed the upset price on land at £1 per acre on a minimum purchase of 340 acres – just the size of land that the average labourer could purchase![38]

And what of the East Indian immigrant? In Demerara the planters were on record as saying that they wanted their immigrants either at work, in hospital or in jail.[39] In Trinidad the same benign formula prevailed. Work was long and hard, and rewards were low. An ordinance of 1847 set out to prescribe wages ranging between a maximum per month of $3.50 for *sirdars*, $2.40 for Indian males, $1.45 for females, and $1.45 for boys under 12 years of age, but it was mercifully disallowed by the imperial government. As a rule, though, immigrant wages were nothing to speak about. In the 1850s they averaged 30 to 40 cents per day; between 1858 and 1875 the wage per task varied between 20 and 25 cents. What was more, labourers were graded and paid proportionately per task according to their assessed ability. By 1899 wages were fixed at between 25 and 16 cents per day depending on whether the immigrant was able-bodied or not.[40] In the period January 1st to December 31st, 1894 and January 1st to December 31st, 1895 only three and six estates respectively out of sixty-nine paid more than an average 6d per day to adult male indentured immigrants employed.[41] In 1910 indentured workers were in some cases receiving as little as 72 cents per week even though the Immigrant Amendment Ordinance of 1872 had long since set their wages at $1.25, the same as that established for free labourers.[42] For compensation, the worker got rations and clothing from the person to whom he was indentured, as well as a place to live. With respect to the former, suffice it to say that food and clothes were not generously issued; as for the latter, the barrack was the standard. And what was the barrack?

According to Lechmere Guppy before the Royal Franchise Commission of 1888,

> The barrack is a long wooden building eleven or twelve feet wide, containing perhaps eight or ten small rooms divided from each other by wooden partitions not reaching to the roof. The roof is galvanised iron, without any ceiling; and the heat of the sun by day and the cold by night take full effect upon the occupants. By standing on a box the occupant of one room can look over the partition into the adjoining one, and can easily climb, over. A family has a single room in which to bring up their boys and girls if they have children. All noises and talking and smells pass through the open space from one end of the barrack to the other. There are no places for cooking, no latrines. The men and women, boys and girls, go together into the

canes or bush when nature requires. Comfort, privacy and decency are impossible under such conditions.[43]

Under indentureship only the ablest and the luckiest of Indian indentured workers managed to stay out of the hospital and the jail. Often he went to the hospital when he was already nearly dead, victim of the overwork and malnutrition that were his lot. In this context 'able-bodied', a description often used in the ordinances of the time, meant simply not sick enough to be hospitalised. Even so, hospital admissions averaged between one and two times per immigrant per year.[44] As for the hospitals themselves, the average was a thorough disgrace, administered by the estate merely to fulfil the requirements of the relevant regulations. Accordingly mortality rates were high, especially in the first year or so of arrival, the period of 'seasoning' as it was called in slavery and was sometimes called in indentureship.

But it was the jailhouse that really emphasised for the immigrant his status in the scheme of things. When one considers that indentureship was supposedly a deliberate alternative to slavery, one is forced to remark upon the excessive domination that coercion exercised over the system. The root cause lay in the planters' determination to extract as much as possible from the labourers for as little as possible. In British Guiana this was accomplished by, among other things, increasing the size of tasks to the point where none but the most able-bodied and indefatigable of workers could fulfil it, with the result that the planters could successfully prove breach of the labour laws against the workers "every week or any week in the year".[45] But whether in Guiana or in Trinidad, the very contract by which the status of the immigrant was supposed to be improved *vis-à-vis* that of the slave, his predecessor, hung like a millstone around his neck. Laws were passed to make breach of contract in its limitless variety a criminal, not a civil offence punishable by fine, but as often as not by imprisonment. As with the slaves in the days of slavery, indentured labourers were strictly confined to the plantations to which they were assigned. Absence from the plantations without permission, manifested by possession of a pass, was regarded as desertion and considered a crime; the punishment was not only fine or imprisonment but forfeiture of wages. In 1862 the standard fine, payable to the employer, was 60 cents per day or sixty days imprisonment.[46] But desertion was not the only "crime"; absence from work without lawful excuse; refusing to begin or finish work; malingering; habitual idleness; vagrancy; using threatening language to persons

10 Labour vs capital after emancipation, 1838-1897

in authority; refusing to obey a lawful order; enticing others away from work and damaging the employer's property were all deemed crimes and the criminal was harshly treated. As a modern critic has concluded that, in all the colonies, "the law was harsh, (but) uneven in its severity".[47]

The severity of the law is reflected in the number of prosecutions as well as in the time spent in jail by the immigrants. By one calculation, out of an indentured population of 11,606 in 1907-1908, 1,869 were convicted under the labour laws.[48] By another, 7,899 prosecutions of immigrants ensued in the period 1909 to 1912.[49] Two investigators into the system of indentureship reported in 1915 that in Trinidad and in British Guiana "reliance on the courts to maintain discipline seems to have grown into a habit of mind with the majority of managers".[50] The Colonial Office was at last driven to observe that such a high rate of prosecutions was a serious indictment of the system: clearly, as one writer puts it, managers had "lost their sense of proportion... in Trinidad".[51] The severity of the law was complemented by the planter's very advantageous position within the society.

Almost as if it had learnt nothing from the experience of slavery, the British government allowed the planter to attain ascendancy in relation to the implementation of the law much akin to that which he had enjoyed in the days of slavery. As with the slave so with the indentured labourer: the planter was employer and magistrate; the worker was employee and accused, and an accused often forbidden to give evidence in his own behalf. To the planter was awarded the right of punishing the worker for a large variety of punishable offenses on the plantation, including even beatings and floggings: the badge of authority was the cattle whip, widely used in the West Indies, supported by the jailhouse.[52] In Ceylon it was said that "Every man is a magistrate on his own estate... and therefore as long as a man is working for you, you have a right to do what you like with him – that is, short of killing".[53] The same grim regime prevailed in Trinidad. As Williams has put it, "Indentured labour was... slavery plus a constable."[54]

As was to be expected, the planter lost no time in modifying the contractual arrangement between himself and the indentured worker to his benefit. Originally, the period of indentureship was conceived as terminal after five years "industrial residence" after which the immigrant was entitled to a free return passage to India. At first a bounty of $50 was established payable to those Indians who chose to extend the period of their indentureship. But since this involved an act of volition on the part of the worker, and did not prove attractive enough to meet the planters' demands, the law was invoked in 1853 to alter the period of indentureship from five to ten years and to require the worker to make a contribution of $35 towards his passage at the end of that period.[55] The unfavourable reaction of intending immigrants to the new law forced the planters to modify these regulations; but the writing was on the wall. A comprehensive ordinance, No. 24 of 1854, recognised two types of immigrants: those who had migrated before January 1st, 1854 and were entitled to a free return passage after five years, and those who had come thereafter and who, therefore, had to complete ten years of 'industrial residence' and received only an assisted return passage afterwards. Both groups could exercise an option after three years had elapsed, the option being that if they chose to opt out of indentureship then they became subject to a lump sum payment of £6 or a monthly tax of five shillings for the unexpired portion of their contract; in 1856, the free passage was again introduced as an inducement, but the tax was raised to £2.10s. per year for those labourers choosing to move out of indentureship. It is a matter of record that in the struggle to free themselves from being tied to the planter by contract many labourers put themselves into the hands of the moneylenders, many of them Indians, who made usurious profits at the expense of the labourers.[56] It seemed to be really and truly a case of being between the devil and the deep blue sea.

A reasonably alert reading of the indentured immigrant's experience would show that the introduction of contract labour into Trinidad in the period after emancipation had three most important consequences: first, the regular supply of Indian labourers saved the sugar plantation system; secondly, it depressed wages generally by introducing competition and, particularly, by reinforcing as a principle the custom that the low level wages paid to immigrants should be paid to other labourers as well; and, finally, it facilitated the extraction of surplus from the labouring population and maximised the level of profits reaped by the planter class at the expense of labour. East Indian indentured labour was the perfect answer paid for at the expense of the entire community, and not only of those who profited from it,[57] to the manifold problems of labour shortage, high wage rates, depression and low income returns experienced by the planter after emancipation. And it was a solution which was, for a long time, destined to make the contest between labour and capital unequal and inequitable. As Henry Alcazar, mayor of Port of Spain, an official member of the Legislative Council, put it in his submission to the Norman Commission in 1897, "Indian immigration... has been

10 Labour vs capital after emancipation, 1838-1897

but a weapon in the hands of the planter *to enable him to obtain at starvation rates the far more efficient labour of local origin.*"[58]
And he continued:

Those who have witnessed the very close struggle between capital and organised labour in Western Europe, must be aware of the irresistible effect which an annual introduction of between 2,000 and 3,000 indentured labourers must have among a population of 240,000 all told; how it must give to employers a complete and uninterrupted command of the labour market, and in Trinidad the more so that facilities for settling on the unoccupied lands of the interior are designedly limited. That this is so admitted facts clearly show...The planters find it more and more difficult to supply the large number of immigrants applied for by them with the contract amount of employment – that is, consistently with their interest, which is that by far the larger part of the work on their estates should be entrusted to the stronger and abler hands of outside labour...It is noticeable in the return of a typical estate supplied by the Honourable G.T. Fenwick to His Excellency the late Sir Napier Broome, that only about one fourth of the work on it is performed by indentured labour... This overcrowding is painfully evident. Lately public works on a large scale have been undertaken in the colony. It is estimated that Government is now employing between 4,000 and 5,000 hands. No difficulty has been experienced in obtaining this amount of labour. And the unemployed are apparently as numerous as ever. During the last year or two hundreds of labourers have, in spite of every warning, left for the canal works at Colon... Wages have during the last 30 years risen all over the civilised world. Even in ultra conservative India there has been a marked increase, as Lord Roberts not long ago reminded us. In Trinidad and the West Indies generally wages have, during the same period fallen greatly, in some occupations by fully one-half, on an average certainly not less than 25 percent. No doubt the price of sugar has also fallen considerably, but so has the price of iron, of wheat, and of every staple product of the very countries in which there has been a rise. *I am justified therefore in contending that the fall in Trinidad is due, not to unavoidable economic causes, but to the operation of a system which places absolute command of the labour market in the hands of the employers.* As far as the workers are concerned, industry is thus kept artificially in a constant state of extreme depression.[59]

The indictment of contract labour has hardly ever been better put. What made that indictment even more pertinent was the fact that the Crown Colony system, much touted as the saviour and bulwark of the rights of the unrepresented masses was more and more glaringly being revealed to be a facade behind which the race and class ascendancy of the sugar planter was made irreversible. By the 1880s that ascendancy had developed to the point where other interests – cocoa, commercial and professional, not labour or petty huckster – were beginning to feel the torture and frustration born of an unequal struggle against an entrenched race and class elite. Out of that frustration was born the Reform Movement of the 1880s and 90s directed against the dictatorship of the plantocracy which was fortified in the Legislative Council by the ceaseless advocacy of a strong and powerful group of Unofficials – a "despotism sweetened by sugar", to turn a contemporary Guianese statement on its head.[60]

Behind the political power lay a very real economic base. Upon that base planter power was secured, Crown Colony or no Crown Colony. Since 1838 a veritable revolution had taken place in the economic fortunes of the planter class in Trinidad. That revolution has as its prime origin the increasing interrelationship of local and metropolitan capital with the spokesmen of such capital emerging as the prime spokesmen of the sugar interest. On the strength of this development, the economy of Trinidad had developed to the point where in terms of revenue, that of Trinidad and Tobago was, at £628,332, higher than that of any other West Indian territory. In terms of total imports and exports that of Trinidad and Tobago's in 1896 was greater than that of all colonies save Jamaica, and in that colony exports were significantly boosted by re-exports. At £3,429,872 it was better than British Guiana by about £200,000, double that of Barbados, and as much as that of Barbados, the Leewards and Windwards taken together.[61] It is true that in the 1880s and 1890s cocoa exports exceeded sugar exports, though not necessarily so if rum, molasses and bitters, by-products of sugar were taken into account.[62] But this fact only emphasised that continuing contradiction inherent in the hegemony of sugar interests over that of all others. Such a situation had one explanation and one explanation only; sugar was supported by imperialism and by metropolitan capitalism as no other interest was supported.

In analysing the interpenetration of local and metropolitan sugar interests, cognisance must be taken of two economic institutions which achieved a position of dominance in the island economy in the second half of the nineteenth century and facilitated the power elite organised around sugar: these organisations were the Colonial Company and the Colonial Bank. Together they reflect the better organisation of capitalism compared with the disorganisation of labour which, only at the end of the century, began to undertake any conscious self-organisation in defence of its interests.

The Colonial Company was incorporated in 1866 to take over

10 Labour vs capital after emancipation, 1838-1897

the holdings of two private firms, one of them named Cavan and Company,[63] operating in British Guiana and Trinidad as well as a large factory in Puerto Rico. It was perhaps the first example of big conglomerate capital in the islands, and marked a decisive shift in interest of such capital away from the older to the newer British West Indian territories. Officers of the company where themselves capitalists of significance in the region and well connected with the ruling circles of the colonial capitalist interest in London. In 1896, for example, Mr (later Sir) Neville Lubbock was shareholder and director in the company and Chairman of the West India Committee in London. Total output on the company's holdings amounted to about 25,000 tons of sugar per year; its estates harboured a resident population of about 11,500 inclusive of 5,000 indentured labourers and 3,000 children. In Trinidad as well as in Guiana the company's activities were associated with the concentration of estate ownership and the modernisation of production processes which were part and parcel of the West Indian sugar industry in the later nineteenth century. In Trinidad, for example, the company owned Usine St Madeleine, then and for a long time the biggest sugar factory in the island. The complex marked the decisive shift from the production of muscovado to centrifugal sugar, and involved substantial investment in factory equipment, railways and rolling stock altogether amounting to £339,342 sterling.[64] In addition, the central not only ground its own canes on fourteen estates spread over 10,340 acres, but also purchased farmers' canes as well. Between 1879 and 1896 such canes totalled 91,154 tons rising from 1,228 tons in 1879 to 19,341 tons in the latter year.[65] By that time, too, the factory was said to have a throughput of 12,000 tons sugar per year.

The Colonial Company was by far the most important of those sugar enterprises which made their appearance in the island in a period when imperative necessity demanded that the sugar planter either expand, consolidate and mechanise or go bust. Only the largest planters were able to survive in those circumstances, planters like Sir Charles Tennant and Company, whose holdings included Malgretoute and la Fortune Estates, comprised 12,925 acres and were said to involve an investment of £400,000;[66] Mr (later, Sir) Norman Lamont of Glasgow, owner of Palmiste, an estate of 2,190 acres in extent and established at an expenditure of £124,600;[67] and Gregor, Turnbull and Company of Glasgow which owned Brechin Castle, Caroni and Lothians comprising all told 12,000 acres. In fact, where by the close of the first half of the nineteenth century more than one hundred individually owned sugar estates were in production, by

1896 eleven combines, either individually or corporately owned, accounted for nearly all the sugar that was produced; almost all the sugar that counted was also being produced by the vacuum pan and centrifugal method, thereby bespeaking the great emphasis on modernisation. Of £700,347 sterling worth of sugar exported £371,661 was produced by the vacuum pan method, £293,177 by the centrifugal method, and only £35,509 was muscovado.[68]

A mournful analysis uttered by F. Lange, Jnr. at a meeting of the Central Agricultural Board held on Friday, June 27th, 1890, spoke volumes on the point of transformation of the island's sugar industry and what was required to stay in it:

> The sugar industry requires such a large expenditure on plant and cultivation that it is beyond the reach of the majority of the inhabitants here and the capital in the Colony which can be devoted to the purpose. This assertion that I make now is confirmed by what we see every day, for year after year we see sugar planters, after years of hard work, obliged to abandon that industry, and with whatever they have been able to save from the wreck, turn their attention to cultivating cocoa. I may say that I may offer myself as an illustration of what has taken place. As we saw last year we shall see this year sugar estates for sale, and, if not disposed of for little or nothing, they will be abandoned. In the annual report of the Colonial Company, published in the European Mail of May last, it was stated that all those estates connected with the Usine for the last thirteen years have made a large profit, something like a sum of 139,000; but all those estates who work their own canes and manufacture them shewed a loss amounting of 89,000. To make the sugar industry a permanent one it is necessary to have large syndicates with sufficient money for developing the estates.[69]

In that sad and doleful situation Lange, failed sugar planter trying his hand at cocoa, could at least claim one consolation: his was not the only neck in the noose; heads were rolling all around. The time would indeed come when even some of the bigger planters would succumb to the increasing pace of the competition. By 1896-97 doubts were being freely expressed about the future viability of even the Tennants and the Burnleys the latter of whose estates were described as being "under the charge of the Royal Bank of Scotland... [and] in danger of abandonment".[70] Indeed Burnley and Company as well as Gregor, Turnbull and Company were soon to go into voluntary liquidation.[71]

The Colonial Bank which was destined to play a very prominent part in the development of capitalism in the island in the nineteenth century was founded in 1836 under royal charter for the purpose

10 Labour vs capital after emancipation, 1838-1897

of carrying on business in the British West Indies. Its offices were located in the city district of London, and its branches were established throughout the islands and British Guiana in the principal localities. It was the principal financial establishment in the region, and took deposits from private individuals and companies as well as from the various island governments. According to policy, it took no deposits in Britain, all its funds derived from the West Indies – planters, merchants and "an enormous number of deposits of small people all over the West Indies, varying from £10 to perhaps £500".[72]

From the very beginning there existed a close connection between the bank and the bigger proprietorships involved in sugar. Sir Neville Lubbock who was born in 1839, three years after the bank was founded, was in due course not only a director of the bank, but also a large shareholder and director of the Colonial Company as well as deputy governor and, from 1904, governor of the Royal Exchange in London, besides being as well director of the London and India Docks Company. He was also, as we have already seen, Chairman of the West India Committee in the closing years of the nineteenth century. H.H. Dobree, who was chairman of the bank in 1896, was a partner in the firm of Samuel Dobree and Sons for about twenty-five years and had an important stake in West Indian sugar. In Trinidad, William Howatson, manager of A. Cumming and Company, the largest plantation firm owned by a resident planter, was also connected with the bank for more than fifteen years. Similarly, in British Guiana, in Jamaica and in Barbados, a close connection existed between the bank and the sugar planting interest. In Jamaica names like Lucie Smith, Ashenheim and Du Quesnay figured prominently and on social occasions the bank's guest lists read like a planters' *Who's Who* in the British West Indies and in London.[73]

Outside of sugar the bank was able to attract the support of many famous and influential individuals and to incorporate them into its circle of friends, supporters and investors. In 1917 its chairman was Lord Beaverbrook; and Silbert Fox, a director of Lever Bros., Liverpool, and Hugh Cunliffe-Owen, deputy chairman of the British American-Tobacco Company, were both on the Board of Directors. So, too, in 1926, was Sir (later Lord) Frederick John Dealtry Lugard, as no doubt befitted a bank which had by then become Barclays Bank (Dominion, Colonial and Overseas).[74]

There can be no overestimation of the role played by the Colonial Bank in the execution of the imperial mission in the West Indies in the nineteenth century. From the very beginning the purpose of the bank was identified as that of establishing the economic foundations upon which British imperialism could rest securely in the West Indies. Put differently, the Colonial Bank was established to promote first and foremost the interest of metropolitan capital and to provide such financial support as the metropolitan interest would need from time to time to facilitate its expansion in the islands. This no doubt explains the favour with which the bank was regarded in the Colonial Office; for example, efforts by local planters and merchants to establish two local banks in Jamaica, the Jamaica Bank and the Planters' Bank, failed in part because of the refusal of the metropolitan government to grant them charters.[75] Also in 1896-97 the Norman Commission fully conscious of the importance of the bank and its activities, received its evidence in private and in confidence in London as well as in British Guiana and in Trinidad.[76]

Under the kind indulgence of successive British governments, the Colonial Bank weathered every storm and vicissitude of the nineteenth century West Indian economic environment and emerged as a power to be reckoned with in the late nineteenth and early twentieth centuries. In 1859 Sewell reckoned that the bank cleared $100,000 in profits.[77] The bank's own records show significant and sustained growth even in the leanest times. By the turn of the century the bank was all set to make its own great leap forward. In 1903 the bank's available assets amounted to £2,749,550 sterling.[78] In 1905 a 'disappointing' year as regards crops the bank still had a net balance of £41,000 and the directors declared a dividend of 3½ per cent.[79] But the war years were to be a period of phenomenal growth. Between 1914 and 1917 assets increased from £3,460,000 to £6,650,000, the profits increased by one-third and the number of branches doubled. Also the bank's operations were no longer restricted to the British West Indies. Between January 1st and November 15th, 1917 new branches were opened up at Kano, Port Harcourt and Jos in Nigeria, at Seccondee on the Gold Coast (Ghana), and at Freetown, Sierra Leone. In the West Indies itself new branches opened at Savanna-la-Mar and Lucea, Jamaica, Speightstown, Barbados and Scarborough, Tobago.[80] The bank's fortunes were such that the authorised share capital was raised from £2 to £5 million sterling in 1917, and doubled again in 1925.[81] In that same year the Colonial Bank Act was made law, the name of the bank was changed to Barclays (DCO) and the Anglo-Egyptian Bank and the National Bank of South Africa were amalgamated with it.[82]

This is what capitalist accumulation had made possible in the West Indies in the nineteenth century. The significance of the Colonial Bank was that, in the context of the exploitation of the labour that

10 Labour vs capital after emancipation, 1838-1897

was taking place, the bank was the final accumulator. Planters and plantations came and went, but the bank was there forever. In the plunder that was taking place the planters plundered the labourers and the bank in turn plundered them. All the evidence is that the bank used its financial leverage to force the weaker capitalists out of business and then provided the finance for the better and larger centralisation of the sugar industry, more often than not in the hands of the Colonial Company. What sometimes is perceived as caution and conservation on the part of the bank was really, on a closer examination, a cunning, tight-fisted policy the object of which was at best to promote the survival only of the fittest firms, and at worst to accumulate as much surplus in currency and in property in the hands of the bank.

According to practice, the bank made few, if any, advances to estates.[83] When advances were given they were made on very short term from fortnight to fortnight and usually on the explicit understanding that the overdrafts would be settled by drafts on London merchants, deductible, of course, from sums held for the account of the Trinidad borrower.[84] This meant, of course that the bank took little risk, never ever, or rarely ever, lost money and gave the ordinary planter what amounted to little or no help. And if that was so for sugar it was several times worse for what was called the 'minor industries', that is, coffee, cocoa, fruit, citrus, rice, livestock, ground provisions and such like which were grown and marketed by the same 'small people' whose deposits the bank was using to increase the imperial stake in the West Indian economy.[85] In 1920, Mr. Charles F. Wood, Chairman of the bank was to recommend to his audience at the 164th half-yearly meeting of the bank the old adage "when you're making money, save it".[86] One would have to go far indeed to find a more apt statement on the activities of the Colonial Bank in the nineteenth and early twentieth centuries.

In this period of imperialist invasion of the domestic economy labour fared badly. In the background was the ever present competition from beet sugar and from lower priced foreign sugars which acted continually to depress the price for West Indian sugar. In the period 1882 to 1895 total British West Indian sugar exports fell from 315,139 tons to 236,770 tons;[87] in the period 1882 to 1896 the value of sugar exports fell from £6,864,000 to £3,251 sterling.[88] The value of all exports in the same period fell from £8,224,000 to £6,102,000.[89] In the same period sugar exports declined from 84 to 53 per cent of total exports.[90] In respect of the British market cane sugar supplied 25 per cent of the market in 1896 compared with 65 per cent in 1882.[91] Of this only 10 per cent was supplied from British sources in 1896 compared with 25 per cent in 1882; in 1882, 40 per cent of British demand was supplied by foreign cane sugar, but only 15 per cent was so supplied in 1896.[92]

The real problem was beet sugar. British imports of raw and refined beet sugar jumped from 35 per cent of all sugar imports in 1882 to 75 per cent in 1896; in value total beet sugar imports, 1882-1896, represented £12,325,000 while cane sugar from British possessions only amounted to £2,616,000.[93] In the period 1840 to 1880 visible world production of beet, principally produced in Europe – in Austria-Hungary, France, Germany and Russia – moved up from 55,000 tons to 1,857,000 metric tons.[94] Between 1880 to 1915, by which time Italy, the Netherlands, Denmark, Sweden, Spain, Roumania, Bulgaria, Switzerland and Britain itself had become producers, total production increased from 2,127,000 to 7,697,000 metric tons.[95]

For the West Indian planter the final solution lay in the alteration of British policy regarding sugar imports on the metropolitan market: countervailing duties should be placed on bounty-fed beet sugar imports. Secondarily, the West Indian islands should be allowed, preferably collectively, to enter into reciprocal tariff arrangements with the United States of America which was, after Britain, the next best market for colonial sugar.[96]

Trinidad and Tobago was not exempt from the tides and buffetings of this period of West Indian sugar crisis. Between 1861 and 1895 exports from Trinidad to Britain fell in value from £783,846 to £660,418 sterling.[97] Exports from Tobago declined in value from £48,186 in 1882 of which sugar accounted for £37,769 to £15,672 of which sugar accounted for £5,988 in 1894.[98]

Caught by imperialist pressure and having a dependent labour force at their disposal, the Trinidad planters tried as best they could to ride the storm. Their chief tactic was to attempt to reduce wages and so pass on the cost of the depression to the labouring population. This they did successfully in 1884 when wages were reduced by about 15 per cent. By 1886-87, however, agricultural wages were back at their old level, low though that was;[99] but the level of wages paid to skilled and semi-skilled labour-artisans, mechanics, etc. remained depressed.[100] Indeed the belief persisted, and was given voice by Messrs. Fenwick and Abel before the 1897 Commission, that wages should be drastically reduced. These two worthies expressed the view that agricultural labourers could easily live on four, five or six cents a day, and argued insistently that wages should be appropriately reduced.[101]

10 Labour vs capital after emancipation, 1838-1897

Another device used was the introduction of cane farming by which means the factory owners were able to obtain canes for grinding at a price cheaper than that at which they could produce it. Also, this method of cultivation limited the cash requirements of the factories outside of the crop since the farmers undertook the costs of growing the canes. Finally, the factory operations were, to some extent, as the delegation from the Cane Farmers' Association frankly admitted to the Norman Commission, 'insured against loss'.[102]

For their part the labourers remained largely unorganised. The chief spokesman for the East Indian indentured workers was the Protector of Immigrants, W.W. Coombs; the Cane Farmers' Association was led not by the small farmers but by people like René de Verteuil and Norman Lamont both, in different times, president of the Association.[103] Elements of self-organisation were, however, beginning to emerge. A memorandum from 78 East Indian immigrants from Princes Town, Couva and St Joseph districts rebutted the outrageous statements made by Fenwick and Abel and proposed that the East Indian immigrant population should be directly represented in the Legislative Council.[104] Also there were the strike actions undertaken by immigrant workers in the period 1883 to 1890. Between 1883 and the end of the century the average number of such actions were seven though as many as twenty-one took place in 1889 and there were serious strikes in 1882, 1883 and 1884 and again on the Colonial Company's Golconda Estate in 1890.[105]

The conscious organisation of the labouring population of Indian and African descent began in 1897, and was in part the consequence of the impact of the investigations of the Norman Commission in that year. However, the gradual rise in consciousness of the Indians as part of the Trinidad society was a factor of some importance. At the census of 1891, there was a resident Indian population of 70,000 persons in the island, about one-third of the population. Of these 24,641 were Trinidad born, and some of them had already started to climb slowly but surely up the social and economic scale. A few East Indians themselves owned estates in Trinidad and one owned a sugar estate in Tobago; eight others owned cocoa estates while hundreds of others were engaged as peasant proprietors, managers, overseers and drivers.[106]

As for the Africans, the intervening period since 1838 had seen the development of many black and coloured men particularly of talent and sometimes, too, of property. Men like Cyrus Prudhomme David and John Jacob (J.J.) Thomas who were black and Michael Maxwell Phillip, Vincent Brown and Henry Alcazar who were coloured were

239

well known and not without impact on the local social and political scene; one would hesitate, though, to say that they were very influential.[107] But they were indicative of the fact that the descendants of slaves were beginning to bestir themselves as became men who were now free.

It was hardly to be expected, therefore, that the 1897 Commission would come and go without some intervention from the African black and coloured population some of whom had been involved in the recent agitation for a reform of the island's constitution. Two separate submissions were made to the Norman Commission, one from the Trinidad Workingmen's Association, whose president, Walter H. Mills appeared in person before the Commission,[108] and the other in writing from the Working Mens' Reform Club whose corresponding secretary described himself, rather immodestly as the "father of labour movements".[109] Both submissions were brief and exposed the weakness of the organised labour movement in the island at that time.

In Tobago, one petition signed by Wm. C. John and presented to the Commission by a Mr Clemens on behalf of a committee of labourers;[110] a letter put in by C. Plagemann, a druggist, a catechist and Anglican lay reader reflecting resolutions adopted at a public meeting of labourers,[111] and a statement submitted after personal examination by David Hatt, a merchant,[112] dealing *inter alia*, with the condition of the labouring population; these represented the total output of the various voices for labour in early 1897.

As in Trinidad, the voices were weak in addition to which no permanent organisation existed to carry forward the hopes and aspirations of the workers. In fact, to judge by the demands made, the workers seemed to endorse the main planter demand, that is, the restoration and the rehabilitation of the sugar industry. The principal demands which seemed genuinely to reflect the labourers' point of view were first, the abolition of the system of *metayage*; secondly, the fostering of the 'minor industries'; and, finally, the enforcement of the Truck Act by which the payment of the workers in kind and not in cash had been prohibited.[113]

What was clear as well was the fact that the large scale migration of adult males to Trinidad in search of employment augured badly for the future organisation of the working class people in Tobago. Indeed, so heavy was that migration, that the Clemens petition specifically requested the adoption of measures aimed at encouraging Barbadians to migrate to the island.[114] Significantly, an analysis of the labour force of Trinidad and Tobago, county by county, in

10 Labour vs capital after emancipation, 1838-1897

1899, which showed that 65,593 persons were engaged in agriculture, 37,654 in manufactures and 4,377 in commerce, did not provide any separate statistics for Tobago.[115] The labouring population of that island apparently was so small, and so indistinguishable because of incessant migration to Trinidad, as to defeat any claim that could have been made for separate attention.

In Trinidad, of the two organisations tendering submissions to the 1897 Commission, one of them was destined to play a major role in the future organisation of labour in the island. Of the Working Men's Reform Club and Charles Phillips, its corresponding secretary and self-styled 'father of labour movements', not much was heard after this time. Further research will have to unravel the circumstances attending its fleeting existence on the public stage. It could well have been a planter inspired organisation which, while advancing a cogent and truthful description of the plight of the labouring population – "Unofficial members nominally representing us (East Indian) immigrants starving us" – nevertheless made its major contribution in proposing the acceptance *in toto* (of) the reforms and aid prayed for by the sugar planters in their petition of 1884, adding only the amendment that land be given at 10s. per acre.[116]

On the other hand, the Trinidad Workingmen's Association (TWA) was to develop into an organisation of significance right down to 1937 and to pave the way by its agitational and organisational work for the outbreak of working class discontent which took place in that year. It was, on all available evidence, the first conscious expression of working class organisation in the British West Indies. Its president, Walter H. Mills, a druggist and "agent for three or four estates"[117] described the Association before the 1897 Commission as comprised of about 50 persons in all: "carpenters, masons, labourers, tailors, and other trades... principally natives of Trinidad, and a few of them... natives of other West India islands".[118]

The programme of the Association as reflected in Mills' contribution amounted to a series of demands for:

1. The mitigation of destitution among the labouring population by putting an end to East Indian immigration, lowering taxes and raising the level of wages;
2. The improvements of the standard of public sanitation and the elimination of diseases attendant on the general insanitary condition of the island's towns, dwellings and estates;
3. The establishment of a free peasantry on five acre plots of land at the end of five years of indentureship or other recognised agricultural work, subject to the condition that the land be

cultivated within five years with one of the minor crops as advised by the state and with plants and transportation of plants freely provided;

4. The further diversification of the economy by the promotion of more 'minor industries' aimed at breaking the domination of sugar and cocoa;

5. The opening of Crown lands for sale in ten or five acre blocks paid for by instalments of 1 per year;

6. The removal of the existing 'oppressive taxation' on food stuffs and commodities commonly used by the poor with the result that, "The very cutlass with which they (the labourers) work in the cane field is taxed, whilst the sugar mill is introduced free... (Taxation) falls very heavily on the poor man who has to pay 4s... for his hut, 1s. for the acre, 1 dollar for his gun, and 1 dollar for his dog".[119] The imposition, instead of a Stamp Act,[120] and a wheel tax;[121]

7. The establishment of a state operated agricultural bank, as distinct from a commercial bank whose operations are secured against loss by government guarantee. "The Poor people cannot get any aid whatever in this colony. The Colonial Bank only deals with merchants..."[122]

8. The improvement of road and rail communications so that the Crown lands could become more accessible;

9. The complete removal of the inequitable export tax placed on cocoa as compared with sugar and the elimination of the duty placed on refined sugar or, else, the establishment of a local sugar refinery;

10. The abolition of the law regulating the capacity of stills for distilling liquors by which "a monopoly (is) granted to the larger sugar estate owners... (thus) virtually destroying an industry which was once in the hands of many proprietors of limited means."[123]

11. The abolition of bounties on sugar or the imposition of countervailing duties;

12. The encouragement of cane-farming 'by every means' as 'the only solution' to the problem of whether sugar will pay in Trinidad or not;

13. The introduction of an elected Legislative Council within which the sugar interest will not predominate.

The class content of the Trinidad Workingmen's Association (TWA) programme is unmistakable; the racial intent is implied. As portrayed by Mills it was a programme devised for black and coloured people falling somewhere between a generalised working

10 Labour vs capital after emancipation, 1838-1897

class position and the petty professional, petty capitalist class from which Mills himself came. Taken in the context of the prevailing realities it was a good programme, but it was destined to remain largely unimplemented. These points were taken up because, even though they were voiced by the TWA, they found answering echoes in the upper reaches of the society. For example, the extension of the system of cane farming which followed on the Report of the Norman Commission is to be explained by the obvious advantages which peasant labour working on its own account had over estate labour in so far as costs of production were concerned.[124] When, at last, even though it was not specifically recommended by the Commission, bounties were internationally abolished it was Sir Neville Lubbock not the likes of Walter Mills or Charles Phillips who was praised for his 'constant and unwearied efforts' to the cause over a period of thirty years. In this context it is certainly not strange that the positive recommendations of the Commission aimed at lessening the dependence on the sugar industry by the substitution of other agricultural industries, and the establishment of a peasant proprietary on the abundance of Crown Lands – two points on which the Commission agreed with Mills – were not implemented. Nor is it strange as well that the frequent representations of the Association on behalf of the workers were very frequently "quietly consigned to the waste-paper basket" in the years to come.[125]

There can be little doubt that the period 1838-1897 constituted one of the most significant in the rise and development of the working people of Trinidad and Tobago. Accordingly, even at the risk of some repetition, it is worth attempting to draw together in succint form the strands of the analysis which we have just completed.

In 1838 the slaves were emancipated. More fundamentally, free wage labour was introduced on a general scale. That is what emancipation meant, where before the slave worked for the master for nothing, now the ex-slave worked for the ex-master for a wage. Qualitatively that meant that whereas under slavery the master took all that the slave produced, under freedom he took most. In addition the ex-slave's social and political position relative to that of his erstwhile master remained largely unchanged.

Between 1838 and the end of the nineteenth century the ex-slave's basic experience remained one of oppression. In Jamaica that oppression reached such a level that actual conflict erupted between the new labouring population and sectors of the planter proprietorship most notably in 1865 at Morant Bay in the parish of St Thomas.[126] That confrontation was to have the most profound impact on the immediate political future of Jamaica and led there, and later nearly everywhere else in the Caribbean, to the introduction of a new form of political despotism known as Crown Colony government. Under this system representative government was abolished and all power was placed in the hands of the colonial governor who was responsible only to the imperial government in London. Touted as a device for treating all sectors of West Indian society with even-handed justice, the Crown Colony system became in fact another form of political oppression, the essence of which was that the representative form of government such as had previously existed in nearly all the islands was denied to the race and class majority of black workers.

Here in Trinidad (and, after union in 1889, in Tobago as well) Crown Colony government was well known. Such a system of government had always existed in Trinidad after the colony was conquered by the British in 1797; in fact so much so that Trinidad had long been recognised as a leading example of that form of government. The power had always been exclusively in the hands of the imperial masters who shared only so much of it as was expedient and then always with the white plantocracy, and urban professionals, that is to say with the race and class minority.

It was the fate of Trinidad to know Crown Colony government inside out: it came earliest to Trinidad and it endured in Trinidad almost to the end. It was not until 1925 that an election was held to determine who should sit in the colonial Legislative Council which had been introduced nearly one hundred years previously in 1831.[127] And it was not until 1946 that an election was held in Trinidad under universal adult suffrage that is to say after Jamaica, Barbados and British Guiana all of which had always been streets ahead of Trinidad politically.

But even more serious than the political subordination was the heightened economic exploitation visited on the labouring population after 1838. Those who thought (and still think) that emancipation meant an end to economic exploitation had (and have) to think again. In the first place, the planters backed by the imperialists continued to behave as if they had a divine right to the labour of the ex-slaves. They demanded that they work for them for next to nothing and when they refused they used all manner of bribery and force to get them to do so. Secondly, both the planters and the imperialists regarded the former as the most important social grouping in the country, the one for whom laws must particularly be made. In fact, as we have seen, the continuation of the plantation system was unashamedly rationalised on the ground that it was in the interests

10 Labour vs capital after emancipation, 1838-1897

of the workers that a European proprietorship should be maintained in the colony in a position of substantial economic and social and, consequently, political privilege. Thirdly, as the logical extension of this blatant partisanship of the planter cause, the imperialists and the planters alike regarded the labouring population as fit only to be exploited and oppressed, as fodder in the struggle between the old society whose epitaph was already being written and the new society which was (and still is) struggling to be born.

In the period between 1838 and the turn of the century the main lines of exploitation had to do: first, with the denial of every conceivable opportunity to blacks to free themselves from plantation labour and to find honourable and gainful employment at other occupations; and second, with the remorseless depression of the level of wages paid to black labourers whether they worked on or off the plantation. Immediately after emancipation even though the planter did his damnedest the workers used their new found independence either to get out of the plantation system completely, to turn to gardening, small trading, squatting and the establishment of new villages on the outskirts of Port of Spain, San Fernando and the north-eastern districts along what is now the Eastern Main Road; or else to demand (and often to get) the highest possible wage for plantation labour.[128]

In this period, and particularly in Trinidad, the planters found themselves faced with an entirely new situation which they had not formerly encountered or had encountered only briefly in the period of apprenticeship between 1834 and 1838. Not only did they have to bargain with the workers to get them to work, but they had to pay them high wages, and in cash as well. The essence of that experience for the planter was that for the first time he faced an adversary who could and did decide if he was going to work, for whom he would work, the hours during which he would work, or, if he wished, that he was not going to work at all. In other words the planter as employer was confronted for the first time with a system wherein the ex-slave could genuinely engage in what might be called a form of industrial bargaining.

For the black worker there was a brief and shortlived advantage in this experience. Between 1838 and the early 1840s when labour was in short supply and land was plentiful and relatively easily acquired the planter found himself in a weaker bargaining position than that of the ex-slave. Workers were able to bargain for a level of wages which, in Trinidad, was higher than anywhere else in the West Indies. Between 1839 and 1846 the wage rate on the sugar plantations in Trinidad averaged between 40 to 50 cents per day. Compare this with 30 cents in Barbados; 28 cents in Grenada; 12 cents in Nevis and 8 cents in Montserrat where, in 1849-50 the rate even fell to 4½ cents. Of the other territories only Jamaica (24 to 36 cents), Guiana (33 to 48 cents) and St Lucia could compare.[129] It was not surprising that W.H. Burnley, complained so bitterly about the greater earning power of the Trinidad worker compared with the worker in Tortola.[130] Unfortunately for the Trinidad worker, history was soon to show that the level of wages then attained was higher than workers were to receive at any time during the next hundred years. By 1937, when the riots and strikes took place, the level of wages at that time was no higher in several instances, and very often lower in most, than those received by workers in the period immediately after 1838.[131]

In attempting to explain this disastrous decline in the wages and consequently in the standard of living of the black worker we must note two important factors.

First of all, we must note the fact that though the worker could bargain he did not bargain collectively. There were no workers' organisations, no trade unions, and consequently no collective bargaining. The worker as an individual bargained with the planter; but the planter because of his higher social awareness often did combine against the worker and sometimes even effectively managed to hold down wages. In these early days, however, he could only do so for a time. The objective situation was against him: there were too few labourers in a country in which labour had always been short, and there was too much idle land and, as a result, too much opportunity for the worker to other wise employ himself.

Secondly, we must note above all the decisive intervention made by British imperialism, the most vigorous imperialism at this time, in altering the objective conditions which had aided the worker in his struggle with the planter. The most decisive intervention of all had the most disastrous impact on the competitive position of the worker. Imperialism intervened to increase the labour supply, at first by permitting, encouraging and facilitating immigration from other parts of the West Indies, parts of Africa, Europe, China, the United States of America, but ultimately and decisively from the sub-continent of India.

Both in Trinidad and in Guiana, and to a far lesser extent in places like Jamaica and Grenada, the labouring population was increased by massive importation of East Indian indentured workers. Where *free wage labour had failed to satisfy the planters' demands compulsory wage labour* (for that is what indentureship was) was made to do so.[132] It is very easy, as some have from time to time attempted to do, to

10 Labour vs capital after emancipation, 1838-1897

present these facts in such a way as to depict East Indian indentured labourers as at best benighted second class workers doing work that the blacks scorned to do, or even as willing agents of British imperialism in its assault on the social and economic position of the black workers.[133]

In this matter as in so much else there is the perspective of race and there is the perspective of class. Imperialism opted for the perspective of race and spent a long time sowing the seeds of racial antagonism. Everything that could be done was done to drive a wedge between the two sectors of the labouring population. This, together with the cultural and religious differences between Africans and Indians, as well as the racial slurs which sprang quickly to the surface in a situation in which one sector of the population saw itself being replaced by the other tended to give an easy permanence to the racial conflict which imperialism stimulated.

But there was (and is) the perspective of class. Where race stresses the differences between the two ethnic groups, class emphasises their similar status as workers. It should also be remembered that the imperial design to divide the labouring population did not begin with the coming of the East Indian. Even in the days of slavery consistent efforts were made to divide the slave population within itself and to stratify the slaves in defiance of geographical origin, family ties, language, religious and cultural practices, and, of course their wishes. Such efforts also came to be associated with the design of introducing other populations into Trinidad before the coming of the East Indian. For example, when the first attempt was made in 1806-7 to introduce a Chinese labouring population important whites felt that the great advantage of such an undertaking was that it would create "a barrier between us, and the negroes with whom they (the Chinese) do not associate; and consequently to whom they will always offer a formidable opposition".[134]

Within this perspective of class it is important to recognise that what was fundamental in the new situation was the capacity of British imperialism to manipulate labour from one British colony to another in order to create precisely the conditions which enabled sugar to survive on the planters' terms. In this manipulation of labour the ethnic identification of the labourer was only incidental. At one time in the distant past the labourer was Amerindian, then he was European, African, Chinese, Madeiran/Portuguese, black American, liberate African, and finally East Indian. The East Indian labourer was the final solution to the continuing search for a work force consistent with the requirements of free (wage) labour as against unfree (slave) labour.

Between 1845 and 1917 a considerable number of East Indian immigrants was imported into the West Indies, creating in the process what even bourgeois historians today describe as "a new slavery", this time of East Indians not of Africans. Into Guyana, 238,000 East Indians were imported within those sixty-odd years; into Trinidad 143,900; into Jamaica 36,400; into Grenada 5,900, all in order to keep the sugar plantations going.[135] Nor was this happening in the British West Indies alone. Wherever the major European powers were involved in economic exploitation, in the French and Spanish colonies as well as in the British, migrant labour, but particularly East Indian labour was the basic work force that created the wealth which the imperialists accumulated. Worldwide, a mass migration of more than seventeen million persons flowed out of India and China, creating in the process the basic new international exploitation of labour undertaken by imperialism in the second half of the nineteenth century.

We, today, have to face this issue squarely. The issue was (and is) not one of race; the issue is also one of immigrant labour in all its manifold complexity. As it is today with the West Indian migrant in Britain, Canada and the USA; as it was with the West Indian migrant in the 1920s and 30s in Cuba, in Costa Rica, in Panama so it was in the 1840s onwards with the East Indian labourer in Trinidad. The conflicts engendered between African and Indian were the conflicts customarily engendered between members of the working population placed in a position of active competition for employment.

In actual fact the ex-slave's advantageous position as a free wage labourer on the morrow of emancipation was destroyed by the influx of new immigrant (East Indian) labour and the planter was soon able to call the tune. But the planter called the tune, not only for the blacks whose wages were depressed but also for the East Indian worker who was underpaid while indentured and underpaid as well when, after serving his indentureship and becoming a free labourer, he, too, became subject to the same low and depressed level of wages to which the black was already accustomed.

Right on down to the last decade of the nineteenth century the working people of African and East Indian descent were unrepresented by any form of working class organisation agitating for the interests of these groups of workers and trying to defend them against exploitation by the planter. In the 1890s, however, a thorough going crisis had the West Indian economies in its grip. In Trinidad and Tobago the crisis was as severe as elsewhere even though Trinidad

10 Labour vs capital after emancipation, 1838-1897

as usual was better placed to cope with crisis than many another West Indian territory. By this time the sugar industry had undergone a significant transformation, a result of the large scale penetration of British capital. The production processes of the industry, with particular reference to the factory operations, had been revolutionised. Estates had been consolidated into larger units. Cane farming had been introduced thereby providing a direct labour subsidy to the larger planters. Moreover, a significant diversification had taken place in the island's economy with the successful development of cocoa as a major export crop.

But the crisis was unrelenting; unrelenting precisely because it was fuelled by imperialism. Free trade and the wholesale importation of beet sugar into Britain all but completely destroyed the market for West Indian sugar in that country. Between 1882 and 1896 British imports of refined beet sugar increased from 35 to 75 per cent of total sugar imports; or, to put it differently cane sugar supplied 65 per cent of the British market in 1882 but only 25 per cent in 1896.[136] Moreover of the 25 per cent being imported in 1896 only ten per cent was supplied by British colonial sources, and within that context West Indian sugar was badly outdistanced by East Indian sugar.[137]

To put it bluntly the period of the 1890s was yet another period of general crisis within the West Indian capitalist economy. To try to deal with the crisis Britain, as usual, appointed a commission, the Norman Commission of 1897; and with the appointment of that Commission the workers, who were already in desperate straits and had seen their wages fall even further from the already depressed levels began to undertake the first conscious act of self-organisation. It was indicative of the weakness of the workers' movement that in some cases their interests were 'represented' by their race and class enemies. Such was the case with the East Indian indentured workers whose chief spokesman was the Protector of Immigrants, W.W. Coombs.[138] Even more scandalously, the Cane Farmers' Association, an organisation in the main consisting of small, struggling farmers, was 'represented' by René de Verteuil and Norman Lamont, the latter being one of the biggest sugar estates proprietors in the country.[139]

It was also indicative of the increasing worker militancy that 78 East Indian immigrants from Princes Town, Couva and St Joseph districts organised a rebuttal of the outrageous falsifications of Fenwick and Abel, managers at Usine Ste Madeleine, who consistently proposed as a solution to all the island's economic ills that wages should be further reduced.[140] On one occasion these two scalawags tried to get the Norman Commission to accept that workers could live on four,

249

five or six cents a day, and urged that workers should be paid accordingly.[141] Undoubtedly the new East Indian militancy, manifested as well in a series of strike actions throughout the period 1882 onwards was indicative of a growing consciousness and self-confidence, no doubt born in part of the growing size of the resident East Indian population and the increasing number among them of Trinidad-born Indians.

But the most advanced reflection of workers' organisation was provided by the Trinidad Workingmen's Association (TWA) which was to develop as the most significant workers' organisation until the agitations of the 1930s led to the emergence of the trade union in its modern form. Moreover it was the first conscious expression of working class organisation in the British West Indies. Why this was so is undoubtedly to be explained by the advanced character of capitalist development in Trinidad at the time and the corresponding development of the working people. Significantly, only in Guyana, like Trinidad an arena of heightened capitalistic penetration, and in Jamaica, did any comparable growth of workers' organisation take place. In Jamaica a shortlived Carpenters, Bricklayers and Painters Union (the Artisans' Union) was formed in 1898. In Guyana Hubert Nathaniel Critchlow, a dockworker, began to agitate among the dockers from as early as 1903 though the British Guiana Labour Union was not formed until 1919.[142]

The programme of the TWA is therefore quite possibly the first articulate statement of working class objectives in the history of the English-speaking Caribbean. Even when one takes into account its weaknesses it remains a remarkable document. Its leadership was middle class: its president was a druggist and "agent for three or four estates".[143] Its membership was small: it comprised about fifty persons mainly carpenters, masons, labourers, tailors and other tradesmen. And basically its demands were moderate. It was a programme devised for black and coloured people belonging to a generalised working class position or the petty professional, petty capitalist class from which Mills himself came. But it was a good programme in that it underscored the completely opposed class and racial aspirations of the majority versus the minority.

Among its main demands were: the ending of East Indian immigration, the source of destitution to all workers alike; the lowering of taxes on food and basic commodities; the raising of the level of wages; the improvement of public sanitation; the establishment of a free peasantry; the diversification of the economy; the sale of Crown Lands in small allotments; the establishment of a state operated agri-

10 Labour vs capital after emancipation, 1838-1897

cultural bank; the improvement of road and rail communications; the abolition of the export tax on cocoa and the import duty on refined sugar; the establishment of a local sugar refinery; the abolition of the big capitalist monopoly on the distillation of rum; the abolition of sugar bounties or, alternatively, the imposition of countervailing duties; the encouragement of cane farming; the introduction of an elected Legislative Council.

Needless to say, this programme was not implemented. Its main provisions had to be fought for. The history of the development of the class struggle between 1897 and 1937 was indeed to be in large part the history of the struggle for the implementation of the TWA programme advanced in 1897. After 1897-98 the TWA itself receded into the background after concluding that the colonial government had no intention whatsoever of listening to its criticisms, pleadings and petitions. For the workers and their organisations it was to be a long and uphill struggle for recognition and achievement.

Notes

1. Donald Wood, *Trinidad in Transition* (Oxford, 1969), p.44. J. Davy, *The West Indies Before and Since Emancipation* (London, 1854), p.245.
2. Wm. G. Sewell, *The Ordeal of Free Labour in the British West Indies* 2nd edn (London, 1861), pp.90, 108. See also Eric Williams, *The History of the People of Trinidad and Tobago* (Trinidad, 1962), pp.83-86.
3. See W.K. Marshall, "Metayage in the Sugar Industry of the British West Indies, 1838-65," *Jamaican Historical Review*, Vol. 5 (1965).
4. *Report of the West India Royal Commission (WIRC)* (1897), Appendix C, Part V (Tobago), p.355.
5. Ibid., p.355.
6. Ibid., p.360.
7. See James Millette, "The Civil Commission of 1802: an Account and an Explanation of an Issue in the Early Constitutional and Political History of Trinidad," *The Jamaican Historical Review*, Vol. VI (1966).
8. Eric Williams, "The British West Indian Slave Trade After its Abolition in 1807," *Journal of Negro History* Vol. XXVII (April 1942), p.178.
9. Williams, ibid., p.180.
10. Williams, *History*, op. cit. p.124. Wood, *Transition*, op. cit., pp.53ff.
11. Wood, ibid., p.53.
12. Ibid., quoting W.H. Burnley.
13. P.D. Curtin, *Two Jamaicas* (Harvard, 1955), passim.
14. James Millette, *The Genesis of Crown Colony Government* (Trinidad, 1970), chap.1.
15. Wood, *Transition*, op. cit., p.54.
16. *British Parliamentary Papers (PP)* (1847-88), XLVI, Lord Harris to Earl Grey, June 19th 1848.
17. Millette, *Genesis*, op. cit., pp.264-66.
18. Douglas Hall, *Five of the Leewards*

(Caribbean Universities Press, 1971), p.176, quoted.
19. F.R. Augier and S. Gordon, *Sources of West Indies History* (London, 1962), p.2, quoted.
20. See for example K.O. Laurence, *Immigration into the West Indies in the 19th Century* (Caribbean Universities Press, 1971), p.13. Wood, *Transition*, op. cit., pp.68ff.
21. W. Emmanuel Riviere, "Labour Shortage in the British West Indies after Emancipation," *The Journal of Caribbean History*, Vol.4 (1972), p.29, Appendix. See also Hall, *Five of the Leewards*, op. cit., p.55.
22. Riviere, ibid.
23. Ibid.
24. Wood, *Transition*, op. cit., p.65. Hall, *Leewards*, op. cit., p.40.
25. Hall, *Leewards*, op. cit., 40-41 and particularly Table 5 (p.41).
26. Millette, *Genesis*, op. cit. pp.134, 215.
27. Ibid., pp.133-34.
28. Wood, *Transition*, op. cit., p.88.
29. Ibid., p.88.
30. Ibid., p.90.
31. Ibid., pp.101ff.
32. Sewell, *Ordeal*, op. cit., pp110-11.
33. PP (1841), XXIX, 379, "Papers Relative to the West Indies," pp.4-5.
34. Judith Weller, *The East Indian Indenture in Trinidad* (Puerto Rico, 1968), passim.
35. Hugh Tinker, *A New System of Slavery* (London, 1974).
36. Laurence, *Immigration*, op. cit., p.26.
37. W.M. Macmillan, *Warning from the West Indies* (London, 1936); Penguin edn, 1938, pp.94-95.
38. Wood, *Transition*, op. cit., pp.92-96
39. Tinker, *New System*, op. cit., p.191; Laurence, *Immigration*, op. cit., p.53.
40. Williams, *History*, op. cit. pp.103ff; Laurence, op. cit., p.88.
41. WIRC (1897), Appendix C, Part IV, Trinidad, p.312.
42. Weller, op. cit., p.47.
43. Williams, *History*, op. cit., p.106.
44. Ibid., p.109.
45. Alan H. Adamson, *Sugar Without Slaves, 1838-1904* (New Haven, 1972), p.112.
46. Weller, op. cit., p.54.
47. Tinker, *New System*, op. cit., p.195.
48. Ibid., p.194.
49. Williams, *History*, op. cit., p.108.
50. Laurence, op. cit., p.56.
51. Ibid.
52. Tinker, *New System*, 191-92; Williams, *History*, op. cit., p.106.
53. Tinker, op. cit., p.192.
54. Williams, *History*, op. cit., p.106.
55. Wood, *Transition*, op. cit., pp.133-35.
56. Ibid., p.135.
57. Howard Johnson, "Immigration and the Sugar Industry in Trinidad during the Last Quarter of the 19th Century," *The Journal of Caribbean History*, Vol. 3 (November 1971), passim.
58. WIRC (1897), Appendix C, Part IV, Trinidad, Memorandum of H.A. Alcazar (No.295), p.319, para.4. My emphasis.
59. Ibid., p.320, para.10. Again, my emphasis.
60. See H.A. Will, *Constitutional Change in the British West Indies, 1880-1903* (Oxford, 1970), Section 3. Also, B. Brereton, "The Reform Movement in Trinidad in the Later 19th Century," paper presented at the Fifth Conference of the Association of Caribbean Historians, 1973. For quotation see Augier and Gordon, *Sources*, op. cit., quoted, p.251 from *Daily Chronicle* (July 10th 1899).
61. WIRC (1897), Appendix A, p.81.
62. Ibid., Appendix A, p.100.
63. Ibid., Appendix C, Part 1, London, p.178. Documents put in by Neville Lubbock. See also Appendix C, Part 1, pp.6ff; and *West India Committee Circular* (WICC) (1904), pp.217-18, Biographical sketch by Sir Neville Lubbock.

The Circular was the official publication of the West India Committee and is an essential source of information on the activities of the leading organisations and individuals attached to

10 Labour vs capital after emancipation, 1838-1897

64 the West Indian interest.
   WIRC (1897), Appendix C, Part 1, London, p.178. See also Appendix C, Part IV, Trinidad, questions 1459-60 and 1548-52. Evidence of P. Abel and Hon. G.T. Fenwick.
65 Ibid., Appendix C, Part 1, London, p.178, Document put in by Neville Lubbock.
66 Ibid., Appendix C, Part IV, Trinidad, p.308, Statistics of Sugar Cultivation. See also pp.310-11. Evidence, G. White, Manager of Messrs C. Tennant and Sons, Estates, Trinidad.
67 Ibid., Appendix C, Part 1, London, pp.182-84, Memorandum by Mr. Norman Lamont of Palmiste, Trinidad.
68 Ibid., Appendix A, p.101, International Sugar Council, *The World Sugar Economy: Structure and Policies*, 2 vols (ISC, 1963), vol.1, p.27.
69 Council Paper No.105, Legislative Council, Trinidad (1890), Secretary of State Knutsford to Governor Robinson, 6 June 1890, No.103, enclosure. See also WIRC (1897), Appendix C, Part IV, Trinidad, p.242, Q.180. Evidence Mr. White.
70 WIRC (1897), Appendix C, Part 1, London, Q.1702-03. Evidence of Norman Lamont.
71 WIRC (1897), Appendix C, Part 1, London, p.24, Q.471. Evidence of H.H. Dobree.
72 Ibid., p.25, Q.505; Evidence of same. See also pp.9-10, Q.82-97. Evidence of N. Lubbock; and p.68, Q.1721-22. Evidence of N. Lamont. See, too, p.74, Q.1990. Evidence of George Carrington in respect of Barbados.
73 See, for example, WICC (1926), p.2 and accompanying photograph.
74 WICC (1926), p.2.
75 Douglas Hall, *Free Jamaica* (New Haven, 1959), 1969 edn, Caribbean Universities Press, pp.112-12, 225.
76 WIRC, Appendix C, Part II, British Guiana, p.73; Part III, Barbados, p.175; Pt. IV, Trinidad, p.265.

77 Op. cit., p.98.
78 WICC (1903), No.95, p.3.
79 Ibid. (1905), p.361.
80 Ibid. (1917), p.446.
81 Ibid. (1925), p.198.
82 Ibid., p.353.
83 WIRC, Appendix C, Part 1, London, p.25. Q.475-77; 486-89. Evidence of H.H. Dobree.
84 Ibid., Appendix C, Part 1, London, p.25. Q.486-87. Evidence of H.H. Dobree. Also, Appendix C, Part IV, Trinidad, p.237. Q.61. Evidence of Henderson and Sanderson.
85 See, for example, WIRC, Appendix C, Part IV, Trinidad, pp.320-23. Evidence of H. Hills.
86 WICC (1920), p.126.
87 WIRC, Appendix B, p.171.
88 Ibid., p.155.
89 Ibid., p.156.
90 Ibid., p.157.
91 Ibid., p.174.
92 Ibid.
93 Ibid., extracted.
94 ISC, p.23.
95 Ibid., p.27.
96 WIRC, Appendix C, Part 1, London, p.59. Q.1766-67. Evidence of N. Lamont.
97 WIRC, Appendix C, Part IV, Trinidad, p.328.
98 Ibid., Part V, Tobago, p.364.
99 Ibid., Part IV, Trinidad, pp.263-64. Evidence of G.W. Mitchell.
100 Ibid., p.349. Evidence of Charles Phillips.
101 Ibid., pp.340-41. Memoranda put in by P. Abel and G.T. Fenwick.
102 Ibid., pp.347-48.
103 Ibid., p.312; see also evidence of Charles Mitchell, late Protector of Immigrants, pp.349-50.
104 Ibid., p.351.
105 Weller, op. cit., pp.49ff.
106 J.C. Jha, "East Indian Pressure Groups in Trinidad, 1897-1921," paper presented to the Fifth Conference of the Association of Caribbean Historians, 1973, passim. See also WIRC, Appendix C, Part V, Tobago, p.361.
107 See, for example, B. Samaroo,

"Cyrus Prudhomme David – A Case Study in the Emergence of the Black Man in Trinidad Politics," *The Journal of Caribbean History*, Vol.3 (Nov. 1971).

[108] *WIRC*, Appendix C, Part IV, Trinidad, pp.301-305.
[109] Ibid., pp.348-49.
[110] Ibid., Part V, Tobago, pp.357-58.
[111] Ibid., p.358.
[112] Ibid., p.359.
[113] See in particular the Clemens petition, p.358.
[114] Ibid.
[115] *Blue Book*, Trinidad and Tobago (1899), Section R.
[116] *WIRC*, Appendix C, Part C, Trinidad, p.349.
[117] Ibid., p.303, Q.1843.
[118] Ibid., p.301, W.1797, 1800.
[119] Ibid., p.302, Q.1836.
[120] Ibid., p.304, Q.1882.
[121] Ibid., pp.304-305, Q.1883.
[122] Ibid., p.302, Q.1837.
[123] Ibid., p.303, Q.1854, 1855.
[124] Ibid., p.303, Q.1858.
[125] B. Samaroo, "The Trinidad Workingmen's Association and the Origins of Popular Protest in a Crown Colony," *Social and Economic Studies*, Vol. 21, No. 2 (June 1972), p.207, quoted.
[126] Douglas Hall, *Free Jamaica, 1838-65* (New Haven 1959); Philip Curtin, op. cit., passim.; Don Robotham, "The Notorious Riot" (Kingston, Jamaica, 1982).
[127] See Hewan Craig, *The Legislative Council of Trinidad & Tobago* (London, 1952); B. Samaroo, "Constitutional and Political Development of Trinidad 1898-1925," PhD thesis, London University (1962).
[128] See Wood, op cit., pp.48-49.
[129] Riviere, op. cit., p.29, Appendix.
[130] Wood, op. cit., p.53.
[131] See for example W.M. Macmillan, *Warning from the West Indies*, op. cit. Also, K. Singh, "Economy and Polity in Trinidad, 1917-1938" (UWI, 1975) published as *Race and Class Struggles in a Colonial State: Trinidad, 1917-1945* (Calgary and Kingston, 1994); W.R. Jacobs, "The Politics of Protest in Trinidad: The Strikes and Disturbances of 1937", paper presented at the Fifth Conference of the Association of Caribbean Historians, Proceedings..., Vol.2 (1973).
[132] See Raphael Sebastien, "The Development of Capitalism in Trinidad, 1845-1917", PhD thesis, Howard University (1978).
[133] Such attempts were particularly prevalent in the late 19th and early 20th centuries when even the best intentioned and most progressive anti-imperialist spokesmen often couched the arguments on the Indian question in purely racial terms. The confusion was between indentureship and the indentured worker, the former being of course the legitimate target, the latter being (though not often seen as such) the hapless victim of a colonial oppression that fell heavily on Indian and African labour alike.
[134] Millette, *Genesis*, op. cit., pp.xiv-xv, quoted.
[135] Laurence, op. cit., p.26.
[136] *WIRC*, Appendix C, Part I, pp.195, 201, 212; Tables of Statistics, Table and Diagram T, p.174.
[137] Ibid., Appendix B, op. cit.
[138] Ibid., Appendix C, Part IV, pp.258-59.
[139] Ibid., pp.273-76, 317-18, 347-48; also, Appendix C, Part I, pp.67ff. See also H. Johnson, "The Origin and Early Development of Cane-Farming in Trinidad," *The Journal of Caribbean History*, Vol.5 (Nov. 1972).
[140] Ibid., p.351.
[141] Ibid., pp.340-41.
[142] See Ashton Chase, *A History of Trade Unionism in Guyana, 1900 to 1961* (Guyana, n.d.).
[143] *WIRC*, Appendix C, Part IV, p.303.

Biographies

Professor **Hilary Beckles,** Pro-Vice Chancellor and Principal of the Cave Hill campus of The University of the West Indies, is also a distinguished historian and author of numerous books on the Caribbean and Barbados.

Bridget Brereton is Professor of History at The University of the West Indies, St Augustine Campus, and is the author or editor of several important books on the history of the post-emancipation Caribbean and of Trinidad & Tobago.

Professor **Selwyn H.H. Carrington** teaches history at Howard University, Washington, DC. He specialises in the economic history of the Caribbean, imperial history, colonial trade and has written on issues related to the historiography of the abolition of the slave trade and slavery.

Mr **H.A.M. Essed** is a well-known researcher and historian of the Maroon communities in Suriname and has worked as an administrator in the educational system of that country.

Dr **Kusha Haraksingh** is Head of the Department of History, and Associate Fellow of the Institute of International Relations at The University of the West Indies, St Augustine. His specialisation is the history of India. He is also a barrister-at-law and actively combines legal and academic work.

Mr **Lloyd King** is a former Senior Lecturer in the Department of French and Spanish Literature, The University of the West Indies, St Augustine, and has published extensively on Latin American Literature.

James Millette is Professor of History in the African American Studies Department, Oberlin College, Ohio. He has researched and published on colonial government, labour movements, political history and Caribbean historiography. He teaches and writes about Caribbean, African-American and African history.

Rhoda Reddock is Professor and Head of the Centre for Gender and Development Studies at The University of the West Indies, St Augustine campus. She has published widely on women in politics, labour and society in the Caribbean, South Africa and elsewhere in the Third World.

Professor **Margaret D. Rouse-Jones** is University Librarian at The University of the West Indies, and an historian. Her areas of special interest and research include historiography, Caribbean bibliography and librarianship.